Anti Inflammatory Cookbook
for Beginners

1800 Days of Affordable & Delicious Recipes with 60-Day Meal Plan to Reduce Inflammation, Balance Hormones and Lose Weight.

Megan Solari

TABLE OF CONTENTS

Chapter 1

The 60-Day Meal Plan

	Breakfast	Lunch	Dinner	Total Calories
DAY 1	Spinach and Egg Breakfast Wraps Calories:434	Butternut Squash and Cauliflower SoupCalories: 415 Rice Pudding with Roasted Orange SoupCalories: 274	Veal Pot Roast (Spanish) Calories: 426 Parmesan Roasted Red Potatoes Calories: 200	1749
DAY 2	Ricotta Toast with Strawberries Calories: 274 Pumpkin Pie Parfait Calories: 263	Cheesy Sweet Potato Burgers Calories: 290 Blueberry and Oat Crisp Calories: 496	Mediterranean Rice and Sausage (Italian) Calories: 650	1973
DAY 3	Egg Bake Calories: 240 Blueberry Smoothie Calories: 459	Baked Rolled Oat with Pears and Pecans Calories: 479	Italian Style Ground Beef (Italian) Calories: 365 Salad Skewers (Greek) Calories: 316	1859
DAY 4	Cauliflower Breakfast Porridge Calories: 381 Tzatziki Calories: 286	Lemon Beef (Spanish) Calories: 355 Guacamole Calories: 81	Macadamia Pork Calories: 436 Lentil-Tahini Dip Calories: 100	1639
DAY 5	Tomato and Egg Scramble Calories: 260 Creamy Peach Smoothie Calories: 212	Delicious Tomato Broth (Spanish) Calories: 460 Chocolate, Almond, and Cherry Clusters Calories: 197	Slow Cooker Salmon in Foil (Italian) Calories: 446 Lemony Blackberry Granita Calories: 183	1758
DAY 6	Quinoa Breakfast Bowls Calories: 219 Cheesy Broccoli and Mushroom Egg Casserole Calories: 326	Lebanese Flavor Broken Thin Noodles Calories: 127 Parsley-Dijon Chicken and Potatoes Calories: 324	Ground Beef, Tomato, and Kidney Bean Chili Calories: 891	1887

DAY 7	Baked Eggs in Avocado Calories: 301 Baked Ricotta with Honey Pears Calories: 329	Ritzy Veggie Chili Calories: 633	Deliciously Simple Beef (Spanish) Calories: 553	1816
DAY 8	Spinach and Egg Breakfast Wraps Calories:434	Butternut Squash and Cauliflower SoupCalories: 415 Rice Pudding with Roasted Orange SoupCalories: 274	Veal Pot Roast (Spanish) Calories: 426 Parmesan Roasted Red Potatoes Calories: 200	1749
DAY 9	Egg Bake Calories: 240 Blueberry Smoothie Calories: 459	Baked Rolled Oat with Pears and Pecans Calories: 479	Italian Style Ground Beef (Italian) Calories: 365 Salad Skewers (Greek) Calories: 316	1859
DAY 10	Ricotta Toast with Strawberries Calories: 274 Pumpkin Pie Parfait Calories: 263	Cheesy Sweet Potato Burgers Calories: 290 Blueberry and Oat Crisp Calories: 496	Mediterranean Rice and Sausage (Italian) Calories: 650	1973
DAY 11	Cauliflower Breakfast Porridge Calories: 381 Tzatziki Calories: 286	Lemon Beef (Spanish) Calories: 355 Guacamole Calories: 81	Macadamia Pork Calories: 436 Lentil-Tahini Dip Calories: 100	1639
DAY 12	Tomato and Egg Scramble Calories: 260 Creamy Peach Smoothie Calories: 212	Delicious Tomato Broth (Spanish) Calories: 460 Chocolate, Almond, and Cherry Clusters Calories: 197	Slow Cooker Salmon in Foil (Italian) Calories: 446 Lemony Blackberry Granita Calories: 183	1758
DAY 13	Quinoa Breakfast Bowls Calories: 219 Cheesy Broccoli and Mushroom Egg Casserole Calories: 326	Lebanese Flavor Broken Thin Noodles Calories: 127 Parsley-Dijon Chicken and Potatoes Calories: 324	Ground Beef, Tomato, and Kidney Bean Chili Calories: 891	1887
DAY 14	Baked Eggs in Avocado Calories: 301 Baked Ricotta with Honey Pears Calories: 329	Ritzy Veggie Chili Calories: 633	Deliciously Simple Beef (Spanish) Calories: 553	1816

DAY 15	Low Carb Bagels (Italian) Calories: 275	Apricot Pork Meat (Spanish) Calories: 332	Baked Cod with Vegetables Calories: 1168	1775
DAY 16	Spinach and Egg Breakfast Wraps Calories:434	Butternut Squash and Cauliflower SoupCalories: 415 Rice Pudding with Roasted Orange SoupCalories: 274	Veal Pot Roast (Spanish) Calories: 426 Parmesan Roasted Red Potatoes Calories: 200	1749
DAY 17	Egg Bake Calories: 240 Blueberry Smoothie Calories: 459	Baked Rolled Oat with Pears and Pecans Calories: 479	Italian Style Ground Beef (Italian) Calories: 365 Salad Skewers (Greek) Calories: 316	1859
DAY 18	Cauliflower Breakfast Porridge Calories: 381 Tzatziki Calories: 286	Lemon Beef (Spanish) Calories: 355 Guacamole Calories: 81	Macadamia Pork Calories: 436 Lentil-Tahini Dip Calories: 100	1639
DAY 19	Tomato and Egg Scramble Calories: 260 Creamy Peach Smoothie Calories: 212	Delicious Tomato Broth (Spanish) Calories: 460 Chocolate, Almond, and Cherry Clusters Calories: 197	Slow Cooker Salmon in Foil (Italian) Calories: 446 Lemony Blackberry Granita Calories: 183	1758
DAY 20	Ricotta Toast with Strawberries Calories: 274 Pumpkin Pie Parfait Calories: 263	Cheesy Sweet Potato Burgers Calories: 290 Blueberry and Oat Crisp Calories: 496	Mediterranean Rice and Sausage (Italian) Calories: 650	1973
DAY 21	Quinoa Breakfast Bowls Calories: 219 Cheesy Broccoli and Mushroom Egg Casserole Calories: 326	Lebanese Flavor Broken Thin Noodles Calories: 127 Parsley-Dijon Chicken and Potatoes Calories: 324	Ground Beef, Tomato, and Kidney Bean Chili Calories: 891	1887
DAY 22	Baked Eggs in Avocado Calories: 301 Baked Ricotta with Honey Pears Calories: 329	Ritzy Veggie Chili Calories: 633	Deliciously Simple Beef (Spanish) Calories: 553	1816

DAY 23	Low Carb Bagels (Italian) Calories: 275	Apricot Pork Meat (Spanish) Calories: 332	Baked Cod with Vegetables Calories: 1168	1775
DAY 24	Quinoa Breakfast Bowls Calories: 219 Cheesy Broccoli and Mushroom Egg Casserole Calories: 326	Lebanese Flavor Broken Thin Noodles Calories: 127 Parsley-Dijon Chicken and Potatoes Calories: 324	Ground Beef, Tomato, and Kidney Bean Chili Calories: 891	1887
DAY 25	Baked Eggs in Avocado Calories: 301 Baked Ricotta with Honey Pears Calories: 329	Ritzy Veggie Chili Calories: 633	Deliciously Simple Beef (Spanish) Calories: 553	1816
DAY 26	Egg Bake Calories: 240 Blueberry Smoothie Calories: 459	Baked Rolled Oat with Pears and Pecans Calories: 479	Italian Style Ground Beef (Italian) Calories: 365 Salad Skewers (Greek) Calories: 316	1859
DAY 27	Tomato and Egg Scramble Calories: 260 Creamy Peach Smoothie Calories: 212	Delicious Tomato Broth (Spanish) Calories: 460 Chocolate, Almond, and Cherry Clusters Calories: 197	Slow Cooker Salmon in Foil (Italian) Calories: 446 Lemony Blackberry Granita Calories: 183	1758
DAY 28	Spinach and Egg Breakfast Wraps Calories:434	Butternut Squash and Cauliflower SoupCalories: 415 Rice Pudding with Roasted Orange SoupCalories: 274	Veal Pot Roast (Spanish) Calories: 426 Parmesan Roasted Red Potatoes Calories: 200	1749
DAY 29	Cauliflower Breakfast Porridge Calories: 381 Tzatziki Calories: 286	Lemon Beef (Spanish) Calories: 355 Guacamole Calories: 81	Macadamia Pork Calories: 436 Lentil-Tahini Dip Calories: 100	1639
DAY 30	Ricotta Toast with Strawberries Calories: 274 Pumpkin Pie Parfait Calories: 263	Cheesy Sweet Potato Burgers Calories: 290 Blueberry and Oat Crisp Calories: 496	Mediterranean Rice and Sausage (Italian) Calories: 650	1973

Please note: refer to the index to find the number of the page corresponding to the recipe. Repeat the nutrition plan for another 30 days, starting again from the beginning.

We trust that this 60-day nutritional plan is to your liking!

Chapter 2
Breakfasts Recipes

Spinach and Egg Breakfast Wraps

Prep time: 10 minutes | **Cook time:** 7 minutes | **Serves:** 2

Ingredients:

1 tablespoon olive oil
¼ cup minced onion
3 to 4 tablespoons minced sun-dried tomatoes in olive oil and herbs
2 (8-inch) whole-wheat tortillas
3 large eggs, whisked
1½ cups packed baby spinach
1 ounce (28 g) crumbled feta cheese
Salt, to taste

Directions:

Heat the olive oil in a large skillet over medium-high heat.

Sauté the onion and tomatoes for about 3 minutes, stirring occasionally, until softened.

Reduce the heat to medium. Add the whisked eggs and stir-fry for 1 to 2 minutes.

Stir in the baby spinach and scatter with the crumbled feta cheese. Season as needed with salt. Remove the egg mixture from the heat to a plate. Set aside.

Working in batches, place 2 tortillas on a microwave-safe dish and microwave for about 20 seconds to make them warm.

Spoon half of the egg mixture into each tortilla. Fold them in half and roll up, then serve.

Per Serving
calories: 434 | fat: 28.1g | protein: 17.2g | carbs: 30.8g

Pumpkin Pie Parfait

Prep time: 5 minutes | **Cook time:** 0 minutes | **Serves:** 4

Ingredients:

1 (15-ounce / 425-g) can pure pumpkin purée
1 teaspoon pumpkin pie spice
2 cups plain Greek yogurt
4 teaspoons honey
1 cup honey granola
¼ teaspoon ground cinnamon

Directions:

Combine the pumpkin purée, honey, pumpkin pie spice, and cinnamon in a large bowl and stir to mix well.

Cover the bowl with plastic wrap and chill in the refrigerator for at least 2 hours.

Make the parfaits: Layer each parfait glass with ¼ cup pumpkin mixture in the bottom. Top with ¼ cup of yogurt and scatter each top with ¼ cup of honey granola. Repeat the layers until the glasses are full. Serve immediately.

Per Serving
calories: 263 | fat: 8.9g | protein: 15.3g | carbs: 34.6g

Ricotta Toast with Strawberries

Prep time: 10 minutes | **Cook time:** 0 minutes | **Serves:** 2

Ingredients:

½ cup crumbled ricotta cheese
1 tablespoon honey, plus additional as needed
Pinch of sea salt, plus additional as needed
4 slices of whole-grain bread, toasted
1 cup sliced fresh strawberries
4 large fresh basil leaves, sliced into thin shreds

Directions:

Mix together the cheese, honey, and salt in a small bowl until well incorporated.

Taste and add additional salt and honey as needed.

Spoon 2 tablespoons of the cheese mixture onto each slice of bread and spread it all over.

Sprinkle the sliced strawberry and basil leaves on top before serving.

Per Serving calories: 274 | fat: 7.9g | protein: 15.1g | carbs: 39.8g

Egg Bake

Prep time: 10 minutes | **Cook time:** 30 minutes | **Serves:** 2

Ingredients:

1 tablespoon olive oil
1 slice whole-grain bread
4 large eggs
3 tablespoons unsweetened almond milk
½ teaspoon onion powder
¼ teaspoon garlic powder
¾ cup chopped cherry tomatoes
¼ teaspoon salt
Pinch freshly ground black pepper

Directions:

Preheat the oven to 375°F (190°C).

Coat two ramekins with the olive oil and transfer to a baking sheet. Line the bottom of each ramekin with ½ of bread slice.

In a medium bowl, whisk together the eggs, almond milk, onion powder, garlic powder, tomatoes, salt, and pepper until well combined.

Pour the mixture evenly into two ramekins. Bake in the preheated oven for 30 minutes, or until the eggs are completely set.

Cool for 5 minutes before serving.

Per Serving
calories: 240 | fat: 17.4g | protein: 9.0g | carbs: 12.2g

Morning Overnight Oats with Raspberries

Prep time: 5 minutes | **Cook time:** 0 minutes | **Serves:** 2

Ingredients:

⅔ cup unsweetened almond milk

¼ cup raspberries

⅓ cup rolled oats

1 teaspoon honey

¼ teaspoon turmeric

⅛ teaspoon ground cinnamon

Pinch ground cloves

Directions:

Place the almond milk, raspberries, rolled oats, honey, turmeric, cinnamon, and cloves in a mason jar. Cover and shake to combine. Transfer to the refrigerator for at least 8 hours, preferably 24 hours. Serve chilled.

Per Serving calories: 81 | fat: 1.9g | protein: 2.1g | carbs: 13.8g

Tomato and Egg Scramble

Prep time: 10 minutes | **Cook time:** 20 minutes | **Serves:** 4

Ingredients:

2 tablespoons extra-virgin olive oil

¼ cup finely minced red onion

1½ cups chopped fresh tomatoes

2 garlic cloves, minced

½ teaspoon dried thyme

½ teaspoon dried oregano

8 large eggs

½ teaspoon salt

¼ teaspoon freshly ground black pepper

¾ cup crumbled feta cheese

¼ cup chopped fresh mint leaves

Directions:

Heat the olive oil in a large skillet over medium heat.

Sauté the red onion and tomatoes in the hot skillet for 10 to 12 minutes, or until the tomatoes are softened. Stir in the garlic, thyme, and oregano and sauté for 2 to 4 minutes, or until the garlic is fragrant. Meanwhile, beat the eggs with the salt and pepper in a medium bowl until frothy. Pour the beaten eggs into the skillet and reduce the heat to low. Scramble for 3 to 4 minutes, stirring constantly, or until the eggs are set. Remove from the heat and scatter with the feta cheese and mint. Serve warm.

Per Serving calories: 260 | fat: 21.9g | protein: 10.2g | carbs: 5.8g

Baked Eggs in Avocado

Prep time: 5 minutes | **Cook time:** 10 to 15 minutes | **Serves:** 2

Ingredients:

1 ripe large avocado

2 large eggs

Salt and freshly ground black pepper, to taste

4 tablespoons jarred pesto, for serving

2 tablespoons chopped tomato, for serving

2 tablespoons crumbled feta cheese, for serving (optional)

Directions:

Preheat the oven to 425°F (220°C).Slice the avocado in half, remove the pit and scoop out a generous tablespoon of flesh from each half to create a hole big enough to fit an egg.

Transfer the avocado halves (cut-side up) to a baking sheet. Crack 1 egg into each avocado half and sprinkle with salt and pepper.

Bake in the preheated oven for 10 to 15 minutes, or until the eggs are cooked to your preferred doneness.

Remove the avocado halves from the oven. Scatter each avocado half evenly with the jarred pesto, chopped tomato, and crumbled feta cheese (if desired). Serve immediately.

Per Serving
calories: 301 | fat: 25.9g | protein: 8.1g | carbs: 9.8g

Crustless Tiropita (Greek Cheese Pie)

Prep time: 10 minutes | **Cook time:** 35 to 40 minutes | **Serves:** 6

Ingredients:

4 tablespoons extra-virgin olive oil, divided

½ cup whole-milk ricotta cheese

1¼ cups crumbled feta cheese

2 tablespoons chopped fresh mint

½ teaspoon lemon zest

¼ teaspoon freshly ground black pepper

2 large eggs

½ teaspoon baking powder

1 tablespoon chopped fresh dill

Directions:

Preheat the oven to 350°F (180°C). Coat the bottom and sides of a baking dish with 2 tablespoons of olive oil. Set aside.Mix together the ricotta and feta cheese in a medium bowl and stir with a fork until well combined. Add the dill, mint, lemon zest, and black pepper and mix well.

In a separate bowl, whisk together the eggs and baking powder. Pour the whisked eggs into the bowl of cheese mixture. Blend well.

Slowly pour the mixture into the coated baking dish and drizzle with the remaining 2 tablespoons of olive oil.

Bake in the preheated oven for about 35 to 40 minutes, or until the pie is browned around the edges and cooked through.Cool for 5 minutes before slicing into wedges.

Per Serving
calories: 181 | fat: 16.6g | protein: 7.0g | carbs: 1.8g

Mediterranean Eggs (Shakshuka)

Prep time: 5 minutes | **Cook time:** 20 minutes | **Serves:**4

Ingredients:

2 tablespoons extra-virgin olive oil
1 cup chopped shallots
1 teaspoon garlic powder
1 cup finely diced potato
1 cup chopped red bell peppers
¼ cup chopped fresh cilantro
1 (14.5-ounce/ 411-g) can diced tomatoes, drained
¼ teaspoon ground cardamom
¼ teaspoon paprika
¼ teaspoon turmeric
4 large eggs

Directions:

Preheat the oven to 350°F (180°C).

Heat the olive oil in an ovenproof skillet over medium-high heat until it shimmers.

Add the shallots and sauté for about 3 minutes, stirring occasionally, until fragrant.

Fold in the garlic powder, potato, and bell peppers and stir to combine. Cover and cook for 10 minutes, stirring frequently. Add the tomatoes, cardamon, paprika, and turmeric and mix well.

When the mixture begins to bubble, remove from the heat and crack the eggs into the skillet.

Transfer the skillet to the preheated oven and bake for 5 to 10 minutes, or until the egg whites are set and the yolks are cooked to your liking.

Remove from the oven and garnish with the cilantro before serving.

Per Serving
calories: 223 | fat: 11.8g | protein: 9.1g | carbs: 19.5g

Creamy Peach Smoothie

Prep time: 15 minutes | **Cook time:** 0 minutes | **Serves:**2

Ingredients:

2 cups packed frozen peaches, partially thawed
½ ripe avocado
½ cup plain or vanilla Greek yogurt
2 tablespoons flax meal
1 tablespoon honey
1 teaspoon orange extract
1 teaspoon vanilla extract

Directions:

Place all the ingredients in a blender and blend until completely mixed and smooth.

Divide the mixture into two bowls and serve immediately.

Per Serving
calories: 212 | fat: 13.1g | protein: 6.0g | carbs: 22.5g

Blueberry Smoothie

Prep time: 5 minutes | **Cook time:** 0 minutes | **Serves:**1

Ingredients:

1 cup unsweetened almond milk, plus additional as needed
¼ cup frozen blueberries
2 tablespoons unsweetened almond butter
1 tablespoon extra-virgin olive oil
1 tablespoon ground flaxseed or chia seeds
1 to 2 teaspoons maple syrup
½ teaspoon vanilla extract
¼ teaspoon ground cinnamon

Directions:

Blend all the ingredients in a blender until smooth and creamy.

You can add additional almond milk to reach your preferred consistency as needed. Serve immediately.

Per Serving
calories: 459 | fat: 40.1g | protein: 8.9g | carbs: 20.0g

Cauliflower Breakfast Porridge

Prep time: 5 minutes | **Cook time:** 5 minutes | **Serves:**2

Ingredients:

2 cups riced cauliflower
¾ cup unsweetened almond milk
4 tablespoons extra-virgin olive oil, divided
2 teaspoons grated fresh orange peel (from ½ orange)
½ teaspoon almond extract or vanilla extract
½ teaspoon ground cinnamon
⅛ teaspoon salt
4 tablespoons chopped walnuts, divided
1 to 2 teaspoons maple syrup (optional)

Directions:

Place the riced cauliflower, almond milk, 2 tablespoons of olive oil, orange peel, almond extract, cinnamon, and salt in a medium saucepan. Stir to incorporate and bring the mixture to a boil over medium-high heat, stirring.

Remove from the heat and add 2 tablespoons of chopped walnuts and maple syrup (if desired).Stir again and divide the porridge into bowls. Sprinkle each bowl evenly with remaining 2 tablespoons of walnuts and olive oil.

Per Serving calories: 381 | fat: 37.8g | protein: 5.2g | carbs: 10.9g

Blackberry-Yogurt Green Smoothie

Prep time: 5 minutes | **Cook time:** 0 minutes | **Serves:**2

Ingredients:

1 cup plain Greek yogurt
1 cup baby spinach
½ cup frozen blackberries
¼ cup chopped pecans
½ cup unsweetened almond milk
½ teaspoon peeled and grated fresh ginger

Directions:

Process the yogurt, baby spinach, blackberries, almond milk, and ginger in a food processor until smoothly blended.

Divide the mixture into two bowls and serve topped with the chopped pecans.

Per Serving

calories: 201 | fat: 14.5g | protein: 7.1g | carbs: 14.9g

Buckwheat Porridge

Prep time: 5 minutes | **Cook time:** 40 minutes | **Serves:**4

Ingredients:

3 cups water
2 cups raw buckwheat groats
Pinch sea salt
1 cup unsweetened almond milk

Directions:

In a medium saucepan, add the water, buckwheat groats, and sea salt and bring to a boil over medium-high heat.

Once it starts to boil, reduce the heat to low. Cook for about 20 minutes, stirring occasionally, or until most of the water is absorbed.

Fold in the almond milk and whisk well. Continue cooking for about 15 minutes, or until the buckwheat groats are very softened. Ladle the porridge into bowls and serve warm.

Per Serving calories: 121 | fat: 1.0g | protein: 6.3g | carbs: 21.5g

Healthy Chia Pudding

Prep time: 5 minutes | **Cook time:** 0 minutes | **Serves:**4

Ingredients:

4 cups unsweetened almond milk
¾ cup chia seeds
1 teaspoon ground cinnamon
Pinch sea salt

Directions:

In a medium bowl, whisk together the almond milk, chia seeds, cinnamon, and sea salt until well incorporated.

Cover and transfer to the refrigerator to thicken for about 1 hour, or until a pudding-like texture is achieved.

Serve chilled.

Per Serving calories: 236 | fat: 9.8g | protein: 13.1g | carbs: 24.8g

Creamy Vanilla Oatmeal

Prep time: 5 minutes | **Cook time:** 40 minutes | **Serves:**4

Ingredients:

4 cups water
Pinch sea salt
1 cup steel-cut oats
¾ cup unsweetened almond milk
2 teaspoons pure vanilla extract

Directions:

Add the water and salt to a large saucepan over high heat and bring to a boil.

Once boiling, reduce the heat to low and add the oats. Mix well and cook for 30 minutes, stirring occasionally.

Fold in the almond milk and vanilla and whisk to combine. Continue cooking for about 10 minutes, or until the oats are thick and creamy.

Ladle the oatmeal into bowls and serve warm.

Per Serving calories: 117 | fat: 2.2g | protein: 4.3g | carbs: 20.0g

Cheesy Broccoli and Mushroom Egg Casserole

Prep time: 10 minutes | **Cook time:** 40 minutes | **Serves:**4

Ingredients:

2 tablespoons extra-virgin olive oil
½ sweet onion, chopped
1 teaspoon minced garlic
1 cup sliced button mushrooms
1 cup chopped broccoli
8 large eggs
¼ cup unsweetened almond milk
1 tablespoon chopped fresh basil
1 cup shredded Cheddar cheese
Sea salt and freshly ground black pepper, to taste

Directions:

Preheat the oven to 375°F (190°C).

Heat the olive oil in a large ovenproof skillet over medium-high heat.

Add the onion, garlic, and mushrooms to the skillet and sauté for about 5 minutes, stirring occasionally.

Stir in the broccoli and sauté for 5 minutes until the vegetables start to soften.

Meanwhile, beat the eggs with the almond milk and basil in a small bowl until well mixed.

Remove the skillet from the heat and pour the egg mixture over the top. Scatter the Cheddar cheese all over.

Bake uncovered in the preheated oven for about 30 minutes, or until the top of the casserole is golden brown and a fork inserted in the center comes out clean.

Remove from the oven and sprinkle with the sea salt and pepper. Serve hot.

Per Serving

calories: 326 | fat: 27.2g | protein: 14.1g | carbs: 6.7g

Baked Ricotta with Honey Pears

Prep time: 5 minutes | **Cook time:** 22 to 25 minutes | **Serves:** 4

Ingredients:

1 (1-pound / 454-g) container whole-milk ricotta cheese
2 large eggs
¼ cup whole-wheat pastry flour
1 teaspoon vanilla extract
¼ teaspoon ground nutmeg
1 pear, cored and diced
2 tablespoons water
1 tablespoon honey
Nonstick cooking spray
1 tablespoon sugar

Directions:

Preheat the oven to 400°F (205°C). Spray four ramekins with nonstick cooking spray.

Beat together the ricotta, eggs, flour, sugar, vanilla, and nutmeg in a large bowl until combined. Spoon the mixture into the ramekins. Bake in the preheated oven for 22 to 25 minutes, or until the ricotta is just set.

Meanwhile, in a small saucepan over medium heat, simmer the pear in the water for 10 minutes, or until slightly softened. Remove from the heat, and stir in the honey.

Remove the ramekins from the oven and cool slightly on a wire rack. Top the ricotta ramekins with the pear and serve.

Per Serving calories: 329 | fat: 19.0g | protein: 17.0g | carbs: 23.0g

Cinnamon Pistachio Smoothie

Prep time: 5 minutes | **Cook time:** 0 minutes | **Serves:** 1

Ingredients:

½ cup unsweetened almond milk, plus more as needed
½ cup plain Greek yogurt
Zest and juice of ½ orange
1 tablespoon extra-virgin olive oil
1 tablespoon shelled pistachios, coarsely chopped
¼ to ½ teaspoon ground allspice
¼ teaspoon vanilla extract
¼ teaspoon ground cinnamon

Directions:

In a blender, combine ½ cup almond milk, yogurt, orange zest and juice, olive oil, pistachios, allspice, vanilla, and cinnamon. Blend until smooth and creamy, adding more almond milk to achieve your desired consistency.

Serve chilled.

Per Serving calories: 264 | fat: 22.0g | protein: 6.0g | carbs: 12.0g

Breakfast Pancakes with Berry Sauce

Prep time: 5 minutes | **Cook time:** 10 minutes | **Serves:** 4

Ingredients:

Pancakes:
1 cup almond flour
1 teaspoon baking powder
¼ teaspoon salt
6 tablespoon extra-virgin olive oil, divided
2 large eggs, beaten
Zest and juice of 1 lemon
½ teaspoon vanilla extract
Berry Sauce:
1 cup frozen mixed berries
1 tablespoon water, plus more as needed
½ teaspoon vanilla extract

Directions:

Make the Pancakes

In a large bowl, combine the almond flour, baking powder, and salt and stir to break up any clumps.

Add 4 tablespoons olive oil, beaten eggs, lemon zest and juice, and vanilla extract and stir until well mixed.

Heat 1 tablespoon of olive oil in a large skillet. Spoon about 2 tablespoons of batter for each pancake. Cook until bubbles begin to form, 4 to 5 minutes. Flip and cook for another 2 to 3 minutes. Repeat with the remaining 1 tablespoon of olive oil and batter.

Make the Berry Sauce

Combine the frozen berries, water, and vanilla extract in a small saucepan and heat over medium-high heat for 3 to 4 minutes until bubbly, adding more water as needed. Using the back of a spoon or fork, mash the berries and whisk until smooth. Serve the pancakes with the berry sauce.

Per Serving calories: 275 | fat: 26.0g | protein: 4.0g | carbs: 8.0g

Banana Corn Fritters

Prep time: 5 minutes | **Cook time:** 10 minutes | **Serves:** 2

Ingredients:

½ cup yellow cornmeal
¼ cup flour
2 small ripe bananas, peeled and mashed
2 tablespoons unsweetened almond milk
1 large egg, beaten
½ teaspoon baking powder
¼ to ½ teaspoon ground chipotle chili
¼ teaspoon ground cinnamon
¼ teaspoon sea salt
1 tablespoon olive oil

Directions:

Stir together all ingredients except for the olive oil in a large bowl until smooth.

Heat a nonstick skillet over medium-high heat. Add the olive oil and drop about 2 tablespoons of batter for each fritter. Cook for 2 to 3 minutes until the bottoms are golden brown, then flip. Continue cooking for 1 to 2 minutes more, until cooked through. Repeat with the remaining batter. Serve warm.

Per Serving calories: 396 | fat: 10.6g | protein: 7.3g | carbs: 68.0g

Quinoa Breakfast Bowls

Prep time: 5 minutes | **Cook time:** 17 minutes | **Serves:** 1

Ingredients:

¼ cup quinoa, rinsed
¾ cup water, plus additional as needed
1 carrot, grated

½ small broccoli head, finely chopped
¼ teaspoon salt
1 tablespoon chopped fresh dill

Directions:

Add the quinoa and water to a small pot over high heat and bring to a boil. Once boiling, reduce the heat to low. Cover and cook for 5 minutes, stirring occasionally.

Stir in the carrot, broccoli, and salt and continue cooking for 1o to 12 minutes, or until the quinoa is cooked though and the vegetables are fork- tender. If the mixture gets too thick, you can add additional water as needed.

Add the dill and serve warm.

Per Serving calories: 219 | fat: 2.9g | protein: 10.0g | carbs: 40.8g

Warm Bulgur Breakfast Bowls with Fruits

Prep time: 5 minutes | **Cook time:** 15 minutes | **Serves:** 6

Ingredients:

2 cups unsweetened almond milk
1½ cups uncooked bulgur
1 cup water
½ teaspoon ground cinnamon

2 cups frozen (or fresh, pitted) dark sweet cherries
8 dried (or fresh) figs, chopped
½ cup chopped almonds
¼ cup loosely packed fresh mint, chopped

Directions:

Combine the milk, bulgur, water, and cinnamon in a medium saucepan, stirring, and bring just to a boil.

Cover, reduce the heat to medium-low, and allow to simmer for 10 minutes, or until the liquid is absorbed.

Turn off the heat, but keep the pan on the stove, and stir in the frozen cherries (no need to thaw), figs, and almonds. Cover and let the hot bulgur thaw the cherries and partially hydrate the figs, about 1 minute.

Fold in the mint and stir to combine, then serve.

Per Serving
calories: 207 | fat: 6.0g | protein: 8.0g | carbs: 32.0g

Spinach Cheese Pie

Prep time: 5 minutes | **Cook time:** 25 minutes | **Serves:** 8

Ingredients:

2 tablespoons extra-virgin olive oil
1 onion, chopped
1 pound (454 g) frozen spinach, thawed
¼ teaspoon ground nutmeg
¼ teaspoon garlic salt
¼ teaspoon freshly ground black pepper

4 large eggs, divided
1 cup grated Parmesan cheese, divided
2 puff pastry doughs, at room temperature
4 hard-boiled eggs, halved
Nonstick cooking spray

Directions:

Preheat the oven to 350°F (180°C). Spritz a baking sheet with nonstick cooking spray and set aside.

Heat a large skillet over medium-high heat. Add the olive oil and onion and sauté for about 5 minutes, stirring occasionally, or until translucent. Squeeze the excess water from the spinach, then add to the skillet and cook, uncovered, so that any excess water from the spinach can evaporate.

Season with the nutmeg, garlic salt, and black pepper. Remove from heat and set aside to cool.

Beat 3 eggs in a small bowl. Add the beaten eggs and ½ cup of Parmesan cheese to the spinach mixture, stirring well. Roll out the pastry dough on the prepared baking sheet. Layer the spinach mixture on top of the dough, leaving 2 inches around each edge.

Once the spinach is spread onto the pastry dough, evenly place the hard-boiled egg halves throughout the pie, then cover with the second pastry dough. Pinch the edges closed. Beat the remaining 1 egg in the bowl. Brush the egg wash over the pastry dough. Bake in the preheated oven for 15 to 20 minutes until golden brown. Sprinkle with the remaining ½ cup of Parmesan cheese. Cool for 5 minutes before cutting and serving.

Per Serving
calories: 417 | fat: 28.0g | protein: 17.0g | carbs: 25.0g

Avocado Smoothie

Prep time: 2 minutes | **Cook time:** 0 minutes | **Serves:** 2

Ingredients:

1 large avocado
1½ cups unsweetened coconut milk

2 tablespoons honey

Directions:

Place all ingredients in a blender and blend until smooth and creamy.

Serve immediately.

Per Serving
calories: 686 | fat: 57.6g | protein: 6.2g | carbs: 35.8g

Café Cooler (Italian)

Preparation Time: 16 minutes **Cooking Time:** 0 minute
Servings: 4

Ingredients:

Ice cubes as needed
½ tsp. pure vanilla extract
2 cups low-fat milk

½ tsp. ground cinnamon
1 cup espresso, cooled to
room temperature
4 tsps. sugar (optional)

Directions:

Fill 4 tall glasses with ice cubes.

In a blender, combine the milk, cinnamon, and vanilla and blend until frothy.

Pour the milk over the ice cubes and top each drink with one-quarter of the espresso. If using sugar, stir it into the espresso until it has dissolved.

Serve immediately, with a chilled teaspoon for stirring.

Per Serving

Calories: 93 Fat: 7 g. Protein: 1 g.

Egg Breakfast Sandwich with Roasted Tomatoes(Greek)

Prep time: 5 minutes **Cooking Time:** 15 minutes
Servings: 1

Ingredients:

Olive oil: 1 tsp. Pesto: 1
tbsp.
Salt & black pepper, to taste
Provolone cheese: 1 to 2
slices 1 whole ciabatta roll

Egg whites: 1/4 cup
Roasted tomatoes: half cup
Chopped fresh herbs: 1 tsp.

Directions:

In a skillet, add oil on medium flame. Add egg whites and salt, pepper.

Sprinkle fresh herbs on top. Cook for 3 to 4 minutes.

Flip only once and toast the ciabatta bread. Spread pesto on both sides and place egg whites on top with cheese.

Add roasted tomatoes on top, sprinkle salt and pepper.

Serve right away.

Per Serving

458 Cal | 24 g Fat | 51 g Carbs | 21 g Protein

Greek Omelet Casserole (Greek)

Prep time: 10 minutes **Cooking Time:** 35-40 mins **Servings:** 12

Ingredients:

12 eggs
Whole milk: 2 cups
Lemon pepper: 1 tsp.
Artichoke with olives,
peppers, chopped without
liquid Tomato (sun dried)
feta cheese: ¾ cup,
crumbled Olive oil: 4 tsp.

Fresh spinach: 1 ½ cups
2 minced garlic cloves Dried
oregano: 1 tsp.
Fresh chopped dill: 1 tbsp.
Salt: 1 tsp.

Directions:

Let the oven preheat to 350 F.

In a skillet, add oil (1 tbsp.), add garlic and spinach, sauté for three minutes.

Take a baking dish (9 by 13") and oil spray it.

Spread the spinach mixture on the bottom evenly.

In a bowl, whisk eggs with the rest of the except for feta cheese.

Pour the mixture over spinach mixture, and spread feta cheese on top.

Bake for 35 to 40 minutes until set.

Per Serving

186 Cal | 13 g Fat | 5 g Carbs | 10 g Protein

Spinach & Goat Cheese Egg Muffins (Greek)

Preparation Time: 10 minutes **Cooking Time:** 35 minutes
Servings: 12

Ingredients:

Olive oil: 1 tbsp. Milk: half
cup
Fresh goat cheese: 1/4 cup,
crumbled
Baby spinach: 1 5-oz.,
chopped

1 red pepper, sliced into ¼"
pieces
2 scallions, diced
Salt & black pepper, to taste
6 eggs

Directions:

Let the oven preheat to 350 F. oil spray a 12-cup muffin tin.

2. In a skillet, add oil on medium flame. Add red pepper, spinach and season with salt and pepper cook for 6-8 minutes.

Turn off the heat and add in scallions.

In a bowl, whisk eggs with salt, pepper and milk. Add spinach mixture and mix.

Pour this mixture into the muffin cups and add goat cheese on top.

Bake for 20-25 minutes until eggs are set.

Cool for five minutes and serve right away

Per Serving

65 Cal | 4.5 g Fat | 2 g Carbs | 4 g Protein

Spinach Feta Breakfast Wraps (Italian)

Preparation Time: 5 minutes **Cooking Time:** 10 minutes
Servings: 4

Ingredients:

Baby spinach: 5 cups	1 cup cherry tomatoes,
4 ounces feta cheese,	halved
crumbled	10 eggs
4 whole-wheat tortillas	Salt & black pepper, to taste

Directions:

In a bowl, whisk eggs well.

Place a skillet on medium flame, spray the pan with oil.

Add eggs and stir occasionally until cooked.

Add black pepper and salt, take out on a plate.

Oil spray the pan again and sauté spinach until wilted. Take out on a plate.

Place tortilla on a surface, add eggs, feta and spinach. Wrap it tightly.

Serve right away.

Per Serving

521 Cal | 27 g Fat | 45 g Carbs | 28.1 g Protein

Pepperoni Eggs (Italian)

Prep time: 10 minutes **Cooking Time:** 20 minutes
Servings: 2

Ingredients:

1 cup of egg substitute	1 egg
3 green onions	minced meat diced
8 slices of pepperoni	1/2 teaspoon of garlic
1 pinch of salt and ground	powder
black pepper to taste	1/4 cup grated Romano
1 teaspoon melted butter	cheese

Directions:

Combine the egg substitute, the egg, the green onions, the pepperoni slices, and the garlic powder in a bowl.

Heat the butter in a non-stick frying pan over low heat; Add the egg mixture, cover the pan and cook until the eggs are set, 10 to 15 minutes. Sprinkle Romano's eggs and season with salt and pepper.

Per Serving

266 calories16.2 g fat 3.7 grams of carbohydrates 25

Low Carb Bagels (Italian)

Preparation Time: 10 minutes **Cooking Time:** 20 minutes
Servings: 4

Ingredients:

1 cups almond flour	2 tbsps. bagel seasoning
3 eggs.	1 tbsp. powder for baking
3 cups mozzarella cheese,	¼ cup cream cheese.
shredded.	

Directions:

Heat your oven in advance at 400 ° c.

Get 2 baking sheets and line them well with paper made from parchment.

Get a large mixing container and in it, mix the almond flour with the powder for baking.

Mix the mozzarella cheese and the cream cheese in a bowl that can be used in a microwave. Place the bowl in a microwave for 2 minutes when the cheese melts and combines.

Get the mixture of cheese from the bowl once out of the microwave and pour it into the mixing container with the flour from almonds and the powder for baking. Mix all the until well mixed.

Take the dough when done and divide it into eight parts that are equal in measure. Using your palms, take each of the eight dough parts and roll them into balls.

Using your fingers, create a hole in each of the balls, and gently stretch the dough to form the shape of a bagel.

Take one egg and beat it in a bowl. Brush the eggs on top of each made bagel following this by sprinkling the bagel seasoning at the top as well.

Place the bagel dough in the oven on its rack, which is in the middle for 25 minutes when they are nice and golden in color.

Remove the bagels from the oven and let them get cold for about 10 minutes before serving them.

Per Serving

Calories: 275 g. Fat: 20 g. Carbs: 8 g. Protein: 20 g.

Chapter 3
Sides Recipes, Salads Recipes, and Soups Recipes

Sumptuous Greek Vegetable Salad

Prep time: 20 minutes | **Cook time:** 0 minutes | **Serves:**6

Ingredients:

Salad:
1 (15-ounce / 425-g) can chickpeas, drained and rinsed
1 (14-ounce / 397-g) can artichoke hearts, drained and halved
1 head Bibb lettuce, chopped (about 2½ cups)
1 cucumber, peeled deseeded, and chopped (about 1½ cups)
1½ cups grape tomatoes, halved
½ cup sliced black olives
½ cup cubed feta cheese

Dressing:
1 tablespoon freshly squeezed lemon juice (from about ½ small lemon)
¼ teaspoon freshly ground black pepper
1 tablespoon chopped fresh oregano
2 tablespoons extra-virgin olive oil
1 tablespoon red wine vinegar
1 teaspoon honey
¼ cup chopped basil leaves

Directions:

Combine the ingredients for the salad in a large salad bowl, then toss to combine well.

Combine the ingredients for the dressing in a small bowl, then stir to mix well. Dress the salad and serve immediately.

Per Serving
calories: 165 | fat: 8.1g | protein: 7.2g | carbs: 17.9g

Brussels Sprout and Apple Slaw

Prep time: 15 minutes | **Cook time:** 0 minutes | **Serves:**4

Ingredients:

Salad:
1 pound (454 g) Brussels sprouts, stem ends removed and sliced thinly
1 apple, cored and sliced thinly
½ red onion, sliced thinly
Dressing:
1 teaspoon Dijon mustard
2 teaspoons apple cider vinegar
1 tablespoon raw honey
1 cup plain coconut yogurt
1 teaspoon sea salt
For Garnish:
½ cup pomegranate seeds
½ cup chopped toasted hazelnuts

Directions:

Combine the ingredients for the salad in a large salad bowl, then toss to combine well.

Combine the ingredients for the dressing in a small bowl, then stir to mix well. Dress the salad let sit for 10 minutes.

Serve with pomegranate seeds and toasted hazelnuts on top.

Per Serving
calories: 248 | fat: 11.2g | protein: 12.7g | carbs: 29.9g

Butternut Squash and Cauliflower Soup

Prep time: 15 minutes | **Cook time:** 4 hours | **Serves:**4 to 6

Ingredients:

1 pound (454 g) butternut squash, peeled and cut into 1-inch cubes
1 small head cauliflower, cut into 1-inch pieces
1 onion, sliced
2 cups unsweetened coconut milk
1 tablespoon curry powder
½ cup no-added-sugar apple juice
4 cups low-sodium vegetable soup
2 tablespoons coconut oil
1 teaspoon sea salt
¼ teaspoon freshly ground white pepper
¼ cup chopped fresh cilantro, divided

Directions:

Combine all the ingredients, except for the cilantro, in the slow cooker. Stir to mix well.

Cook on high heat for 4 hours or until the vegetables are tender.

Pour the soup in a food processor, then pulse until creamy and smooth.

Pour the puréed soup in a large serving bowl and garnish with cilantro before serving.

Per Serving
calories: 415 | fat: 30.8g | protein: 10.1g | carbs: 29.9g

Cherry, Plum, Artichoke, and Cheese Board

Prep time: 15 minutes | **Cook time:** 0 minutes | **Serves:**4

Ingredients:

2 cups rinsed cherries
2 cups rinsed and sliced plums
2 cups rinsed carrots, cut into sticks
1 cup canned low-sodium artichoke hearts, rinsed and drained
1 cup cubed feta cheese

Directions:

Arrange all the ingredients in separated portions on a clean board or a large tray, then serve with spoons, knife, and forks.

Per Serving
calories: 417 | fat: 13.8g | protein: 20.1g | carbs: 56.2g

Pumpkin Soup with Crispy Sage Leaves

Prep time: 15 minutes | **Cook time:** 10 minutes | **Serves:**4

Ingredients:

1 tablespoon olive oil

2 garlic cloves, cut into ⅛-inch-thick slices

1 onion, chopped

2 cups freshly puréed pumpkin

4 cups low-sodium vegetable soup

2 teaspoons chipotle powder

1 teaspoon sea salt

½ teaspoon freshly ground black pepper

½ cup vegetable oil

12 sage leaves, stemmed

Directions:

Heat the olive oil in a stockpot over high heat until shimmering.

Add the garlic and onion, then sauté for 5 minutes or until the onion is translucent.

Pour in the puréed pumpkin and vegetable soup in the pot, then sprinkle with chipotle powder, salt, and ground black pepper. Stir to mix well.

Bring to a boil. Reduce the heat to low and simmer for 5 minutes.

Meanwhile, heat the vegetable oil in a nonstick skillet over high heat.

Add the sage leaf to the skillet and sauté for a minute or until crispy. Transfer the sage on paper towels to soak the excess oil.

Gently pour the soup in three serving bowls, then divide the crispy sage leaves in bowls for garnish. Serve immediately.

Per Serving

calories: 380 | fat: 20.1g | protein: 8.9g | carbs: 45.2g

Arugula and Fig Salad

Prep time: 15 minutes | **Cook time:** 0 minutes | **Serves:**2

Ingredients:

3 cups arugula

4 fresh, ripe figs (or 4 to 6 dried figs), stemmed and sliced

2 tablespoons olive oil

¼ cup lightly toasted pecan halves

2 tablespoons crumbled blue cheese

1 to 2 tablespoons balsamic glaze

Directions:

Toss the arugula and figs with the olive oil in a large bowl until evenly coated. Add the pecans and blue cheese to the bowl. Toss the salad lightly.

Drizzle with the balsamic glaze and serve immediately.

Per Serving calories: 517 | fat: 36.2g | protein: 18.9g | carbs: 30.2g

Mushroom Barley Soup

Prep time: 5 minutes | **Cook time:** 20 to 23 minutes **Serves:**6

Ingredients:

2 tablespoons extra-virgin olive oil

1 cup chopped carrots

1 cup chopped onion

5½ cups chopped mushrooms

6 cups no-salt-added vegetable broth

1 cup uncooked pearled barley

¼ cup red wine

2 tablespoons tomato paste

4 sprigs fresh thyme or ½ teaspoon dried thyme

1 dried bay leaf

6 tablespoons grated Parmesan cheese

Directions:

In a large stockpot over medium heat, heat the oil. Add the onion and carrots and cook for 5 minutes, stirring frequently. Turn up the heat to medium-high and add the mushrooms. Cook for 3 minutes, stirring frequently.

Add the broth, barley, wine, tomato paste, thyme, and bay leaf. Stir, cover, and bring the soup to a boil. Once it's boiling, stir a few times, reduce the heat to medium-low, cover, and cook for another 12 to 15 minutes, until the barley is cooked through.

Remove the bay leaf and serve the soup in bowls with 1 tablespoon of cheese sprinkled on top of each.

Per Serving

calories: 195 | fat: 4.0g | protein: 7.0g | carbs: 34.0g

Parmesan Roasted Red Potatoes

Prep time: 10 minutes | **Cook time:** 55 minutes | **Serves:**2

Ingredients:

12 ounces (340 g) red potatoes (3 to 4 small potatoes), scrubbed and diced into 1-inch pieces

1 tablespoon olive oil

½ teaspoon garlic powder

¼ teaspoon salt

1 tablespoon grated Parmesan cheese

1 teaspoon minced fresh rosemary (from 1 sprig)

Directions:

Preheat the oven to 425ºF (220ºC). Line a baking sheet with parchment paper. In a mixing bowl, combine the potatoes, olive oil, garlic powder, and salt. Toss well to coat. Lay the potatoes on the parchment paper and roast for 10 minutes. Flip the potatoes over and roast for another 10 minutes. Check the potatoes to make sure they are golden brown on the top and bottom. Toss them again, turn the heat down to 350ºF (180ºC), and roast for 30 minutes more. When the potatoes are golden brown, scatter the Parmesan cheese over them and toss again. Return to the oven for 3 minutes to melt the cheese.

Remove from the oven and sprinkle with the fresh rosemary before serving.

Per Serving calories: 200 fat: 8.2g protein: 5.1g | carbs: 30.0g

Rich Chicken and Small Pasta Broth

Prep time: 10 minutes | **Cook time:** 4 hours | **Serves:**6

6 boneless, skinless chicken thighs
4 stalks celery, cut into ½-inch pieces
4 carrots, cut into 1-inch pieces
1 medium yellow onion, halved
2 garlic cloves, minced
2 bay leaves
Sea salt and freshly ground black pepper, to taste
6 cups low-sodium chicken stock
½ cup stelline pasta
¼ cup chopped fresh flat-leaf parsley

Directions:

Combine the chicken thighs, celery, carrots, onion, and garlic in the slow cooker. Spread with bay leaves and sprinkle with salt and pepper. Toss to mix well.

Pour in the chicken stock. Put the lid on and cook on high for 4 hours or until the internal temperature of chicken reaches at least 165°F (74°C).

In the last 20 minutes of the cooking, remove the chicken from the slow cooker and transfer to a bowl to cool until ready to reserve.

Discard the bay leaves and add the pasta to the slow cooker. Put the lid on and cook for 15 minutes or until al dente. Meanwhile, slice the chicken, then put the chicken and parsley in the slow cooker and cook for 5 minutes or until well combined. Pour the soup in a large bowl and serve immediately.

Per Serving calories: 285 | fat: 10.8g | protein: 27.4g | carbs: 18.8g

Orange-Honey Glazed Carrots

Prep time: 10 minutes | **Cook time:** 15 to 20 minutes
Serves:2

Ingredients:

½ pound (227 g) rainbow carrots, peeled
2 tablespoons fresh orange juice
1 tablespoon honey
½ teaspoon coriander
Pinch salt

Directions:

Preheat the oven to 400°F (205°C).

Cut the carrots lengthwise into slices of even thickness and place in a large bowl. Stir together the orange juice, honey, coriander, and salt in a small bowl. Pour the orange juice mixture over the carrots and toss until well coated.

Spread the carrots in a baking dish in a single layer. Roast for 15 to 20 minutes until fork-tender.

Let cool for 5 minutes before serving.

Per Serving
calories: 85 | fat: 0g | protein: 1.0g | carbs: 21.0g

Roasted Root Vegetable Soup

Prep time: 10 minutes | **Cook time:** 35 minutes | **Serves:**6

Ingredients:

2 parsnips, peeled and sliced
2 carrots, peeled and sliced
2 sweet potatoes, peeled and sliced
1 teaspoon chopped fresh rosemary
1 teaspoon chopped fresh thyme
1 teaspoon sea salt
½ teaspoon freshly ground black pepper
2 tablespoons extra-virgin olive oil
4 cups low-sodium vegetable soup
½ cup grated Parmesan cheese, for garnish (optional)

Directions:

Preheat the oven to 400°F (205°C). Line a baking sheet with aluminum foil.

Combine the parsnips, carrots, and sweet potatoes in a large bowl, then sprinkle with rosemary, thyme, salt, and pepper, and drizzle with olive oil. Toss to coat the vegetables well.

Arrange the vegetables on the baking sheet, then roast in the preheated oven for 30 minutes or until lightly browned and soft. Flip the vegetables halfway through the roasting.

Pour the roasted vegetables with vegetable broth in a food processor, then pulse until creamy and smooth.

Pour the puréed vegetables in a saucepan, then warm over low heat until heated through. Spoon the soup in a large serving bowl, then scatter with Parmesan cheese. Serve immediately.

Per Serving calories: 192 | fat: 5.7g | protein: 4.8g | carbs: 31.5g

Lemon-Tahini Hummus

Prep time: 15 minutes | **Cook time:** 0 minutes | **Serves:**6

1 (15-ounce / 425-g) can chickpeas, drained and rinsed
4 tablespoons extra-virgin olive oil, divided
2 lemons, juiced
1 lemon, zested, divided
1 tablespoon minced garlic
Pinch salt
4 to 5 tablespoons tahini (sesame seed paste)

Directions:

In a food processor, combine the chickpeas, 2 tablespoons of olive oil, tahini, lemon juice, half of the lemon zest, and garlic and pulse for up to 1 minute, scraping down the sides of the food processor bowl as necessary.

Taste and add salt as needed. Feel free to add 1 teaspoon of water at a time to thin the hummus to a better consistency. Transfer the hummus to a serving bowl. Serve drizzled with the remaining 2 tablespoons of olive oil and remaining half of the lemon zest.

Per Serving calories: 216 | fat: 15.0g | protein: 5.0g | carbs: 17.0g

Rosemary Red Quinoa (Greek)

Preparation Time: 10 minutes **Cooking Time:** 25 minutes
Servings: 6

Ingredients:

4 cups chicken stock
2 tablespoons olive oil
1 teaspoon lemon zest, grated
2 tablespoons lemon juice
1 red onion, chopped

2 cups red quinoa, rinsed
1 tablespoon garlic, minced
Salt and black pepper to the taste
2 tablespoons rosemary, chopped

Directions:

Heat up a pan with the oil over medium heat, add the onion and the garlic and sauté for 5 minutes.

Add the quinoa, the stock and the rest of the , bring to a simmer and cook for 20 minutes stirring from time to time.

Divide the mix between plates and serve.

Per Serving
calories 193, fat 7.9, carbs 5.4, protein 1.3

Olives and Carrots Sauté (Greek)

Preparation Time: 10 minutes **Cooking Time:** 20 minutes
Servings: 4

Ingredients:

1 tablespoon green olives, pitted and sliced
½ teaspoon lemon zest, grated
¼ teaspoon rosemary, dried
Salt and black pepper to the taste
2 pounds carrots, sliced
1 tablespoon parsley, chopped

2 teaspoons capers, drained and chopped
1 and ½ teaspoons balsamic vinegar
¼ cup veggie stock
2 spring onions, chopped
3 tablespoons olive oil

Directions:

Heat up a pan with the oil over medium heat, add the carrots and brown for 5 minutes.

Add green olives, capers and the rest of the except the parsley and the chives, stir and cook over medium heat for 15 minutes.

Add the chives and parsley, toss, divide the mix between plates and serve as a side dish.

Per Serving
calories 244, fat 11, carbs 5.6, protein 6.3

Lemon Endives (Greek)

Preparation Time: 10 minutes **Cooking Time:** 35 minutes
Servings: 4

Ingredients:

Juice of 1 and ½ lemons
3 tablespoons olive oil
¼ cup veggie stock

Salt and black pepper to the taste
4 endives, halved lengthwise
1 tablespoon dill, chopped

Directions:

In a roasting pan, combine the endives with the rest of the, introduce in the oven and cook at 375 degrees F for 35 minutes.

Divide the endives between plates and serve as a side dish.

Per Serving
calories 221, fat 5.4, carbs 15.4, protein 14.3

Leeks Sauté (Greek)

Preparation Time: 10 minutes **Cooking Time:** 15 minutes
Servings: 4

Ingredients:

2 pounds leeks, sliced
Salt and black pepper to the taste

2 tablespoons chicken stock
2 tablespoons tomato paste
1 tablespoon olive oil

Directions:

Heat up a pan with the oil over medium heat, add the leeks and brown for 5 minutes.

Add the rest of the toss, increase the heat to medium-high and cook for 10 minutes more. Divide everything between plates and serve as a side dish.

Per Serving
calories 200, fat 11.4, carbs 16.4, protein 3.6

Oregano Potatoes (Spanish)

Preparation Time: 10 minutes **Cooking Time:** 40 minutes
Servings: 4

Ingredients:

6 red potatoes, peeled and cut into wedges
1 teaspoon lemon zest, grated
1 teaspoon oregano, dried

2 tablespoons olive oil ½ cup chicken stock
1 tablespoon chives, chopped
Salt and black pepper to the taste

Directions:

In a roasting pan, combine the potatoes with salt, pepper, the oil and the rest of the except the chives, toss, introduce in the oven and cook at 425 degrees F for 40 minutes.

Divide the mix between plates, sprinkle the chives on top and serve as a side dish.

Per Serving
calories 245, fat 4.5, carbs 7.1, protein 6.4

Cranberry Bulgur Mix (Greek)

Preparation Time: 10 minutes **Cooking Time:** 0 minutes
Servings: 4

Ingredients:

1 1/2 cups hot water 1 cup bulgur	Juice of 1/2 lemon
4 tablespoons cilantro, chopped	1/2 cup red bell peppers
1/2 cup cranberries	1 1/2 teaspoons curry powder
1/2 cup carrots, grated	1/4 cup green onions
	1 tablespoon olive oil

Directions:

Put bulgur into a bowl, add the water, stir, cover, leave aside for 10 minutes, fluff, and transfer to a bowl. Merge the rest of the , toss, and serve cold.

Per Serving
Calories: 300 Fat: 6.4 g Protein: 13 g

Chickpeas Corn and Black Beans Salad

Preparation Time: 10 minutes **Cooking Time:** 0 minutes
Servings: 4

Ingredients:

1 1/2 cups black beans	1/2 teaspoon garlic powder
1 1/2 cups canned chickpeas	1 avocado, pitted, peeled, and chopped
1 cup baby spinach	1 cup corn kernels, chopped
2 tablespoons lemon juice	1 tablespoon apple cider vinegar
1 tablespoon olive oil	
2 teaspoons chili powder	1 teaspoon chives, chopped

Directions:

Mix the black beans with the garlic powder, chili powder, and the rest of the in a bowl, toss and serve cold.

Per Serving
Calories: 300 Fat: 13.4 g Protein: 13 g

Green Beans and Peppers Mix (Greek)

Preparation Time: 10 minutes **Cooking Time:** 10 minutes
Servings: 4

Ingredients:

2 tablespoons olive oil	1 and ½ pounds green beans, trimmed and halved
Salt and black pepper to the taste	
1 tablespoon dill, chopped	
2 red bell peppers, cut into strips	2 tablespoons rosemary, chopped
1 tablespoon lime juice	

Directions:

Heat up a pan with the oil over medium heat, add the bell peppers and the green beans, toss and cook for 5 minutes.

Add the rest of the , toss, cook for 5 minutes more, divide between plates and serve as a side dish.

Per Serving
calories 222, fat 8.6, carbs 8.6, protein 3.4

Garlic Snap Peas Mix (Greek)

Preparation Time: 10 minutes **Cooking Time:** 10 minutes
Servings: 4

Ingredients:

½ cup walnuts, chopped	¼ cup olive oil
1 and ½ teaspoons garlic, minced	½ cup veggie stock
	1 tablespoon chives, chopped
1 pound sugar snap peas	Salt and black pepper to the taste
2 teaspoons lime juice	

Directions:

Heat up a pan with the stock over medium heat, add the snap peas and cook for 5 minutes.

Add the rest of the except the chives, cook for 5 minutes more and divide between plates.

Sprinkle the chives on top and serve as a side dish.

Per Serving
calories 200, fat 7.6, carbs 8.5, protein 4.3

Corn and Olives (Spanish)

Preparation Time: 5 minutes **Cooking Time:** 0 minutes
Servings: 4

Ingredients:

2 cups corn	4 ounces green olives, pitted and halved
2 tablespoons extra virgin olive oil	
	1 teaspoon thyme, chopped
½ teaspoon balsamic vinegar	1 tablespoon oregano, chopped
Salt and black pepper to the taste	

Directions:

In a bowl, combine the corn with the olives and the rest of the , toss and serve as a side dish.

Per Serving
calories 154, fat 10, carbs 17, protein 9.3

Thyme Corn and Cheese Mix (Greek)

Preparation Time: 5 minutes **Cooking Time:** 0 minutes
Servings: 4

Ingredients:

1 tablespoon olive oil	1 teaspoon thyme, chopped
2 cups corn	Salt and black pepper to the taste
1 cup scallions, sliced	
2 tablespoons blue cheese, crumbled	1 tablespoon chives, chopped

Directions:

In a salad bowl, combine the corn with scallions, thyme and the rest of the , toss, divide between plates and serve.

Per Serving
calories 183, fat 5.5, carbs 14.5

Chapter 4
Sandwiches Recipes, Pizzas Recipes, & Wraps Recipes

Falafel Balls with Tahini Sauce

Prep time: 2 hours 20 minutes | **Cook time:** 20 minutes | Serves:4

Ingredients:

Tahini Sauce:
½ cup tahini
2 tablespoons lemon juice
¼ cup finely chopped flat-leaf parsley
2 cloves garlic, minced
½ cup cold water, as needed

Falafel:
1 cup dried chickpeas, soaked overnight, drained
¼ cup chopped flat-leaf parsley
¼ cup chopped cilantro
1 large onion, chopped
1 teaspoon cumin
½ teaspoon chili flakes
4 cloves garlic
1 teaspoon sea salt
5 tablespoons almond flour
1½ teaspoons baking soda, dissolved in 1 teaspoon water
2 cups peanut oil
1 medium bell pepper, chopped
1 medium tomato, chopped
4 whole-wheat pita breads

Directions:

Make the Tahini Sauce

Combine the ingredients for the tahini sauce in a small bowl. Stir to mix well until smooth.

Wrap the bowl in plastic and refrigerate until ready to serve.

Make the Falafel

Put the chickpeas, parsley, cilantro, onion, cumin, chili flakes, garlic, and salt in a food processor. Pulse to mix well but not puréed.

Add the flour and baking soda to the food processor, then pulse to form a smooth and tight dough.

Put the dough in a large bowl and wrap in plastic. Refrigerate for at least 2 hours to let it rise.

Divide and shape the dough into walnut-sized small balls.

Pour the peanut oil in a large pot and heat over high heat until the temperature of the oil reaches 375°F (190°C).

Drop 6 balls into the oil each time, and fry for 5 minutes or until golden brown and crispy. Turn the balls with a strainer to make them fried evenly.

Transfer the balls on paper towels with the strainer, then drain the oil from the balls.

Roast the pita breads in the oven for 5 minutes or until golden brown, if needed, then stuff the pitas with falafel balls and top with bell peppers and tomatoes. Drizzle with tahini sauce and serve immediately.

Per Serving

calories: 574 | fat: 27.1g | protein: 19.8g | carbs: 69.7g

Glazed Mushroom and Vegetable Fajitas

Prep time: 20 minutes | **Cook time:** 20 minutes | Makes 6

Ingredients:

Spicy Glazed Mushrooms:
1 teaspoon olive oil
1 (10- to 12-ounce / 284- to 340-g) package cremini mushrooms, rinsed and drained, cut into thin slices
½ to 1 teaspoon chili powder
Sea salt and freshly ground black pepper, to taste
1 teaspoon maple syrup

Fajitas:
2 teaspoons olive oil
1 onion, chopped
Sea salt, to taste
1 bell pepper, any color, deseeded and sliced into long strips
1 zucchini, cut into large matchsticks
6 whole-grain tortilla
2 carrots, grated
3 to 4 scallions, sliced
½ cup fresh cilantro, finely chopped

Directions:

Make the Spicy Glazed Mushrooms

Heat the olive oil in a nonstick skillet over medium heat until shimmering.

Add the mushrooms and sauté for 10 minutes or until tender.

Sprinkle the mushrooms with chili powder, salt, and ground black pepper. Drizzle with maple syrup. Stir to mix well and cook for 5 to 7 minutes or until the mushrooms are glazed. Set aside until ready to use.

Make the Fajitas

Heat the olive oil in the same skillet over medium heat until shimmering.

Add the onion and sauté for 5 minutes or until translucent. Sprinkle with salt.

Add the bell pepper and zucchini and sauté for 7 minutes or until tender.

Meanwhile, toast the tortilla in the oven for 5 minutes or until golden brown.

Allow the tortilla to cool for a few minutes until they can be handled, then assemble the tortilla with glazed mushrooms, sautéed vegetables and remaining vegetables to make the fajitas. Serve immediately.

Per Serving

calories: 403 | fat: 14.8g | protein: 11.2g | carbs: 7.9g

Ritzy Garden Burgers

Prep time: 1 hour 30 minutes | **Cook time:** 30 minutes
Serves: 6

Ingredients:

1 tablespoon avocado oil
1 yellow onion, diced
½ cup shredded carrots
4 garlic cloves, halved
1 (15 ounces / 425 g) can black beans, rinsed and drained
1 cup gluten-free rolled oats
¼ cup oil-packed sun-dried tomatoes, drained and chopped
½ cup sunflower seeds, toasted
1 teaspoon chili powder
1 teaspoon paprika
½ cup fresh parsley, stems removed

¼ teaspoon ground red pepper flakes
¾ teaspoon sea salt
¼ teaspoon ground black pepper
¼ cup olive oil

For Serving:

6 whole-wheat buns, split in half and toasted
2 ripe avocados, sliced
1 cup kaiware sprouts or mung bean sprouts
1 ripe tomato, sliced
1 teaspoon ground cumin

Directions:

1. Line a baking sheet with parchment paper.

   Heat 1 tablespoon of avocado oil in a nonstick skillet over medium heat.

   Add the onion and carrots and sauté for 10 minutes or until the onion is caramelized.

   Add the garlic and sauté for 30 seconds or until fragrant.

   Transfer them into a food processor, then add the remaining ingredients, except for the olive oil. Pulse until chopped fine and the mixture holds together. Make sure not to purée the mixture.

   Divide and form the mixture into six 4-inch diameter and ½-inch thick patties.

   Arrange the patties on the baking sheet and wrap the sheet in plastic. Put the baking sheet in the refrigerator and freeze for at least an hour until firm.

   Remove the baking sheet from the refrigerator, let them sit under room temperature for 10 minutes.

   Heat the olive oil in a nonstick skillet over medium-high heat until shimmering.

   Fry the patties in the skillet for 15 minutes or until lightly browned and crispy. Flip the patties halfway through the cooking time. You may need to work in batches to avoid overcrowding.

   Assemble the buns with patties, avocados, sprouts, and tomato slices to make the burgers.

Per Serving

calories: 613 | fat: 23.1g | protein: 26.2g | carbs: 88.3g

Alfalfa Sprout and Nut Rolls

Prep time: 40 minutes | **Cook time:** 0 minutes
Makes 16 bite-size pieces

Ingredients:

1 cup alfalfa sprouts
2 tablespoons Brazil nuts
½ cup chopped fresh cilantro
2 tablespoons flaked coconut
1 garlic clove, minced
2 tablespoons ground flaxseeds

Zest and juice of 1 lemon
Pinch cayenne pepper
Sea salt and freshly ground black pepper, to taste
1 tablespoon melted coconut oil
2 tablespoons water
2 whole-grain wraps

Directions:

Combine all ingredients, except for the wraps, in a food processor, then pulse to combine well until smooth.

Unfold the wraps on a clean work surface, then spread the mixture over the wraps.

Roll the wraps up and refrigerate for 30 minutes until set.

Remove the rolls from the refrigerator and slice into 16 bite-sized pieces, if desired, and serve.

Per Serving (1 piece)

calories: 67 | fat: 7.1g | protein: 2.2g | carbs: 2.9g

Roasted Tomato Panini

Prep time: 15 minutes | **Cook time:** 3 hours 6 minutes
Serves: 2

Ingredients:

2 teaspoons olive oil
4 Roma tomatoes, halved
4 cloves garlic
1 tablespoon Italian seasoning

Sea salt and freshly ground pepper, to taste
4 slices whole-grain bread
4 basil leaves
2 slices fresh Mozzarella cheese

Directions:

Preheat the oven to 250ºF (121ºC). Grease a baking pan with olive oil.

Place the tomatoes and garlic in the baking pan, then sprinkle with Italian seasoning, salt, and ground pepper. Toss to coat well.

Roast in the preheated oven for 3 hours or until the tomatoes are lightly wilted.

Preheat the panini press.

Make the panini: Place two slices of bread on a clean work surface, then top them with wilted tomatoes. Sprinkle with basil and spread with Mozzarella cheese. Top them with remaining two slices of bread.

Cook the panini for 6 minutes or until lightly browned and the cheese melts. Flip the panini halfway through the cooking. Serve immediately.

Per Serving

calories: 323 | fat: 12.0g | protein: 17.4g | carbs: 37.5mg

Turkish Eggplant and Tomatoes Pide with Mint

Prep time: 1 day 40 minutes | **Cook time:** 20 minutes
Makes 6 pides

Ingredients:

Dough:
3 cups almond flour
2 teaspoons raw honey
½ teaspoon instant or rapid-rise yeast
1⅓ cups ice water
1 tablespoon extra-virgin olive oil
1½ teaspoons sea salt

Eggplant and Tomato Toppings:
28 ounces (794 g) whole tomatoes, peeled and puréed

5 tablespoons extra-virgin olive oil, divided
1 pound (454 g) eggplant, cut into ½-inch pieces
½ red bell pepper, chopped
Sea salt and ground black pepper, to taste
3 garlic cloves, minced
¼ teaspoon red pepper flakes
½ teaspoon smoked paprika
6 tablespoons minced fresh mint, divided
1½ cups crumbled feta cheese

Directions:

Make the Dough

Combine the flour, yeast, and honey in a food processor, pulse to combine well. Gently add water while pulsing. Let the dough sit for 10 minutes.

Mix the olive oil and salt in the dough and knead the dough until smooth. Wrap in plastic and refrigerate for at least 1 day.

Make the Toppings

Heat 2 tablespoons of olive oil in a nonstick skillet over medium-high heat until shimmering.

Add the bell pepper, eggplant, and ½ teaspoon of salt. Sauté for 6 minutes or until the eggplant is lightly browned.

Add the red pepper flakes, paprika, and garlic. Sauté for 1 minute or until fragrant. Pour in the puréed tomatoes. Bring to a simmer, then cook for 10 minutes or until the mixture is thickened into about 3½ cups. Turn off the heat and mix in 4 tablespoons of mint, salt, and ground black pepper. Set them aside until ready to use.

Make the Turkish Pide

Preheat the oven to 500°F (260°C). Line three baking sheets with parchment papers.

On a clean work surface, divide and shape the dough into six 14 by 5- inch ovals. Transfer the dough to the baking sheets. Brush them with 3 tablespoons of olive oil and spread the eggplant mixture and feta cheese on top.

Bake in the preheated oven for 12 minutes or until golden brown. Rotate the pide halfway through the baking time.

Remove the pide from the oven and spread with remaining mint and serve immediately.

Per Serving (1 pide)
calories: 500 | fat: 22.1g | protein: 8.0g | carbs: 69.7g

Veg Mix and Blackeye Pea Burritos

Prep time: 15 minutes | **Cook time:** 40 minutes
Makes 6 burritos

Ingredients:

1 teaspoon olive oil
1 red onion, diced
2 garlic cloves, minced
1 zucchini, chopped
1 tomato, diced
1 bell pepper, any color, deseeded and diced

1 (14-ounce / 397-g) can blackeye peas
2 teaspoons chili powder
Sea salt, to taste
6 whole-grain tortillas

Directions:

Preheat the oven to 325°F (160°C).

Heat the olive oil in a nonstick skillet over medium heat or until shimmering.

Add the onion and sauté for 5 minutes or until translucent.

Add the garlic and sauté for 30 seconds or until fragrant. Add the zucchini and sauté for 5 minutes or until tender. Add the tomato and bell pepper and sauté for 2 minutes or until soft.

Fold in the black peas and sprinkle them with chili powder and salt. Stir to mix well.

Place the tortillas on a clean work surface, then top them with sautéed vegetables mix.

Fold one ends of tortillas over the vegetable mix, then tuck and roll them into burritos.

Arrange the burritos in a baking dish, seam side down, then pour the juice remains in the skillet over the burritos.

Bake in the preheated oven for 25 minutes or until golden brown. Serve immediately.

Per Serving
calories: 335 | fat: 16.2g | protein: 12.1g | carbs: 8.3g

Za'atar Pizza

Prep time: 10 minutes | **Cook time:** 1o to 12 minutes | **Serves:** 4 to 6

Ingredients:

1 sheet puff pastry
¼ cup extra-virgin olive oil

⅓ cup za'atar seasoning

Directions:

Preheat the oven to 350°F (180°C). Line a baking sheet with parchment paper.

Place the puff pastry on the prepared baking sheet. Cut the pastry into desired slices.

Brush the pastry with the olive oil. Sprinkle with the za'atar seasoning.

Put the pastry in the oven and bake for 10 to 12 minutes, or until edges are lightly browned and puffed up. Serve warm.

Per Serving
calories: 374 | fat: 30.0g | protein: 3.0g | carbs: 20.0g

Salmon Salad Wraps

Prep time: 10 minutes | **Cook time:** 0 minutes | **Serves:** 6

Ingredients:

1 pound (454 g) salmon fillets, cooked and flaked
½ cup diced carrots
½ cup diced celery
3 tablespoons diced red onion
3 tablespoons chopped fresh dill
2 tablespoons capers

1½ tablespoons extra-virgin olive oil
1 tablespoon aged balsamic vinegar
¼ teaspoon kosher or sea salt
½ teaspoon freshly ground black pepper
4 whole-wheat flatbread wraps or soft whole-wheat tortillas

Directions:

In a large bowl, stir together all the ingredients, except for the wraps.

On a clean work surface, lay the wraps. Divide the salmon mixture evenly among the wraps. Fold up the bottom of the wraps, then roll up the wrap. Serve immediately.

Per Serving

calories: 194 | fat: 8.0g | protein: 18.0g | carbs: 13.0g

Samosas in Potatoes

Prep time: 20 minutes | **Cook time:** 30 minutes | **Makes 8**

Ingredients:

4 small potatoes
1 teaspoon coconut oil
1 small onion, finely chopped
1 small piece ginger, minced
2 garlic cloves, minced
2 to 3 teaspoons curry powder

Sea salt and freshly ground black pepper, to taste
¼ cup frozen peas, thawed
2 carrots, grated
¼ cup chopped fresh cilantro

Directions:

Preheat the oven to 350°F (180°C). Poke small holes into potatoes with a fork, then wrap with aluminum foil.

Bake in the preheated oven for 30 minutes until tender.

Meanwhile, heat the coconut oil in a nonstick skillet over medium-high heat until melted. Add the onion and sauté for 5 minutes or until translucent. Add the ginger and garlic to the skillet and sauté for 3 minutes or until fragrant.

Add the curry powder, salt, and ground black pepper, then stir to coat the onion. Remove them from the heat.

When the cooking of potatoes is complete, remove the potatoes from the foil and slice in half.

Hollow to potato halves with a spoon, then combine the potato fresh with sautéed onion, peas, carrots, and cilantro in a large bowl. Stir to mix well.

Spoon the mixture back to the tomato skins and serve immediately.

Per Serving (1 samosa)

calories: 131 | fat: 13.9g | protein: 3.2g | carbs: 8.8g

Eggplant, Spinach, and Feta Sandwiches

Prep time: 10 minutes | **Cook time:** 6 to 8 minutes | **Serves:** 2

Ingredients:

1 medium eggplant, sliced into ½-inch-thick slices
2 tablespoons olive oil
Sea salt and freshly ground pepper, to taste

5 to 6 tablespoons hummus
4 slices whole-wheat bread, toasted
1 cup baby spinach leaves
2 ounces (57 g) feta cheese, softened

Directions:

Preheat the grill to medium-high heat.

Salt both sides of the sliced eggplant, and let sit for 20 minutes to draw out the bitter juices.

Rinse the eggplant and pat dry with a paper towel.

Brush the eggplant slices with olive oil and season with sea salt and freshly ground pepper to taste.

Grill the eggplant until lightly charred on both sides but still slightly firm in the middle, about 3 to 4 minutes per side.

Spread the hummus on the bread slices and top with the spinach leaves, feta cheese, and grilled eggplant. Top with the other slice of bread and serve immediately.

Per Serving

calories: 493 | fat: 25.3g | protein: 17.1g | carbs: 50.9g

Zucchini Hummus Wraps

Prep time: 15 minutes | **Cook time:** 6 minutes | **Serves:** 2

Ingredients:

1 zucchini, ends removed, thinly sliced lengthwise
¼ teaspoon freshly ground black pepper
¼ cup hummus
2 Roma tomatoes, cut lengthwise into slices
2 tablespoons chopped red onion

½ teaspoon dried oregano
¼ teaspoon garlic powder
2 whole wheat tortillas
1 cup chopped kale
½ teaspoon ground cumin

Directions:

In a skillet over medium heat, add the zucchini slices and cook for 3 minutes per side. Sprinkle with the oregano, pepper, and garlic powder and remove from the heat.

Spread 2 tablespoons of hummus on each tortilla. Lay half the zucchini in the center of each tortilla. Top with tomato slices, kale, red onion, and ¼ teaspoon of cumin. Wrap tightly and serve.

Per Serving

calories: 248 | fat: 8.1g | protein: 9.1g | carbs: 37.1g

Baked Parmesan Chicken Wraps

Prep time: 10 minutes | **Cook time:** 18 minutes | **Serves:**6

Ingredients:

1 pound (454 g) boneless, skinless chicken breasts
1 large egg
¼ cup unsweetened almond milk
⅔ cup whole-wheat bread crumbs
½ cup grated Parmesan cheese
¾ teaspoon garlic powder, divided
1 cup canned low-sodium or no-salt-added crushed tomatoes
1 teaspoon dried oregano
6 (8-inch) whole-wheat tortillas, or whole-grain spinach wraps
1 cup fresh Mozzarella cheese, sliced
1½ cups loosely packed fresh flat-leaf (Italian) parsley, chopped
Cooking spray

Directions:

1. Preheat the oven to 425ºF (220ºC). Line a large, rimmed baking sheet with aluminum foil. Place a wire rack on the aluminum foil, and spritz the rack with nonstick cooking spray. Set aside.
2. Place the chicken breasts into a large plastic bag. With a rolling pin, pound the chicken so it is evenly flattened, about ¼ inch thick. Slice the chicken into six portions.
3. In a bowl, whisk together the egg and milk. In another bowl, stir together the bread crumbs, Parmesan cheese and ½ teaspoon of the garlic powder.
4. Dredge each chicken breast portion into the egg mixture, and then into the Parmesan crumb mixture, pressing the crumbs into the chicken so they stick. Arrange the chicken on the prepared wire rack.
5. Bake in the preheated oven for 15 to 18 minutes, or until the internal temperature of the chicken reads 165ºF (74ºC) on a meat thermometer and any juices run clear.
6. Transfer the chicken to a cutting board, and cut each portion diagonally into ½-inch pieces.
7. In a small, microwave-safe bowl, stir together the tomatoes, oregano, and the remaining ¼ teaspoon of the garlic powder. Cover the bowl with a paper towel and microwave for about 1 minute on high, until very hot. Set aside.
8. Wrap the tortillas in a damp paper towel and microwave for 30 to 45 seconds on high, or until warmed through.
9. Assemble the wraps: Divide the chicken slices evenly among the six tortillas and top with the sliced Mozzarella cheese. Spread 1 tablespoon of the warm tomato sauce over the cheese on each tortilla, and top each with about ¼ cup of the parsley.
10. Wrap the tortilla: Fold up the bottom of the tortilla, then fold one side over and fold the other side over the top.
11. Serve the wraps warm with the remaining sauce for dipping.

Per Serving
calories: 358 | fat: 12.0g | protein: 21.0g | carbs: 41.0g

Grilled Caesar Salad Sandwiches

Prep time: 5 minutes | **Cook time:** 5 minutes | **Serves:**2

Ingredients:

¾ cup olive oil, divided
2 romaine lettuce hearts, left intact
3 to 4 anchovy fillets
Juice of 1 lemon
2 to 3 cloves garlic, peeled
1 teaspoon Dijon mustard
¼ teaspoon Worcestershire sauce
Sea salt and freshly ground pepper, to taste
2 slices whole-wheat bread, toasted
Freshly grated Parmesan cheese, for serving

Directions:

Preheat the grill to medium-high heat and oil the grates.

On a cutting board, drizzle the lettuce with 1 to 2 tablespoons of olive oil and place on the grates.

Grill for 5 minutes, turning until lettuce is slightly charred on all sides. Let lettuce cool enough to handle.

In a food processor, combine the remaining olive oil with the anchovies, lemon juice, garlic, mustard, and Worcestershire sauce.

Pulse the ingredients until you have a smooth emulsion. Season with sea salt and freshly ground pepper to taste. Chop the lettuce in half and place on the bread.

Drizzle with the dressing and serve, sprinkle of Parmesan cheese.

Per Serving
calories: 949 | fat: 85.6g | protein: 12.9g | carbs: 34.1g

Mediterranean Greek Salad Wraps

Prep time: 15 minutes | **Cook time:** 0 minutes | **Serves:**4

Ingredients:

1½ cups seedless cucumber, peeled and chopped
1 cup chopped tomato
½ cup finely chopped fresh mint
¼ cup diced red onion
1 (2.25-ounce / 64-g) can sliced black olives, drained
2 tablespoons extra-virgin olive oil
1 tablespoon red wine vinegar
¼ teaspoon kosher salt
¼ teaspoon freshly ground black pepper
½ cup crumbled goat cheese
4 whole-wheat flatbread wraps or soft whole-wheat tortillas

Directions:

In bowl, stir together the cucumber, tomato, mint, onion & olives.

In a small bowl, whisk together the oil, vinegar, salt, and pepper. Spread the dressing over the salad. Toss gently to combine.

On a clean work surface, lay the wraps. Divide the goat cheese evenly among the wraps. Scoop a quarter of the salad filling down the center of each wrap.

Fold up each wrap: Start by folding up the bottom, then fold one side over and fold the other side over the top. Repeat with the remaining wraps.Serve immediately.

Per Serving calories: 225 | fat: 12.0g | protein: 12.0g | carbs: 18.0g

Green Veggie Sandwiches

Prep time: 20 minutes | **Cook time:** 0 minutes | **Serves:**2

Ingredients:

Spread:

1 (15-ounce / 425-g) can cannellini beans, drained and rinsed

⅓ cup packed fresh basil leaves

⅓ cup packed fresh parsley

⅓ cup chopped fresh chives

2 garlic cloves, chopped

Zest and juice of ½ lemon

1 tablespoon apple cider vinegar

Sandwiches:

4 whole-grain bread slices, toasted

8 English cucumber slices

1 large beefsteak tomato, cut into slices

1 large avocado, halved, pitted, and cut into slices

1 small yellow bell pepper, cut into slices

2 handfuls broccoli sprouts

2 handfuls fresh spinach

Directions:

Make the Spread

In a food processor, combine the cannellini beans, basil, parsley, chives, garlic, lemon zest and juice, and vinegar. Pulse a few times, scrape down the sides, and purée until smooth. You may need to scrape down the sides again to incorporate all the basil and parsley. Refrigerate for at least 1 hour to allow the flavors to blend.

Assemble the Sandwiches

Build your sandwiches by spreading several tablespoons of spread on each slice of bread. Layer two slices of bread with the cucumber, tomato, avocado, bell pepper, broccoli sprouts, and spinach. Top with the remaining bread slices and press down lightly. Serve immediately.

Per Serving

calories: 617 | fat: 21.1g | protein: 28.1g | carbs: 86.1g

Mushroom-Pesto Baked Pizza

Prep time: 5 minutes | **Cook time:** 15 minutes | **Serves:**2

Ingredients:

1 teaspoon extra-virgin olive oil

½ cup sliced mushrooms

½ red onion, sliced

Salt and freshly ground black pepper

¼ cup store-bought pesto sauce

2 whole-wheat flatbreads

¼ cup shredded Mozzarella cheese

Directions:

Preheat the oven to 350°F (180°C). In a small skillet, heat the oil over medium heat. Add the mushrooms and onion, and season with salt and pepper. Sauté for 3 to 5 minutes until the onion and mushrooms begin to soften. Spread 2 tablespoons of pesto on each flatbread. Divide the mushroom-onion mixture between the two flatbreads. Top each with 2 tablespoons of cheese. Place the flatbreads on a baking sheet and bake for 10 to 12 minutes until the cheese is melted and bubbly. Serve warm.

Per Serving calories: 348 | fat: 23.5g | protein: 14.2g | carbs: 28.1g

Tuna and Hummus Wraps

Prep time: 10 minutes | **Cook time:** 0 minutes | **Serves:**2

Ingredients:

Hummus:

1 cup from 1 (15-ounce / 425-g) can low-sodium chickpeas, drained and rinsed

2 tablespoons tahini

1 tablespoon extra-virgin olive oil

1 garlic clove

Juice of ½ lemon

2 tablespoons water

Wraps:

4 large lettuce leaves

1 (5-ounce / 142-g) can chunk light tuna packed in water, drained

1 red bell pepper, seeded and cut into strips

1 cucumber, sliced

¼ teaspoon salt

Directions:

Make the Hummus

In a blender jar, combine the chickpeas, tahini, olive oil, garlic, lemon juice, salt, and water. Process until smooth. Taste and adjust with additional lemon juice or salt, as needed.

Make the Wraps

On each lettuce leaf, spread 1 tablespoon of hummus, and divide the tuna among the leaves. Top each with several strips of red pepper and cucumber slices.

Roll up the lettuce leaves, folding in the two shorter sides and rolling away from you, like a burrito. Serve immediately.

Per Serving calories: 192 | fat: 5.1g | protein: 26.1g | carbs: 15.1g

Chickpea Lettuce Wraps

Prep time: 15 minutes | **Cook time:** 0 minutes | **Serves:**2

Ingredients:

1 (15-ounce / 425-g) can chickpeas, drained and rinsed well

1 celery stalk, diced

½ shallot, minced

1 green apple, cored and diced

3 tablespoons tahini (sesame paste)

2 teaspoons freshly squeezed lemon juice

1 teaspoon raw honey

1 teaspoon Dijon mustard

Dash salt

Filtered water, to thin

4 romaine lettuce leaves

Directions:

In a medium bowl, stir together the chickpeas, celery, shallot, apple, tahini, lemon juice, honey, mustard, and salt. If needed, add some water to thin the mixture.

Place the romaine lettuce leaves on a plate. Fill each with the chickpea filling, using it all. Wrap the leaves around the filling. Serve immediately.

Per Serving calories: 397 | fat: 15.1g | protein: 15.1g | carbs: 53.1g

Brown Rice and Black Bean Burgers

Prep time: 20 mins | **Cook time:** 40 mins | **Makes 8 burgers**

Ingredients:

1 cup cooked brown rice
1 (15-ounce / 425-g) can black beans, drained and rinsed
1 tablespoon olive oil
2 tablespoons taco or Harissa seasoning
½ yellow onion, finely diced
1 beet, peeled and grated
1 carrot, peeled and grated
2 tablespoons no-salt-added tomato paste

2 tablespoons apple cider vinegar
3 garlic cloves, minced
¼ teaspoon sea salt
Ground black pepper, to taste
8 whole-wheat hamburger buns

Toppings:
16 lettuce leaves, rinsed well
8 tomato slices, rinsed well
Whole-grain mustard, to taste

Directions:

Line a baking sheet with parchment paper. Put the brown rice and black beans in a food processor and pulse until mix well. Pour the mixture in a large bowl and set aside. Heat the olive oil in a nonstick skillet over medium heat until shimmering. Add the taco seasoning and stir for 1 minute or until fragrant. Add the onion, beet, and carrot and sauté for 5 minutes or until the onion is translucent and beet and carrot are tender. Pour in the tomato paste and vinegar, then add the garlic and cook for 3 minutes or until the sauce is thickened. Sprinkle with salt and ground black pepper. Transfer the vegetable mixture to the bowl of rice mixture, then stir to mix well until smooth. Divide and shape the mixture into 8 patties, then arrange the patties on the baking sheet and refrigerate for at least 1 hour. Preheat the oven to 400°F (205°C).

Remove the baking sheet from the refrigerator and allow to sit under room temperature for 10 minutes.

Bake in the preheated oven for 40 minutes or until golden brown on both sides. Flip the patties halfway through the cooking time. Remove the patties from the oven and allow to cool for 10 minutes. Assemble the buns with patties, lettuce, and tomato slices. Top the filling with mustard and serve immediately.

Per Serving (1 burger)
calories: 544 | fat: 20.0g | protein: 15.8g | carbs: 76.0g

Classic Socca

Prep time: 10 minutes | **Cook time:** 10 minutes | **Serves:** 4

Ingredients:

1½ cups chickpea flour
½ teaspoon ground turmeric
½ teaspoon sea salt

½ teaspoon ground black pepper
2 tablespoons plus 2 teaspoons extra-virgin olive oil
1½ cups water

Directions:

Combine the chickpea flour, turmeric, salt, and black pepper in a bowl. Stir to mix well, then gently mix in 2 tablespoons of olive oil and water. Stir to mix until smooth.

Heat 2 teaspoons of olive oil in an 8-inch nonstick skillet over medium- high heat until shimmering. Add half cup of the mixture into the skillet and swirl the skillet so the mixture coat the bottom evenly. Cook for 5 minutes or until lightly browned and crispy. Flip the socca halfway through the cooking time. Repeat with the remaining mixture. Slice and serve warm.

Per Serving calories: 207 | fat: 10.2g | protein: 7.9g | carbs: 20.7g

Artichoke and Cucumber Hoagies

Prep time: 10 minutes | **Cook time:** 15 minutes
Servings: 1

Ingredients:

1 (12-ounce / 340-g) whole grain baguette, sliced in half horizontally
1 cup frozen and thawed artichoke hearts, roughly chopped
1 cucumber, sliced
2 tomatoes, sliced
1 red bell pepper, sliced

⅓ cup Kalamata olives, pitted and chopped
¼ small red onion, thinly sliced
Sea salt and ground black pepper, to taste
2 tablespoons pesto
Balsamic vinegar, to taste

Directions:

range the baguette halves on a clean work surface, then cut off the top third from each half. Scoop some insides of the bottom half out and reserve as breadcrumbs.

Toast the baguette in a baking pan in the oven for 1 minute to brown lightly. Put the artichokes, cucumber, tomatoes, bell pepper, olives, and onion in a large bowl. Sprinkle with salt and ground black pepper. Toss to combine well.

Spread the bottom half of the baguette with the vegetable mixture and drizzle with balsamic vinegar, then smear the cut side of the baguette top with pesto. Assemble the two baguette halves. Wrap the hoagies in parchment paper and let sit for at least an hour before serving.

Per Serving (1 hoagies) calories: 1263 | fat: 37.7g | protein: 56.3g | carbs: 180.1g

Chapter 5
Beans Recipes, Grains Recipes, & Pastas Recipes

Baked Rolled Oat with Pears and Pecans

Prep time: 15 minutes | **Cook time:** 30 minutes | **Serves:**6

Ingredients:

2 tablespoons coconut oil, melted, plus more for greasing the pan
3 ripe pears, cored and diced
2 cups unsweetened almond milk
1 tablespoon pure vanilla extract
¼ cup pure maple syrup
2 cups gluten-free rolled oats
½ cup raisins
¾ cup chopped pecans
¼ teaspoon ground nutmeg
1 teaspoon ground cinnamon
½ teaspoon ground ginger
¼ teaspoon sea salt

Directions:

Preheat the oven to 350°F (180°C). Grease a baking dish with melted coconut oil, then spread the pears in a single layer on the baking dish evenly.

Combine the almond milk, vanilla extract, maple syrup, and coconut oil in a bowl. Stir to mix well.

Combine the remaining ingredients in a separate large bowl. Stir to mix well. Fold the almond milk mixture in the bowl, then pour the mixture over the pears.

Place the baking dish in the preheated oven and bake for 30 minutes or until lightly browned and set. Serve immediately.

Per Serving
calories: 479 | fat: 34.9g | protein: 8.8g | carbs: 50.1g

Curry Apple Couscous with Leeks and Pecans

Prep time: 10 minutes | **Cook time:** 8 minutes | **Serves:**4

Ingredients:

2 teaspoons extra-virgin olive oil
2 leeks, white parts only, sliced
1 apple, diced
2 cups cooked couscous
2 tablespoons curry powder
½ cup chopped pecans

Directions:

Heat the olive oil in a skillet over medium heat until shimmering.

Add the leeks and sauté for 5 minutes or until soft. Add the diced apple and cook for 3 more minutes until tender.

Add the couscous and curry powder. Stir to combine.

Transfer them in a large serving bowl, then mix in the pecans and serve.

Per Serving
calories: 254 | fat: 11.9g | protein: 5.4g | carbs: 34.3g

Brown Rice Pilaf with Pistachios and Raisins

Prep time: 5 minutes | **Cook time:** 15 minutes | **Serves:**6

Ingredients:

1 tablespoon extra-virgin olive oil
1 cup chopped onion
½ cup shredded carrot
½ teaspoon ground cinnamon
1 teaspoon ground cumin
2 cups brown rice
1¾ cups pure orange juice
¼ cup water
½ cup shelled pistachios
1 cup golden raisins
½ cup chopped fresh chives

Directions:

Heat the olive oil in a saucepan over medium-high heat until shimmering. Add the onion, sauté for 5 minutes or until translucent.

Add the carrots, cinnamon, and cumin, then sauté for 1 minutes or until aromatic.

Pour int the brown rice, orange juice, and water. Bring to a boil. Reduce the heat to medium-low and simmer for 7 minutes or until the liquid is almost absorbed.

Transfer the rice mixture in a large serving bowl, then spread with pistachios, raisins, and chives. Serve immediately.

Per Serving
calories: 264 | fat: 7.1g | protein: 5.2g | carbs: 48.9g

Black Bean Chili with Mangoes

Prep time: 10 minutes | **Cook time:** 10 minutes | **Serves:**4

Ingredients:

2 tablespoons coconut oil
1 onion, chopped
2 (15-ounce / 425-g) cans black beans, drained and rinsed
1 tablespoon chili powder
1 teaspoon sea salt
¼ teaspoon freshly ground black pepper
1 cup water
2 ripe mangoes, sliced thinly
¼ cup chopped fresh cilantro, divided
¼ cup sliced scallions, divided

Directions:

Heat the coconut oil in a pot over high heat until melted.

Put the onion in the pot and sauté for 5 minutes or until translucent. Add the black beans to the pot. Sprinkle with chili powder, salt, and ground black pepper. Pour in the water. Stir to mix well.Bring to a boil. Reduce the heat to low, then simmering for 5 minutes or until the beans are tender.

Turn off the heat and mix in the mangoes, then garnish with scallions and cilantro before serving.

Per Serving
calories: 430 | fat: 9.1g | protein: 20.2g | carbs: 71.9g

Chickpea, Vegetable, and Fruit Stew

Prep time: 20 minutes | **Cook time:** 6 hours 4 minutes | **Serves:** 6

Ingredients:

1 large bell pepper, any color, chopped
6 ounces (170 g) green beans, trimmed and cut into bite-size pieces
3 cups canned chickpeas, rinsed and drained
1 (15-ounce / 425-g) can diced tomatoes, with the juice
1 large carrot, cut into ¼-inch rounds
2 large potatoes, peeled and cubed
1 large yellow onion, chopped
1 teaspoon grated fresh ginger
2 garlic cloves, minced
1¾ cups low-sodium vegetable soup
1 teaspoon ground cumin
1 tablespoon ground coriander
¼ teaspoon ground red pepper flakes
Sea salt and ground black pepper, to taste
8 ounces (227 g) fresh baby spinach
¼ cup diced dried figs
¼ cup diced dried apricots
1 cup plain Greek yogurt

Directions:

Place the bell peppers, green beans, chicken peas, tomatoes and juice, carrot, potatoes, onion, ginger, and garlic in the slow cooker. Pour in the vegetable soup and sprinkle with cumin, coriander, red pepper flakes, salt, and ground black pepper. Stir to mix well.

Put the slow cooker lid on and cook on high for 6 hours or until the vegetables are soft. Stir periodically.

Open the lid and fold in the spinach, figs, apricots, and yogurt. Stir to mix well.

Cook for 4 minutes or until the spinach is wilted. Pour them in a large serving bowl. Allow to cool for at least 20 minutes, then serve warm.

Per Serving

calories: 611 | fat: 9.0g | protein: 30.7g | carbs: 107.4g

Quinoa and Chickpea Vegetable Bowls

Prep time: 20 minutes | **Cook time:** 15 minutes | **Serves:** 4

Ingredients:

1 cup red dry quinoa, rinsed and drained
2 cups low-sodium vegetable soup
2 cups fresh spinach
2 cups finely shredded red cabbage
1 (15-ounce / 425-g) can chickpeas, drained and rinsed
1 ripe avocado, thinly sliced
1 cup shredded carrots
1 red bell pepper, thinly sliced
½ cup fresh cilantro,

Mango Sauce:

1 mango, diced
¼ cup fresh lime juice
½ teaspoon ground turmeric
1 teaspoon finely minced fresh ginger
¼ teaspoon sea salt
Pinch of ground red pepper
1 teaspoon pure maple syrup
2 tablespoons extra-virgin olive oil
4 tablespoons Mango Sauce

Directions:

Pour the quinoa and vegetable soup in a saucepan. Bring to a boil. Reduce the heat to low. Cover and cook for 15 minutes or until tender. Fluffy with a fork.

Divide the quinoa, spinach, and cabbage into 4 serving bowls, then top with chickpeas, avocado, carrots, and bell pepper. Dress them with the mango sauce and spread with cilantro. Serve immediately.

Per Serving calories: 366 | fat: 11.1g | protein: 15.5g | carbs: 55.6g

Ritzy Veggie Chili

Prep time: 15 minutes | **Cook time:** 5 hours | **Serves:** 4

Ingredients:

1 (28-ounce / 794-g) can chopped tomatoes, with the juice
1 (15-ounce / 425-g) can black beans, drained and rinsed
1 (15-ounce / 425-g) can redly beans, drained and rinsed
1 medium green bell pepper, chopped
1 yellow onion, chopped
1 tablespoon onion powder
1 teaspoon paprika
1 teaspoon cayenne pepper
1 teaspoon garlic powder
½ teaspoon sea salt
½ teaspoon ground black pepper
1 tablespoon olive oil
1 large hass avocado, pitted, peeled, and chopped, for garnish

Directions:

Combine all the ingredients, except for the avocado, in the slow cooker. Stir to mix well.

Put the slow cooker lid on and cook on high for 5 hours or until the vegetables are tender and the mixture has a thick consistency.

Pour the chili in a large serving bowl. Allow to cool for 30 minutes, then spread with chopped avocado and serve.

Per Serving

calories: 633 | fat: 16.3g | protein: 31.7g | carbs: 97.0g

Cherry, Apricot, and Pecan Brown Rice Bowl

Prep time: 15 minutes | **Cook time:** 1 hour 1 minutes | **Serves:** 2

Ingredients:
2 tablespoons olive oil
2 green onions, sliced
½ cup brown rice
1 cup low -sodium chicken stock
2 tablespoons dried cherries
4 dried apricots, chopped
2 tablespoons pecans, toasted and chopped
Sea salt and freshly ground pepper, to taste

Directions:
Heat the olive oil in a medium saucepan over medium-high heat until shimmering.

Add the green onions and sauté for 1 minutes or until fragrant.

Add the rice. Stir to mix well, then pour in the chicken stock.

Bring to a boil. Reduce the heat to low. Cover and simmer for 50 minutes or until the brown rice is soft.

Add the cherries, apricots, and pecans, and simmer for 10 more minutes or until the fruits are tender.

Pour them in a large serving bowl. Fluff with a fork. Sprinkle with sea salt and freshly ground pepper. Serve immediately.

Per Serving
calories: 451 | fat: 25.9g | protein: 8.2g | carbs: 50.4g

Rice and Blueberry Stuffed Sweet Potatoes

Prep time: 15 minutes | **Cook time:** 20 minutes | **Serves:** 4

Ingredients:
2 cups cooked wild rice
½ cup dried blueberries
½ cup chopped hazelnuts
½ cup shredded Swiss chard
1 teaspoon chopped fresh thyme
1 scallion, white and green parts, peeled and thinly sliced
Sea salt and freshly ground black pepper, to taste
4 sweet potatoes, baked in the skin until tender

Directions:
Preheat the oven to 400°F (205°C).

Combine all the ingredients, except for the sweet potatoes, in a large bowl. Stir to mix well.

Cut the top third of the sweet potato off length wire, then scoop most of the sweet potato flesh out.

Fill the potato with the wild rice mixture, then set the sweet potato on a greased baking sheet.

Bake in the preheated oven for 20 minutes or until the sweet potato skin is lightly charred.

Serve immediately.

Per Serving
calories: 393 | fat: 7.1g | protein: 10.2g | carbs: 76.9g

Lebanese Flavor Broken Thin Noodles

Prep time: 10 minutes | **Cook time:** 25 minutes | **Serves:** 6

Ingredients:
1 tablespoon extra-virgin olive oil
1 (3-ounce / 85-g) cup vermicelli, broken into 1- to 1½-inch pieces
3 cups shredded cabbage
1 cup brown rice
3 cups low-sodium vegetable soup
½ cup water
2 garlic cloves, mashed
¼ teaspoon sea salt
⅛ teaspoon crushed red pepper flakes
½ cup coarsely chopped cilantro
Fresh lemon slices, for serving

Directions:
Heat the olive oil in a saucepan over medium-high heat until shimmering.

Add the vermicelli and sauté for 3 minutes or until toasted.

Add the cabbage and sauté for 4 minutes or until tender.

Pour in the brown rice, vegetable soup, and water. Add the garlic and sprinkle with salt and red pepper flakes.

Bring to a boil over high heat. Reduce the heat to medium low. Put the lid on and simmer for another 10 minutes.

Turn off the heat, then let sit for 5 minutes without opening the lid.

Pour them on a large serving platter and spread with cilantro. Squeeze the lemon slices over and serve warm.

Per Serving
calories: 127 | fat: 3.1g | protein: 4.2g | carbs: 22.9g

Italian Sautéd Cannelliqni Beans

Prep time: 10 minutes | **Cook time:** 15 minutes | **Serves:** 6

Ingredients:
2 teaspoons extra-virgin olive oil
½ cup minced onion
¼ cup red wine vinegar
1 (12-ounce / 340-g) can no-salt-added tomato paste
2 tablespoons raw honey
½ cup water
¼ teaspoon ground cinnamon

Directions:
2 (15-ounce / 425-g) cans cannellini beans

Heat the olive oil in saucepan over medium heat until shimmering.

Add the onion and sauté for 5 minutes or until translucent.

Pour in the red wine vinegar, tomato paste, honey, and water. Sprinkle with cinnamon. Stir to mix well.

Reduce the heat to low, then pour all the beans into the saucepan. Cook for 10 more minutes. Stir constantly. Serve immediately.

Per Serving
calories: 435 | fat: 2.1g | protein: 26.2g | carbs: 80.3g

Chicken and Spaghetti Ragù Bolognese

Prep time: 15 minutes | **Cook time:** 42 minutes | **Serves:**8

Ingredients:

2 tablespoons olive oil
6 ounces (170 g) bacon, cubed
1 onion, minced
1 carrot, minced
1 celery stalk, minced
2 garlic cloves, crushed
¼ cup tomato paste
¼ teaspoon crushed red pepper flakes
1½ pounds (680 g) ground chicken
½ cup white wine
1 cup milk
1 cup chicken broth
Salt, to taste
1 pound (454 g) spaghetti

Directions:

Warm oil on Sauté. Add bacon and fry for 5 minutes until crispy. Add celery, carrot, garlic and onion and cook for 5 minutes until fragrant. Mix in red pepper flakes and tomato paste, and cook for 2 minutes. Break chicken into small pieces and place in the pot.

Cook for 10 minutes, as you stir, until browned. Pour in wine and simmer for 2 minutes. Add chicken broth and milk. Seal the lid and cook for 15 minutes on High Pressure. Release the pressure quickly.

Add the spaghetti and stir. Seal the lid, and cook on High Pressure for another 5 minutes.

Release the pressure quickly. Check the pasta for doneness. Taste, adjust the seasoning and serve hot.

Per Serving calories: 477 | fat: 20.6g | protein: 28.1g | carbs: 48.5g

Cheesy Tomato Linguine

Prep time: 15 minutes | **Cook time:** 11 minutes | **Serves:**4

Ingredients:

2 tablespoons olive oil
1 small onion, diced
2 garlic cloves, minced
1 cup cherry tomatoes, halved
1½ cups vegetable stock
¼ cup julienned basil leaves
1 teaspoon salt
½ teaspoon ground black pepper
¼ teaspoon red chili flakes
1 pound (454 g) Linguine noodles, halved
Fresh basil leaves for garnish
½ cup Parmigiano-Reggiano cheese, grated

Directions:

Warm oil on Sauté. Add onion and Sauté for 2 minutes until soft. Mix garlic and tomatoes and sauté for 4 minutes. To the pot, add vegetable stock, salt, julienned basil, red chili flakes and pepper.

Add linguine to the tomato mixture until covered. Seal the lid and cook on High Pressure for 5 minutes.

Naturally release the pressure for 5 minutes. Stir the mixture to ensure it is broken down.

Divide into plates. Top with basil and Parmigiano-Reggiano cheese and serve.

Per Serving calories: 311 fat: 11.3g protein: 10.3g carbs: 42.1g

Parmesan Squash Linguine

Prep time: 15 minutes | **Cook time:** 5 minutes | **Serves:**4

Ingredients:

1 cup flour
2 teaspoons salt
2 eggs
4 cups water
1 cup seasoned breadcrumbs
½ cup grated Parmesan cheese, plus more for garnish
1 yellow squash, peeled and sliced
1 pound (454 g) linguine
24 ounces (680 g) canned seasoned tomato sauce
2 tablespoons olive oil
1 cup shredded Mozzarella cheese
Minced fresh basil, for garnish

Directions:

Break the linguine in half. Put it in the pot and add water and half of salt. Seal the lid and cook on High Pressure for 5 minutes. Combine the flour and 1 teaspoon of salt in a bowl. In another bowl, whisk the eggs and 2 tablespoons of water. In a third bowl, mix the breadcrumbs and Mozzarella cheese.

Coat each squash slices in the flour. Shake off excess flour, dip in the egg wash, and dredge in the bread crumbs. Set aside. Quickly release the pressure. Remove linguine to a serving bowl and mix in the tomato sauce and sprinkle with fresh basil. Heat oil on Sauté and fry breaded squash until crispy.

Serve the squash topped Mozzarella cheese with the linguine on side.

Per Serving

calories: 857 | fat: 17.0g | protein: 33.2g | carbs: 146.7g

Italian Chicken Pasta (Italian)

Preparation Time: 10 minutes **Cooking Time:** 9 minutes
Servings: 8

Ingredients:

1 lb. chicken breast, skinless, boneless, and cut into chunks
1 tsp garlic, minced
1/2 cup cream cheese
2 tomatoes, diced 2 cups of water
1 cup mozzarella cheese, shredded
1 1/2 tsp Italian seasoning
1 cup mushrooms, diced
1/2 onion, diced
16 oz whole wheat penne pasta Pepper, Salt

Directions:

Add all except cheeses into the inner pot of instant pot and stir well.

Seal pot with lid and cook on high for 9 minutes.

Once done, allow to release pressure naturally for 5 minutes then release remaining using quick release. Remove lid.

Add cheeses and stir well and serve.

Per Serving

Calories 328 Fat 8.5 g Carbohydrates 42.7 g Sugar 1.4 g Protein 23.7 g Cholesterol 55 mg

Red Bean Curry

Prep time: 10 minutes | **Cook time:** 24 minutes | **Serves:** 4

Ingredients:

½ cup raw red beans
1½ tablespoons cooking oil
½ cup chopped onions
1 bay leaf
½ tablespoon grated garlic
¼ tablespoon grated ginger
¾ cup water
1 cup fresh tomato purée
Boiled white rice or quinoa, for serve

½ green chili, finely chopped
¼ teaspoon turmeric
½ teaspoon coriander powder
1 teaspoon chili powder
1 cup chopped baby spinach
Salt, to taste

Directions:

Add the oil and onions to the Instant Pot. Sauté for 5 minutes.

Stir in ginger, garlic paste, green chili and bay leaf. Cook for 1 minute, then add all the spices.

Add the red beans, tomato purée and water to the pot.

Cover and secure the lid. Turn its pressure release handle to the sealing position.

Cook on the Manual function with High Pressure for 15 minutes. After the beep, do a Natural release for 20 minutes.

Stir in spinach and cook for 3 minutes on the Sauté setting.

Serve hot with boiled white rice or quinoa.

Per Serving

calories: 159 | fat: 5.6g | protein: 6.8g | carbs: 22.5g

Easy Simple Pesto Pasta (Italian)

Preparation Time: 10 minutes **Cooking Time:** 8 minutes
Servings: 4 to 6

Ingredients:

1-pound (454 g) spaghetti
3 cloves garlic
1 teaspoon salt
1/2 cup toasted pine nuts
1/4 cup lemon juice
1 cup extra-virgin olive oil

4 cups fresh basil leaves, stems removed
1/2 teaspoon freshly ground black pepper
1/2 cup grated Parmesan cheese

Directions:

Bring a large pot of salted water to a boil. Add the spaghetti to the pot and cook for 8 minutes. In a food processor, place the remaining , except for the olive oil, and pulse.

While the processor is running, slowly drizzle the olive oil through the top opening. Process until all the olive oil has been added. Reserve ½ cup of the cooking liquid. Drain the pasta and put it into a large bowl. Add the pesto and cooking liquid to the bowl of pasta and toss everything together. Serve immediately.

Per Serving

calories: 1067 fat: 72.0g protein: 23.0g carbs: 91.0g

Pesto Chicken Pasta (Italian)

Preparation Time: 10 minutes **Cooking Time:** 10 minutes
Servings: 6

Ingredients:

1 lb. chicken breast, skinless, boneless, and diced
3 tbsp olive oil
1/4 cup heavy cream
3 1/2 cups water Pepper
6 oz basil pesto

1/2 cup parmesan cheese, shredded
1 tsp Italian seasoning
16 oz whole wheat pasta
Salt

Directions:

Season chicken with Italian seasoning, pepper, and salt.

Add oil into the inner pot of instant pot and set the pot on sauté mode.

Add chicken to the pot and sauté until brown.

Add remaining except for parmesan cheese, heavy cream, and pesto and stir well.

Seal pot with lid and cook on high for 5 minutes.

Once done, release pressure using quick release. Remove lid.

Stir in parmesan cheese, heavy cream, and pesto and serve.

Per Serving

Calories 475 Fat 14.7 g Carbohydrates 57 g Sugar 2.8 g Protein 28.7 g Cholesterol 61 mg

Mac & Cheese (Italian)

Preparation Time: 10 minutes **Cooking Time:** 4 minutes
Servings: 8

Ingredients:

1 lb. whole grain pasta
4 cups cheddar cheese, shredded
1/4 tsp garlic powder
1/2 tsp ground mustard
2 tbsp olive oil

1/2 cup parmesan cheese, grated
1 cup milk
4 cups of water Pepper
Salt

Directions:

Add pasta, garlic powder, mustard, oil, water, pepper, and salt into the instant pot. Seal pot with lid and cook on high for 4 minutes. Once done, release pressure using quick release. Remove lid. Add remaining and stir well and serve.

Per Serving

Calories 509 Fat 25.7 g Carbohydrates 43.8 g Sugar 3.8 g Protein 27.3 g Cholesterol 66 mg

Lentil and Mushroom Pasta

Prep time: 10 minutes | **Cook time:** 50 minutes | **Serves:**2

Ingredients:

2 tablespoons olive oil
1 large yellow onion, finely diced
2 portobello mushrooms, trimmed and chopped finely
2 tablespoons tomato paste
3 garlic cloves, chopped
1 teaspoon oregano
2½ cups water

1 cup brown lentils
1 (28-ounce / 794-g) can diced tomatoes with basil (with juice if diced)
1 tablespoon balsamic vinegar
Salt and black pepper, to taste
Chopped basil, for garnish
8 ounces (227 g) pasta of choice, cooked

Directions:

Place a large stockpot over medium heat and add the olive oil. Once the oil is hot, add the onion and mushrooms. Cover and cook until both are soft, about 5 minutes. Add the tomato paste, garlic, and oregano and cook 2 minutes, stirring constantly. Stir in the water and lentils. Bring to a boil, then reduce the heat to medium-low and cook covered for 5 minutes. Add the tomatoes (and juice if using diced) and vinegar. Reduce the heat to low and cook until the lentils are tender, about 30 minutes.

Remove from the heat and season with salt and pepper to taste. Garnish with the basil and serve over the cooked pasta.

Per Serving

calories: 463 | fat: 15.9g | protein: 12.5g | carbs: 70.8g

Lentil Risotto

Prep time: 10 minutes | **Cook time:** 20 minutes | **Serves:**2

Ingredients:

½ tablespoon olive oil
½ medium onion, chopped
½ cup dry lentils, soaked overnight
½ celery stalk, chopped

1 sprig parsley, chopped
½ cup Arborio (short-grain Italian) rice
1 garlic clove, lightly mashed
2 cups vegetable stock

Directions:

Press the Sauté button to heat your Instant Pot.

Add the oil and onion to the Instant Pot and sauté for 5 minutes.

Add the remaining ingredients to the Instant Pot, stirring well.

Secure the lid. Select the Manual mode and set the cooking time for 15 minutes at High Pressure.

Once cooking is complete, do a natural pressure release for 20 minutes, then release any remaining pressure. Carefully open the lid. Stir and serve hot.

Per Serving

calories: 261 | fat: 3.6g | protein: 10.6g | carbs: 47.1g

Tomato Basil Pasta

Prep time: 3 minutes | **Cook time:** 2 minutes | **Serves:**2

Ingredients:

2 cups dried campanelle or similar pasta
1¾ cups vegetable stock
½ teaspoon salt, plus more as needed
2 tomatoes, cut into large dices

1 or 2 pinches red pepper flakes
½ teaspoon garlic powder
½ teaspoon dried oregano
10 to 12 fresh sweet basil leaves
Freshly ground black pepper, to taste

Directions:

In your Instant Pot, stir together the pasta, stock, and salt. Scatter the tomatoes on top (do not stir).

Secure the lid. Select the Manual mode and set the cooking time for 2 minutes at High Pressure.

Once cooking is complete, do a quick pressure release. Carefully open the lid.

Stir in the red pepper flakes, oregano, and garlic powder. If there's more than a few tablespoons of liquid in the bottom, select Sauté and cook for 2 to 3 minutes until it evaporates.

When ready to serve, chiffonade the basil and stir it in. Taste and season with more salt and pepper, as needed. Serve warm.

Per Serving

calories: 415 | fat: 2.0g | protein: 15.2g | carbs: 84.2g

Pork and Spinach Spaghetti

Prep time: 15 minutes | **Cook time:** 16 minutes | **Serves:**4

Ingredients:

2 tablespoons olive oil
½ cup onion, chopped
1 garlic clove, minced
1 pound (454 g) ground pork
2 cups water
1 (14-ounce / 397-g) can diced tomatoes, drained
½ cup sun-dried tomatoes

1 tablespoon dried oregano
1 teaspoon Italian seasoning
1 fresh jalapeño chile, stemmed, seeded, and minced
1 teaspoon salt
8 ounces (227 g) dried spaghetti, halved
1 cup spinach

Directions:

Warm oil onSauté. Add onion and garlic and cook for 2 minutes until softened. Stir in pork and cook for 5 minutes. Stir in jalapeño, water, sun- dried tomatoes, Italian seasoning, oregano, diced tomatoes, and salt with the chicken; mix spaghetti and press to submerge into the sauce.

Seal the lid and cook on High Pressure for 9 minutes. Release the pressure quickly. Stir in spinach, close lid again, and simmer on Keep Warm for 5 minutes until spinach is wilted.

Per Serving

calories: 621 | fat: 32.2g | protein: 29.1g | carbs: 53.9g

Rigatoni and Zucchini Minestrone

Prep time: 20 minutes | **Cook time:** 7 minutes | **Serves:**4

Ingredients:

3 tablespoons olive oil
1 onion, diced
1 celery stalk, diced
1 large carrot, peeled and diced
14 ounces (397 g) canned chopped tomatoes
4 ounces (113 g) rigatoni
3 cups water
1 cup chopped zucchini
1 bay leaf
1 teaspoon mixed herbs
¼ teaspoon cayenne pepper
½ teaspoon salt
¼ cup shredded Pecorino Romano cheese
1 garlic clove, minced
⅓ cup olive oil-based pesto

Directions:

Heat oil on Sauté and cook onion, celery, garlic, and carrot for 3 minutes, stirring occasionally until the vegetables are softened. Stir in rigatoni, tomatoes, water, zucchini, bay leaf, herbs, cayenne, and salt. Seal the lid and cook on High for 4 minutes. Do a natural pressure release for 5 minutes. Adjust the taste of the soup with salt and black pepper, and remove the bay leaf. Ladle the soup into serving bowls and drizzle the pesto over. Serve with the garlic toasts.

Per Serving

calories: 278 | fat: 23.4g | protein: 6.7g | carbs: 12.2g

Asparagus and Broccoli Primavera Farfalle

Prep time: 15 minutes | **Cook time:** 12 minutes | **Serves:**4

Ingredients:

1 bunch asparagus, trimmed, cut into 1-inch pieces
2 cups broccoli florets
3 tablespoons olive oil
3 teaspoons salt
10 ounces (283 g) egg noodles
3 garlic cloves, minced
2½ cups vegetable stock
½ cup heavy cream
1 cup small tomatoes, halved
¼ cup chopped basil
½ cup grated Parmesan cheese

Directions:

Pour 2 cups of water, add the noodles, 2 tablespoons of olive oil, garlic and salt. Place a trivet over the water. Combine asparagus, broccoli, remaining olive oil and salt in a bowl. Place the vegetables on the trivet.Seal the lid and cook on Steam for 12 minutes on High. Do a quick release. Remove the vegetables to a plate. Stir the heavy cream and tomatoes in the pasta. Press Sauté and simmer the cream until desired consistency.

Gently mix in the asparagus and broccoli. Garnish with basil and Parmesan, to serve.

Per Serving

calories: 544 | fat: 23.8g | protein: 18.5g | carbs: 66.1g

Chickpea Curry

Prep time: 10 minutes | **Cook time:** 24 minutes | **Serves:**4

Ingredients:

½ cup raw chickpeas
1½ tablespoons cooking oil
½ cup chopped onions
1 bay leaf
½ tablespoon grated garlic
¼ tablespoon grated ginger
¾ cup water
Boiled white rice, for serving
1 cup fresh tomato purée
½ green chili, finely chopped
¼ teaspoon turmeric
½ teaspoon coriander powder
1 teaspoon chili powder
1 cup chopped baby spinach
Salt, to taste

Directions:

Add the oil and onions to the Instant Pot. Sauté for 5 minutes.

Stir in ginger, garlic paste, green chili and bay leaf. Cook for 1 minute, then add all the spices.

Add the chickpeas, tomato purée and the water to the pot.

Cover and secure the lid. Turn its pressure release handle to the sealing position.

Cook on the Manual function with High Pressure for 15 minutes.

After the beep, do a Natural release for 20 minutes.

Stir in spinach and cook for 3 minutes on the Sauté setting. Serve hot with boiled white rice.

Per Serving

calories: 176 | fat: 6.8g | protein: 6.7g | carbs: 24.1g

Cumin Quinoa Pilaf

Prep time: 5 minutes | **Cook time:** 5 minutes | **Serves:**2

Ingredients:

2 tablespoons extra virgin olive oil
2 cloves garlic, minced
3 cups water
2 cups quinoa, rinsed
2 teaspoons ground cumin
2 teaspoons turmeric
Salt, to taste
1 handful parsley, chopped

Directions:

Press the Sauté button to heat your Instant Pot.

Once hot, add the oil and garlic to the pot, stir and cook for 1 minute. Add water, quinoa, cumin, turmeric, and salt, stirring well. Lock the lid. Select the Manual mode and set the cooking time for 1 minute at High Pressure.

When the timer beeps, perform a natural pressure release for 10 minutes, then release any remaining pressure. Carefully remove the lid.Fluff the quinoa with a fork. Season with more salt, if needed.

Sprinkle the chopped parsley on top and serve.

Per Serving

calories: 384 | fat: 12.3g | protein: 12.8g | carbs: 57.4g

Turkey and Bell Pepper Tortiglioni

Prep time: 20 minutes | **Cook time:** 10 minutes | **Serves:**6

Ingredients:

2 teaspoons chili powder
1 teaspoon salt
1 teaspoon cumin
1 teaspoon onion powder
1 teaspoon garlic powder
½ teaspoon thyme
1½ pounds (680 g) turkey breast, cut into strips
1 tablespoon olive oil
1 red onion, cut into wedges
4 garlic cloves, minced
3 cups chicken broth
1 cup salsa
1 pound (454 g) tortiglioni
1 red bell pepper, chopped diagonally
1 yellow bell pepper, chopped diagonally
1 green bell pepper, chopped diagonally
1 cup shredded Gouda cheese
½ cup sour cream
½ cup chopped parsley

Directions:

In a bowl, mix chili powder, cumin, garlic powder, onion powder, salt, and oregano. Reserve 1 teaspoon of seasoning. Coat turkey with the remaining seasoning.

Warm oil on Sauté. Add turkey strips and sauté for 4 to 5 minutes until browned. Place the turkey in a bowl. Sauté the onion and garlic for 1 minute in the cooker until soft. Press Cancel. Mix in salsa, broth, and scrape the bottom of any brown bits. Into the broth mixture, stir in tortiglioni pasta and cover with bell peppers and chicken.

Seal lid, cook for 5 minutes , HighPressure.1 quick Pressure release.

Open the lid and sprinkle with shredded gouda cheese and reserved seasoning, and stir well. Divide into plates and top with sour cream. Add parsley for garnishing and serve.

Per Serving

calories: 646 | fat: 21.7g | protein: 41.1g | carbs: 72.9g

Carrot Risoni

Prep time: 5 minutes | **Cook time:** 11 minutes | **Serves:**6

Ingredients:

1 cup orzo, rinsed
2 cups water
2 carrots, cut into sticks
1 large onion, chopped
2 tablespoons olive oil
Salt, to taste
Fresh cilantro, chopped, for garnish

Directions:

Heat oil on Sauté. Add onion and carrots and stir-fry for about 10 minutes until tender and crispy. Remove to a plate and set aside. Add water, salt and orzo in the instant pot.

Seal the lid and cook on High Pressure for 1 minute. Do a quick release. Fluff the cooked orzo with a fork. Transfer to a serving plate and top with the carrots and onion. Serve scattered with cilantro.

Per Serving

calories: 121 | fat: 4.9g | protein: 1.7g | carbs: 18.1g

Roasted Butternut Squash and Rice

Prep time: 15 minutes | **Cook time:** 15 minutes | **Serves:**4

Ingredients:

½ cup water
2 cups vegetable broth
1 small butternut squash, peeled and sliced
2 tablespoons olive oil, divided
1 teaspoon salt
1 teaspoon freshly ground black pepper
1 cup feta cheese, cubed
1 tablespoon coconut aminos
2 teaspoons arrowroot starch
1 cup jasmine rice, cooked

Directions:

Pour the rice and broth in the pot and stir to combine. In a bowl, toss butternut squash with 1 tablespoon of olive oil and season with salt and black pepper.

In another bowl, mix the remaining olive oil, water and coconut aminos. Toss feta in the mixture, add the arrowroot starch, and toss again to combine well. Transfer to a greased baking dish.

Lay a trivet over the rice and place the baking dish on the trivet. Seal the lid and cook on High for 15 minutes. Do a quick pressure release. Fluff the rice with a fork and serve with squash and feta.

Per Serving

calories: 258 | fat: 14.9g | protein: 7.8g | carbs: 23.2g

Pesto Arborio Rice and Veggie Bowls

Prep time: 10 minutes | **Cook time:** 1 minute | **Serves:**2

Ingredients:

1 cup arborio rice, rinsed and drained
2 cups vegetable broth
Salt and black pepper to taste
1 potato, peeled, cubed
1 head broccoli, cut into small florets
1 bunch baby carrots, peeled
¼ cabbage, chopped
2 eggs
¼ cup pesto sauce
Lemon wedges, for serving

Directions:

In the pot, mix broth, pepper, rice and salt. Set trivet to the inner pot on top of rice and add a steamer basket to the top of the trivet. Mix carrots, potato, eggs and broccoli in the steamer basket. Add pepper and salt for seasoning.

Seal the lid and cook for 1 minute on High Pressure. Quick release the pressure. Take away the trivet and steamer basket from the pot.

Set the eggs in a bowl of ice water. Then peel and halve the eggs. Use a fork to fluff rice.

Adjust the seasonings. In two bowls, equally divide rice, broccoli, eggs, carrots, sweet potatoes, and a dollop of pesto. Serve alongside a lemon wedge.

Per Serving calories: 858 | fat: 24.4g | protein: 26.4g | carbs: 136.2g

Rice and Bean Stuffed Zucchini

Prep time: 10 minutes | **Cook time:** 15 minutes | **Serves:** 4

Ingredients:

2 small zucchinis, halved lengthwise

½ cup cooked rice

½ cup canned white beans, drained and rinsed

½ cup chopped tomatoes

½ cup chopped toasted cashew nuts

½ cup grated Parmesan cheese

1 tablespoon olive oil

½ teaspoon salt

½ teaspoon freshly ground black pepper

Directions:

Pour 1 cup of water in the instant pot and insert a trivet. Scoop out the pulp of zucchini and chop roughly.

In a bowl, mix the zucchini pulp, rice, tomatoes, cashew nuts, ¼ cup of Parmesan, olive oil, salt, and black pepper. Fill the zucchini boats with the mixture, and arrange the stuffed boats in a single layer on the trivet. Seal the lid and cook for 15 minutes on Steam on High. Do a quick release and serve.

Per Serving calories: 239 | fat: 14.7g | protein: 9.4g

Chard and Mushroom Risotto

Prep time: 15 minutes | **Cook time:** 20 minutes | **Serves:** 4

Ingredients:

3 tablespoons olive oil

1 onion, chopped

2 Swiss chard, stemmed and chopped

1 cup risotto rice

⅓ cup white wine

3 cups vegetable stock

½ teaspoon salt

½ cup mushrooms

4 tablespoons pumpkin seeds, toasted

⅓ cup grated Pecorino Romano cheese

Directions:

Heat oil on Sauté, and cook onion and mushrooms for 5 minutes, stirring, until tender. Add the rice and cook for a minute. Stir in wine and cook for 2 to 3 minutes until almost evaporated.

Pour in stock and season with salt. Seal the lid and cook on High Pressure for 10 minutes.

Do a quick release. Stir in chard until wilted, mix in cheese to melt, and serve scattered with pumpkin seeds.

Per Serving
calories: 420 | fat: 17.7g | protein: 11.8g | carbs: 54.9g

Beef and Bean Stuffed Pasta Shells

Prep time: 15 minutes | **Cook time:** 17 minutes | **Serves:** 4

Ingredients:

2 tablespoons olive oil

1 pound (454 g) ground beef

1 pound (454 g) pasta shells

2 cups water

15 ounces (425 g) tomato sauce

1 (15-ounce / 425-g) can black beans, drained and rinsed

15 ounces (425 g) canned corn, drained (or 2 cups frozen corn)

10 ounces (283 g) red enchilada sauce

4 ounces (113 g) diced green chiles

1 cup shredded Mozzarella cheese

Salt and ground black pepper to taste

Additional cheese for topping

Finely chopped parsley for garnish

Directions:

Heat oil on Sauté. Add ground beef and cook for 7 minutes until it starts to brown.

Mix in pasta, tomato sauce, enchilada sauce, black beans, water, corn, and green chiles and stir to coat well. Add more water if desired.

Seal the lid and cook on High Pressure for 10 minutes. Do a quick Pressure release. Into the pasta mixture, mix in Mozzarella cheese until melted; add black pepper and salt. Garnish with parsley to serve.

Per Serving
calories: 1006 | fat: 30.0g | protein: 53.3g | carbs: 138.9g

Caprese Fusilli

Prep time: 15 minutes | **Cook time:** 7 minutes | **Serves:** 3

Ingredients:

1 tablespoon olive oil

1 onion, thinly chopped

6 garlic cloves, minced

1 teaspoon red pepper flakes

2½ cups dried fusilli

1 (15-ounce / 425-g) can tomato sauce

1 cup tomatoes, halved

1 cup water

¼ cup basil leaves

1 teaspoon salt

1 cup Ricotta cheese, crumbled

2 tablespoons chopped fresh basil

Directions:

Warm oil on Sauté. Add red pepper flakes, garlic and onion and cook for 3 minutes until soft.

Mix in fusilli, tomatoes, half of the basil leaves, water, tomato sauce, and salt. Seal the lid, and cook on High Pressure for 4 minutes. Release the pressure quickly.

Transfer the pasta to a serving platter and top with the crumbled ricotta and remaining chopped basil.

Per Serving
calories: 589 | fat: 17.7g | protein: 19.5g | carbs: 92.8g

Pasta with Lemon and Artichokes (Italian)

Preparation Time: 10 minutes **Cooking Time:** 15 minutes
Servings: 4

Ingredients:

16 ounces linguine or angel hair pasta
2 (15-ounce) jars water-packed artichoke hearts, drained and quartered
2 tablespoons freshly squeezed lemon juice
Freshly ground black pepper
8 garlic cloves, finely minced or pressed
1/4 cup thinly sliced fresh basil
1 teaspoon of sea salt
1/4 cup extra-virgin olive oil

Directions:

Boil a pot of water on high heat and cook the pasta.

While the pasta is cooking, heat the oil in a skillet over medium heat and cook the garlic, stirring often, for 1 to 2 minutes until it just begins to brown. Toss the garlic with the artichokes in a large bowl.

When the pasta is cooked, drain it very carefully and add it to the artichoke mixture, then add the lemon juice, basil, salt, and pepper. Gently stir and serve.

Per Serving
Calories: 423 Protein: 15 g Fat: 14 g

Spinach Beef Pasta (Italian)

Preparation Time: 30 minutes **Cooking Time:** 10 minutes
Servings: 4

Ingredients:

1 ¼ cups uncooked orzo pasta
1 ½ lb. beef tenderloin
1 cup cherry tomatoes, halved
¾ cup baby spinach
2 tbsp. olive oil
¾ cup feta cheese
¼ tsp. Salt
2 quarts water

Directions:

Rub the meat with pepper and cut into small cubes.

Over medium stove flame; heat the oil in a deep saucepan (preferably of medium size).

Add and stir-fry the meat until it is evenly brown.

Add the water and boil the mixture; stir in the orzo and salt.

Cook the mixture for 7-8 minutes. Add the spinach and cook until it wilts.

Add the tomatoes and cheese; combine and serve warm.

Per Serving
Calories 334 | Fat 13g | Carbs 36g | Protein 16g

Chickpea Pasta Salad (Italian)

Preparation Time: 10 minutes **Cooking Time:** 15 minutes
Servings: 6

Ingredients:

2 Tablespoons Olive Oil 16 Ounces Rotelle Pasta
2 Tablespoons Oregano, Fresh & Minced
Pepper to Taste
15 Ounces Canned Garbanzo Beans, Drained & Rinsed
½ Cup Cured Olives, Chopped
¼ Cup Red Wine Vinegar
1 Bunch Green Onions, Chopped
½ Cup Parmesan Cheese, Grated Sea Salt & Black
2 Tablespoons Parsley, Fresh & Chopped

Directions:

Bring a pot of water to a boil and cook your pasta al dente per package instructions. Drain it and rinse it using cold water.

Get out a skillet and heat up your olive oil over medium heat. Add in your scallions, chickpeas, parsley, oregano and olives. Lower the heat to low, and cook for twenty minutes more. Allow this mixture to cool.

Toss your chickpea mixture with your pasta, and then add in your grated cheese, salt, pepper and vinegar. Let it chill for four hours or overnight before serving.

Per Serving
Calories: 424 Protein: 16 g Fat: 10 g Carbs: 69 g

Spaghetti with Pine Nuts and Cheese (Italian)

Preparation Time: 10 minutes **Cooking Time:** 11 minutes
Servings: 4 to 6

Ingredients:

8 ounces (227 g) spaghetti
4 tablespoons almond butter
1 cup fresh grated Parmesan cheese, divided
1 teaspoon freshly ground black pepper
1/2 cup pine nuts

Directions:

Bring a large pot of salted water to a boil. Add the pasta and cook for 8 minutes.

In a large saucepan over medium heat, combine the butter, black pepper, and pine nuts. Cook for 2 to 3 minutes, or until the pine nuts are lightly toasted.

Reserve ½ cup of the pasta water. Drain the pasta and place it into the pan with the pine nuts.

Add ¾ cup of the Parmesan cheese and the reserved pasta water to the pasta and toss everything together to coat the pasta evenly.

Transfer the pasta to a serving dish and top with the remaining ¼ cup of the Parmesan cheese. Serve immediately.

Per Serving
calories: 542 fats: 32.0g protein: 20.0g carbs: 46.0g

Fresh Sauce Pasta (Italian)

Preparation Time: 15 minutes **Cooking Time:** 15 minutes
Servings: 4

Ingredients:

1/8 teaspoon salt, plus more for cooking the pasta
1 garlic clove, crushed
3 tomatoes, diced
2 tablespoons chopped fresh basil
1/4 cup olive oil
1-pound penne pasta
3 cups chopped scallions, white and green parts
1/8 teaspoon freshly ground black pepper
Freshly grated Parmesan cheese, for serving

Directions:

Bring a large pot of salted water to a boil over high heat. Drop in the pasta, stir, and return the water to a boil. Boil the pasta for about 6 minutes or until al dente.

A couple minutes before the pasta is completely cooked, in a medium saucepan over medium heat, heat the olive oil.

Add the garlic and cook for 30 seconds.

Stir in the scallions and tomatoes. Cover the pan and cook for 2 to 3 minutes.

Drain the pasta and add it to the vegetables. Stir in the basil and season with the salt and pepper. Top with the Parmesan cheese.

Per Serving

Calories: 477; Total Fat: 16g; Saturated Fat: 2g; Carbohydrates: 72g; Protein: 15g

Caprese Fusilli

Prep time: 15 minutes | **Cook time:** 7 minutes | **Serves:** 3

Ingredients:

1 tablespoon olive oil
1 onion, thinly chopped
6 garlic cloves, minced
1 teaspoon red pepper flakes
2½ cups dried fusilli
1 (15-ounce / 425-g) can tomato sauce
1 cup tomatoes, halved
1 cup water
¼ cup basil leaves
1 teaspoon salt
1 cup Ricotta cheese, crumbled
2 tablespoons chopped fresh basil

Directions:

Warm oil on Sauté. Add red pepper flakes, garlic and onion and cook for 3 minutes until soft.

Mix in fusilli, tomatoes, half of the basil leaves, water, tomato sauce, and salt. Seal the lid, and cook on High Pressure for 4 minutes. Release the pressure quickly.

Transfer the pasta to a serving platter and top with the crumbled ricotta and remaining chopped basil.

Per Serving

calories: 589 | fat: 17.7g | protein: 19.5g | carbs: 92.8g

Broccoli Pesto Spaghetti (Italian)

Preparation Time: 5 minutes **Cooking Time:** 35 minutes
Servings: 4

Ingredients:

8 oz. Spaghetti
2 tablespoons olive oil
4 garlic cloves, chopped
4 basil leaves
Salt and pepper to taste
1-pound broccoli, cut into florets
2 tablespoons blanched almonds
1 lemon, juiced

Directions:

For the pesto, combine the broccoli, oil, garlic, basil, lemon juice and almonds in a blender and pulse until well mixed and smooth.

Cook the spaghetti in a large pot of salty water for 8 minutes or until al dente. Drain well.

Mix the warm spaghetti with the broccoli pesto and serve right away.

Per Serving

Calories: 284, Fat:10.2g, Protein:10.4g, Carbohydrates:40.2g

Very Vegan Patras Pasta (Italian)

Prep time: 5 minutes **Cooking Time:** 10 mins **Servings:** 6

Ingredients:

4 quarts salted water
10 oz. gluten-free and whole-grain pasta
5 cloves garlic, minced
½ cup walnuts
2 tbsp dried cranberries (optional)
1 cup hummus Salt and pepper
1/3 cup water
½ cup olives

Directions:

Bring the salted water to a boil for cooking the pasta.

In the meantime, prepare for the hummus sauce. Combine the garlic, hummus, salt, and pepper with water in a mixing bowl. Add the walnuts, olive, and dried cranberries, if desired. Set aside.

Add the pasta in the boiling water. Cook the pasta following the manufacturer's specifications until attaining an al dente texture. Drain the pasta.

Transfer the pasta to a large serving bowl and combine with the sauce.

Per Serving

Calories: 329 Protein: 12 g Fat: 13 g Carbs: 43 g

Cheesy Spaghetti with Pine Nuts (Italian)

Prep time: 10 minutes **Cooking Time:** 10 mins **Servings:** 4

Ingredients:

8 oz. spaghetti	4 tbsp. (½ stick) unsalted butter
1 tsp. freshly ground black pepper	½ cup pine nuts
1 cup fresh grated Parmesan cheese, divided	

Directions:

Bring a large pot of salted water to a boil. Add the pasta and cook for 8 minutes.

In a large saucepan over medium heat, combine the butter, black pepper, and pine nuts. Cook for 2 to 3 minutes or until the pine nuts are lightly toasted.

Reserve ½ cup of the pasta water. Drain the pasta and put it into the pan with the pine nuts.

Add ¾ cup of Parmesan cheese and the reserved pasta water to the pasta and toss everything together to coat the pasta evenly.

To serve, put the pasta in a serving dish and top with the remaining ¼ cup of Parmesan cheese.

Per Serving

Calories: 238; Protein: 12.3g; Carbs: 3.4g; Fat: 6.3g

Italian Mac & Cheese (Italian)

Prep time: 10 minutes **Cooking Time:** 6 mins **Servings:** 4

Ingredients:

1 lb. whole grain pasta	4 cups of water
2 tsp Italian seasoning	1 cup sour cream
4 oz parmesan cheese, shredded	Pepper Salt
12 oz ricotta cheese	1 1/2 tsp onion powder
	1 1/2 tsp garlic powder

Directions:

Add all except ricotta cheese into the inner pot of instant pot and stir well.

Seal pot with lid and cook on high for 6 minutes.

Once done, allow to release pressure naturally for 5 minutes then release remaining using quick release. Remove lid.

Add ricotta cheese and stir well and serve.

Per Serving

Calories 388 Fat 25.8 g Carbohydrates 18.1 g Sugar 4 g Protein 22.8 g Cholesterol 74 mg

Penne Bolognese Pasta (Italian)

Preparation Time: 15 minutes **Cooking Time:** 20 minutes **Servings:** 2

Ingredients:

Penne pasta 7 oz. Beef 5 oz.	Parmesan Cheese 1 oz..
Shallots 26 g	Carrot 1.5 oz.
Garlic 1 clove	Thyme 1 g
Tomatoes in own juice 6 oz.	Oregano 1 g
Parsley 3 g	Celery Stalk 1 oz
Butter 20 g	Dry white wine 50 ml Olive oil 40 ml

Directions:

Pour the penne into boiling salted water and cook for 9 minutes.

Roll the beef through a meat grinder.

Dice onion, celery, carrots and garlic in a small cube.

Fry the chopped vegetables in a heated frying pan in olive oil with minced meat for 4–5 minutes, salt and pepper.

Add oregano to the fried minced meat and vegetables, pour 50 ml of wine, add the tomatoes along with the juice and simmer for 10 minutes until the tomatoes are completely softened.

Add the boiled penne and butter to the sauce and simmer for 1-2 minutes, stirring continuously.

Put in a plate, sprinkle with grated Parmesan and chopped parsley, decorate with a sprig of thyme and serve.

Per Serving

Calories: 435 Protein: 18 g Fat: 14 g Carbs: 33 g

Spaghetti all 'Olio (Italian)

Preparation Time: 5 minutes **Cooking Time:** 30 minutes **Servings:** 4

Ingredients:

8 oz. Spaghetti	2 tablespoons olive oil
4 garlic cloves, minced	2 red peppers, sliced
1 tablespoon lemon juice	½ cup grated parmesan cheese
Salt and pepper to taste	

Directions:

Heat the oil in a skillet and add the garlic. Cook for 30 seconds then stir in the red peppers and cook for 1 more minute on low heat, making sure only to infuse them, not to burn or fry them.

Add the lemon juice and remove off heat.

Cook the spaghetti in a large pot of salty water for 8 minutes or as stated on the package, just until they become al dente.

Drain the spaghetti well and mix them with the garlic and pepper oil.

Serve right away.

Per Serving

Calories:268, Fat:11.9g, Protein:7.1g, Carbohydrates:34.1g

Mediterranean Pasta with Tomato Sauce and Vegetables (Italian)

Preparation Time: 15 minutes **Cooking Time:** 25 minutes
Servings: 8

Ingredients:

8 oz. linguine or spaghetti, cooked	1 (28 oz.) can whole peeled tomatoes, drained and sliced
1 tsp. garlic powder	1 tbsp. olive oil
1 (8 oz.) can tomato sauce	½ tsp. Italian seasoning
8 oz. mushrooms, sliced	8 oz. zucchini, sliced
8 oz. yellow squash, sliced	½ tsp. sugar
½ cup grated Parmesan cheese	

Directions:

In a medium saucepan, mix tomato sauce, tomatoes, sugar, Italian seasoning, and garlic powder. Bring to boil on medium heat. Reduce heat to low. Cover and simmer for 20 minutes.

In a large skillet, heat olive oil on medium-high heat. Add squash, mushrooms, and zucchini. Cook, stirring, for 4 minutes or until tender-crisp. Stir vegetables into the tomato sauce.

Place pasta in a serving bowl. Spoon vegetable mixture over pasta and toss to coat. Top with grated Parmesan cheese.

Per Serving Calories: 154 Protein: 6 g Fat: 2 g Carbs: 28 g

Penne Pasta with Tomato Sauce and MitzithraCheese (Italian)

Preparation Time: 15 minutes **Cooking Time:** 20 minutes
Servings: 5

Ingredients:

2 tablespoons olive oil	2 scallion stalks, chopped
2 green garlic stalks, minced	1/3 teaspoon ground black pepper, to taste Sea salt, to taste
10 ounces penne	
1/2 teaspoon dried oregano	
1/4 teaspoon cayenne pepper	1/2 cup marinara sauce
1/2 teaspoon dried basil	2 cups vegetable broth
1 cup Mitzithra cheese, grated	1/4 teaspoon dried marjoram
2 overripe tomatoes, pureed	

Directions:

Press the "Sauté" button to preheat your Instant Pot. Heat the oil until sizzling. Now, sauté the scallions and garlic until just tender and fragrant.

Secure the lid. Choose the "Manual" mode and cook for 7 minutes at High pressure. Once cooking is complete, use a natural pressure release for 5 minutes; carefully remove the lid.

Fold in the cheese and seal the lid. Let it sit in the residual heat until the cheese melts. Bon appetite

Per Serving
395 Calories; 15.6g Fat; 51.8g Carbs; 14.9g Protein; 2.5g Sugars;

Lentil and Mushroom Pasta (Italian)

Preparation Time: 10 minutes **Cooking Time:** 50 minutes
Servings: 2

Ingredients:

2 tablespoons olive oil	1 large yellow onion, finely diced
2 tablespoons tomato paste	
2 portobello mushrooms, trimmed and chopped finely	3 garlic cloves, chopped
2½ cups water	1 teaspoon oregano
1 (28-ounce / 794-g) can diced tomatoes with basil (with juice if diced)	1 cup brown lentils
	8 ounces (227 g) pasta of choice, cooked Salt and black pepper, to taste
1 tablespoon balsamic vinegar	Chopped basil, for garnish

Directions:

Place a large stockpot over medium heat. Add the oil. Once the oil is hot, add the onion and mushrooms. Cover and cook until both are soft, about 5 minutes. Add the tomato paste, garlic, and oregano and cook 2 minutes, stirring constantly.

Stir in the water and lentils. Bring to a boil, then reduce the heat to medium-low and cook for 5 minutes, covered.

Add the tomatoes (and juice if using diced) and vinegar. Replace the lid, reduce the heat to low and cook until the lentils are tender, about 30 minutes.

Remove the sauce from the heat and season with salt and pepper to taste. Garnish with the basil and serve over the cooked pasta.

Per Serving
calories: 463 fats: 15.9g protein: 12.5g carbs: 70.0g

Chapter 6
Vegetable Recipes

Stuffed Portobello Mushrooms with Spinach

Prep time: 5 minutes | **Cook time:** 20 minutes | **Serves:** 4

Ingredients:

8 large portobello mushrooms, stems removed
3 teaspoons extra-virgin olive oil, divided
1 medium red bell pepper, diced
4 cups fresh spinach
¼ cup crumbled feta cheese

Directions:

Preheat the oven to 450ºF (235ºC).

Using a spoon to scoop out the gills of the mushrooms and discard them. Brush the mushrooms with 2 teaspoons of olive oil.

Arrange the mushrooms (cap-side down) on a baking sheet. Roast in the preheated oven for 20 minutes.

Meantime, in a medium skillet, heat the remaining olive oil over medium heat until it shimmers.

Add the bell pepper and spinach and saut é for 8 to 10 minutes, stirring occasionally, or until the spinach is wilted.

Remove the mushrooms from the oven to a paper towel-lined plate. Using a spoon to stuff each mushroom with the bell pepper and spinach mixture. Scatter the feta cheese all over. Serve immediately.

Per Serving (2 mushrooms)
calories: 115 | fat: 5.9g | protein: 7.2g | carbs: 11.5g

Chickpea Lettuce Wraps with Celery

Prep time: 10 minutes | **Cook time:** 0 minutes | **Serves:** 4

Ingredients:

1 (15-ounce / 425-g) can low-sodium chickpeas, drained and rinsed
1 celery stalk, thinly sliced
2 tablespoons finely chopped red onion
2 tablespoons unsalted tahini
3 tablespoons honey mustard
1 tablespoon capers, undrained
12 butter lettuce leaves

Directions:

In a bowl, mash the chickpeas with a potato masher or the back of a fork until mostly smooth.

Add the celery, red onion, tahini, honey mustard, and capers to the bowl and stir until well incorporated.

For each serving, place three overlapping lettuce leaves on a plate and top with ¼ of the mashed chickpea filling, then roll up. Repeat with the remaining lettuce leaves and chickpea mixture.

Per Serving
calories: 182 | fat: 7.1g | protein: 10.3g | carbs: 19.6g

Zoodles with Walnut Pesto

Prep time: 10 minutes | **Cook time:** 10 minutes | **Serves:** 4

Ingredients:

4 medium zucchinis, spiralized
¼ cup extra-virgin olive oil, divided
1 teaspoon minced garlic, divided
½ teaspoon crushed red pepper
¼ teaspoon freshly ground black pepper, divided
¼ teaspoon kosher salt, divided
2 tablespoons grated Parmesan cheese, divided
1 cup packed fresh basil leaves
¾ cup walnut pieces, divided

Directions:

In a large bowl, stir together the zoodles, 1 tablespoon of the olive oil, ½ teaspoon of the minced garlic, red pepper, ⅛ teaspoon of the black pepper and ⅛ teaspoon of the salt. Set aside.

Heat ½ tablespoon of the oil in a large skillet over medium-high heat. Add half of the zoodles to the skillet and cook for 5 minutes, stirring constantly. Transfer the cooked zoodles into a bowl. Repeat with another ½ tablespoon of the oil and the remaining zoodles. When done, add the cooked zoodles to the bowl.

Make the pesto: In a food processor, combine the remaining ½ teaspoon of the minced garlic, ⅛ teaspoon of the black pepper and ⅛ teaspoon of the salt, 1 tablespoon of the Parmesan, basil leaves and ¼ cup of the walnuts. Pulse until smooth and then slowly drizzle the remaining 2 tablespoons of the oil into the pesto. Pulse again until well combined.

Add the pesto to the zoodles along with the remaining 1 tablespoon of the Parmesan and the remaining ½ cup of the walnuts. Toss to coat well.

Serve immediately.

Per Serving
calories: 166 | fat: 16.0g | protein: 4.0g | carbs: 3.0g

Mushroom and Spinach Stuffed Peppers

Prep time: 15 minutes | **Cook time:** 8 minutes | **Serves:**7

Ingredients:

7 mini sweet peppers

1 cup button mushrooms, minced

5 ounces (142 g) organic baby spinach

½ teaspoon fresh garlic

½ teaspoon coarse sea salt

¼ teaspoon cracked mixed pepper

2 tablespoons water

1 tablespoon olive oil

Organic Mozzarella cheese, diced

Directions:

Put the sweet peppers and water in the instant pot and Sauté for 2 minutes.

Remove the peppers and put the olive oil into the pot.

Stir in the mushrooms, garlic, spices and spinach.

Cook on Sauté until the mixture is dry. Stuff each sweet pepper with the cheese and spinach mixture. Bake the stuffed peppers in an oven for 6 minutes at 400ºF (205ºC).

Once done, serve hot.

Per Serving

calories: 81 | fat: 2.4g | protein: 4.1g | carbs: 13.2g

Black Bean and Corn Tortilla Bowls

Prep time: 10 minutes | **Cook time:** 8 minutes | **Serves:**4

Ingredients:

1½ cups vegetable broth

½ cup tomatoes, undrained diced

1 small onion, diced

2 garlic cloves, finely minced

1 teaspoon chili powder

1 teaspoon cumin

½ teaspoon paprika

½ teaspoon ground coriander

Salt and pepper to taste

2 small potatoes, cubed

½ cup bell pepper, chopped

½ can black beans, drained and rinsed

1 cup frozen corn kernels

½ tablespoon lime juice

2 tablespoons cilantro for topping, chopped

Whole-wheat tortilla chips

½ cup carrots, diced

Directions:

Add the oil and all the vegetables into the instant pot and Sauté for 3 minutes.

Add all the spices, corn, lime juice, and broth, along with the beans, to the pot.

Seal the lid and cook on Manual setting at High Pressure for 5 minutes.

Once done, natural release the pressure when the timer goes off. Remove the lid.

To serve, put the prepared mixture into a bowl.

Top with tortilla chips and fresh cilantro. Serve.

Per Serving

calories: 183 | fat: 0.9g | protein: 7.1g | carbs: 39.8g

Cauliflower and Broccoli Bowls

Prep time: 5 minutes | **Cook time:** 7 minutes | **Serves:**3

Ingredients:

½ medium onion, diced

2 teaspoons olive oil

1 garlic clove, minced

½ cup tomato paste

½ pound (227 g) frozen cauliflower

½ pound (227 g) broccoli florets

½ cup vegetable broth

½ teaspoon paprika

¼ teaspoon dried thyme

2 pinches sea salt

Directions:

Add the oil, onion and garlic into the instant pot and Sauté for 2 minutes.

Add the broth, tomato paste, cauliflower, broccoli, and all the spices, to the pot.

Secure the lid. Cook on the Manual setting at with pressure for 5 minutes.

After the beep, Quick release the pressure and remove the lid.

Stir well and serve hot.

Per Serving

calories: 109 | fat: 3.8g | protein: 6.1g | carbs: 16.7g

Potato and Broccoli Medley

Prep time: 10 minutes | **Cook time:** 20 minutes | **Serves:**3

Ingredients:

1 tablespoon olive oil

½ white onion, diced

1½ cloves garlic, finely chopped

1 pound (454 g) potatoes, cut into chunks

1 pound (454 g) broccoli florets, diced

1 pound (454 g) baby carrots, cut in half

¼ cup vegetable broth

½ teaspoon Italian seasoning

½ teaspoon Spike original seasoning

Fresh parsley for garnishing

Directions:

Put the oil and onion into the instant pot and Sauté for 5 minutes. Stir in the carrots, and garlic and stir-fry for 5 minutes. Add the remaining ingredients and secure the lid.

Cook on the Manual function for 10 minutes at High Pressure. After the beep, Quick release the pressure and remove the lid. Stir gently and garnish with fresh parsley , then serve.

Per Serving

calories: 256 | fat: 5.6g | protein: 9.1g | carbs: 46.1g

Mushroom Swoodles

Prep time: 5 minutes | **Cook time:** 3 minutes | **Serves:** 4

Ingredients:

2 tablespoons coconut aminos
1 tablespoon white vinegar
2 teaspoons olive oil
1 teaspoon sesame oil
1 tablespoon honey
¼ teaspoon red pepper flakes

3 cloves garlic, minced
1 large sweet potato, peeled and spiraled
1 pound (454 g) shiitake mushrooms, sliced
1 cup vegetable broth
¼ cup chopped fresh parsley

Directions:

In a large bowl, whisk together coconut aminos, vinegar, olive oil, sesame oil, honey, red pepper flakes, and garlic.

Toss sweet potato and shiitake mushrooms in sauce. Refrigerate covered for 30 minutes.

Pour vegetable broth into Instant Pot. Add trivet. Lower steamer basket onto trivet and add the sweet potato mixture to the basket. Lock lid.

Press the Manual button and adjust time to 3 minutes. When timer beeps, let pressure release naturally for 5 minutes. Quick release any additional pressure until float valve drops and then unlock lid.

Remove basket from the Instant Pot and distribute sweet potatoes and mushrooms evenly among four bowls; pour liquid from the Instant Pot over bowls and garnish with chopped parsley.

Per Serving

calories: 127 | fat: 4.0g | protein: 4.2g | carbs: 20.9g

Carrot and Turnip Purée

Prep time: 10 minutes | **Cook time:** 10 minutes | **Serves:** 6

Ingredients:

2 tablespoons olive oil, divided
3 large turnips, peeled and quartered
4 large carrots, peeled and cut into 2-inch pieces

2 cups vegetable broth
1 teaspoon salt
½ teaspoon ground nutmeg
2 tablespoons sour cream

Directions:

Press the Sauté button on Instant Pot. Heat 1 tablespoon olive oil. Toss turnips and carrots in oil for 1 minute. Add broth. Lock lid. Press the Manual button and adjust time to 8 minutes. When timer beeps, quick release pressure until float valve drops and then unlock lid.

Drain vegetables and reserve liquid; set liquid aside. Add 2 tablespoons of reserved liquid plus remaining ingredients to vegetables in the Instant Pot.

Use an immersion blender to blend until desired smoothness. If too thick, add more liquid 1 tablespoon at a time. Serve warm.

Per Serving

calories: 95 | fat: 5.2g | protein: 1.4g | carbs: 11.8g

Rice, Corn, and Bean Stuffed Peppers

Prep time: 15 minutes | **Cook time:** 15 minutes | **Serves:** 4

Ingredients:

4 large bell peppers
2 cups cooked white rice
1 medium onion, peeled and diced
3 small Roma tomatoes, diced
¼ cup marinara sauce
1 cup corn kernels (cut from the cob is preferred)
¼ cup sliced black olives

¼ cup canned cannellini beans, rinsed and drained
¼ cup canned black beans, rinsed and drained
1 teaspoon sea salt
1 teaspoon garlic powder
½ cup vegetable broth
2 tablespoons grated Parmesan cheese

Directions:

Cut off the bell pepper tops as close to the tops as possible. Hollow out and discard seeds. Poke a few small holes in the bottom of the peppers to allow drippings to drain.

In a medium bowl, combine remaining ingredients except for broth and Parmesan cheese. Stuff equal amounts of mixture into each of the bell peppers.

Place trivet into the Instant Pot and pour in the broth. Set the peppers upright on the trivet. Lock lid.

Press the Manual button and adjust time to 15 minutes. When timer beeps, let pressure release naturally until float valve drops and then unlock lid.

Serve immediately and garnish with Parmesan cheese.

Per Serving

calories: 265 | fat: 3.0g | protein: 8.1g | carbs: 53.1g

Zoodles

Prep time: 10 minutes | **Cook time:** 5 minutes | **Serves:** 2

Ingredients:

2 tablespoons avocado oil
2 medium zucchini, spiralized

¼ teaspoon salt
Freshly ground black pepper, to taste

Directions:

Heat the avocado oil in a large skillet over medium heat until it shimmers.

Add the zucchini noodles, salt, and black pepper to the skillet and toss to coat. Cook for 1 to 2 minutes, stirring constantly, until tender.

Serve warm.

Per Serving

calories: 128 | fat: 14.0g | protein: 0.3g | carbs: 0.3g

Cheesy Sweet Potato Burgers

Prep time: 10 minutes | **Cook time:** 19 to 20 minutes | **Serves:** 4

Ingredients:

1 large sweet potato (about 8 ounces / 227 g)
2 tablespoons extra-virgin olive oil, divided
1 cup chopped onion
1 large egg
¼ teaspoon kosher salt
1 garlic clove
1 cup old-fashioned rolled oats
1 tablespoon dried oregano
1 tablespoon balsamic vinegar
½ cup crumbled Gorgonzola cheese

Directions:

Using a fork, pierce the sweet potato all over and microwave on high for 4 to 5 minutes, until softened in the center. Cool slightly before slicing in half.

Meanwhile, in a large skillet over medium-high heat, heat 1 tablespoon of the olive oil. Add the onion and sauté for 5 minutes.

Spoon the sweet potato flesh out of the skin and put the flesh in a food processor. Add the cooked onion, egg, garlic, oats, oregano, vinegar and salt. Pulse until smooth. Add the cheese and pulse four times to barely combine.

Form the mixture into four burgers. Place the burgers on a plate, and press to flatten each to about ¾-inch thick.

Wipe out the skillet with a paper towel. Heat the remaining 1 tablespoon of the oil over medium-high heat for about 2 minutes. Add the burgers to the hot oil, then reduce the heat to medium. Cook the burgers for 5 minutes per side.

Transfer the burgers to a plate and serve.

Per Serving

calories: 290 | fat: 12.0g | protein: 12.0g | carbs: 43.0g

Radish and Cabbage Congee

Prep time: 5 minutes | **Cook time:** 20 minutes | **Serves:** 3

Ingredients:

1 cup carrots, diced
½ cup radish, diced
6 cups vegetable broth
Salt, to taste
1½ cups short grain rice, rinsed
1 tablespoon grated fresh ginger
4 cups cabbage, shredded
Green onions for garnishing, chopped

Directions:

Add all the ingredients, except the cabbage and green onions, into the instant pot.

Select the Porridge function and cook on the default time and settings.

After the beep, Quick release the pressure and remove the lid Stir in the shredded cabbage and cover with the lid.

Serve after 10 minutes with chopped green onions on top.

Per Serving

calories: 438 | fat: 0.8g | protein: 8.7g | carbs: 98.4g

Mushroom and Potato Teriyaki

Prep time: 10 minutes | **Cook time:** 18 minutes | **Serves:** 4

Ingredients:

¾ large yellow or white onion, chopped
1½ medium carrots, diced
1½ ribs celery, chopped
1 medium portabella mushroom, diced
¾ tablespoon garlic, chopped
2 cups water
1 pound (454 g) white potatoes, peeled and diced
¼ cup tomato paste
½ tablespoon sesame oil
2 teaspoons sesame seeds
½ tablespoon paprika
1 teaspoon fresh rosemary
¾ cups peas
¼ cup fresh parsley for garnishing, chopped

Directions:

Add the oil, sesame seeds, and all the vegetables in the instant pot and Sauté for 5 minutes.

Stir in the remaining ingredients and secure the lid. Cook on Manual function for 13 minutes at High Pressure.

After the beep, natural release the pressure and remove the lid. Garnish with fresh parsley and serve hot.

Per Serving

calories: 160 | fat: 3.0g | protein: 4.7g | carbs: 30.6g

Cauliflower with Sweet Potato

Prep time: 15 minutes | **Cook time:** 8 minutes | **Serves:** 8

Ingredients:

1 small onion
4 tomatoes
4 garlic cloves, chopped
2-inch ginger, chopped
2 teaspoons olive oil
1 teaspoon turmeric
2 teaspoons ground cumin
Salt, to taste
1 teaspoon paprika
2 medium sweet potatoes, cubed small
2 small cauliflowers, diced
2 tablespoons fresh cilantro for topping, chopped

Directions:

Blend the tomatoes, garlic, ginger and onion in a blender.

Add the oil and cumin in the instant pot and Sauté for 1 minute.

Stir in the blended mixture and the remaining spices.

Add the sweet potatoes and cook for 5 minutes on Sauté

Add the cauliflower chunks and secure the lid.

Cook on Manual for 2 minutes at High Pressure.

Once done, Quick release the pressure and remove the lid.

Stir and serve with cilantro on top.

Per Serving

calories: 76 | fat: 1.6g | protein: 2.7g | carbs: 14.4g

Fried Eggplant Rolls

Prep time: 20 minutes | **Cook time:** 10 mins | **Serves:** 4 to 6

Ingredients:

1 large eggplants, trimmed and cut lengthwise into ¼-inch-thick slices
1 teaspoon salt
1 cup ricotta cheese
Olive oil spray
4 ounces (113 g) goat cheese, shredded
¼ cup finely chopped fresh basil
½ teaspoon freshly ground black pepper

Directions:

Add the eggplant slices to a colander and season with salt. Set aside for 15 to 20 minutes.

Mix together the ricotta and goat cheese, basil, and black pepper in a large bowl and stir to combine. Set aside.

Dry the eggplant slices with paper towels and lightly mist them with olive oil spray.

Heat a large skillet over medium heat and lightly spray it with olive oil spray.

Arrange the eggplant slices in the skillet and fry each side for 3 minutes until golden brown.

Remove from the heat to a paper towel-lined plate and rest for 5 minutes.

Make the eggplant rolls: Lay the eggplant slices on a flat work surface and top each slice with a tablespoon of the prepared cheese mixture. Roll them up and serve immediately.

Per Serving

calories: 254 | fat: 14.9g | protein: 15.3g | carbs: 18.6g

Cauliflower Hash with Carrots

Prep time: 10 minutes | **Cook time:** 10 minutes | **Serves:** 4

Ingredients:

3 tablespoons extra-virgin olive oil
1 large onion, chopped
1 tablespoon minced garlic
2 cups diced carrots
4 cups cauliflower florets
½ teaspoon ground cumin
1 teaspoon salt

Directions:

In a large skillet, heat the olive oil over medium heat.

Add the onion and garlic and sauté for 1 minute. Stir in the carrots and stir-fry for 3 minutes.

Add the cauliflower florets, cumin, and salt and toss to combine.

Cover and cook for 3 minutes until lightly browned. Stir well and cook, uncovered, for 3 to 4 minutes, until softened.

Remove from the heat and serve warm.

Per Serving

calories: 158 | fat: 10.8g | protein: 3.1g | carbs: 14.9g

Roasted Veggies and Brown Rice Bowl

Prep time: 15 minutes | **Cook time:** 20 minutes | **Serves:** 4

Ingredients:

2 cups cauliflower florets
2 cups broccoli florets
1 (15-ounce / 425-g) can chickpeas, drained and rinsed
1 cup carrot slices (about 1 inch thick)
2 to 3 tablespoons extra-virgin olive oil, divided
Salt and freshly ground black pepper, to taste
Nonstick cooking spray
2 cups cooked brown rice
2 to 3 tablespoons sesame seeds, for garnish
Dressing:
3 to 4 tablespoons tahini
2 tablespoons honey
1 lemon, juiced
1 garlic clove, minced
Salt and freshly ground black pepper, to taste

Directions:

Preheat the oven to 400ºF (205ºC). Spritz two baking sheets with nonstick cooking spray.

Spread the cauliflower and broccoli on the first baking sheet and the second with the chickpeas and carrot slices.

Drizzle each sheet with half of the olive oil and sprinkle with salt and pepper. Toss to coat well.

Roast the chickpeas and carrot slices in the preheated oven for 10 minutes, leaving the carrots tender but crisp, and the cauliflower and broccoli for 20 minutes until fork-tender. Stir them once halfway through the cooking time.

Meanwhile, make the dressing: Whisk together the tahini, honey, lemon juice, garlic, salt, and pepper in a small bowl.

Divide the cooked brown rice among four bowls. Top each bowl evenly with roasted vegetables and dressing. Sprinkle the sesame seeds on top for garnish before serving.

Per Serving

calories: 453 | fat: 17.8g | protein: 12.1g | carbs: 61.8g

Wilted Dandelion Greens with Sweet Onion

Prep time: 15 minutes | **Cook time:** 15 minutes | **Serves:** 4

Ingredients:

1 tablespoon extra-virgin olive oil
2 garlic cloves, minced
1 Vidalia onion, thinly sliced
½ cup low-sodium vegetable broth
2 bunches dandelion greens, roughly chopped
Freshly ground black pepper, to taste

Directions:

Heat the olive oil in a large skillet over low heat.

Add the garlic and onion and cook for 2 to 3 minutes, stirring occasionally, or until the onion is translucent.

Fold in the vegetable broth and dandelion greens and cook for 5 to 7 minutes until wilted, stirring frequently.

Sprinkle with the black pepper and serve on a plate while warm.

Per Serving

calories: 81 | fat: 3.9g | protein: 3.2g | carbs: 10.8g

Zucchini and Artichokes Bowl with Farro

Prep time: 15 minutes | **Cook time:** 10 mins | **Serves:** 4 to 6

Ingredients:

⅓ cup extra-virgin olive oil
⅓ cup chopped red onions
½ cup chopped red bell pepper
2 garlic cloves, minced
1 cup zucchini, cut into ½-inch-thick slices
½ cup coarsely chopped artichokes
½ cup canned chickpeas, drained and rinsed
3 cups cooked farro

Salt and freshly ground black pepper, to taste
½ cup crumbled feta cheese, for serving (optional)
¼ cup sliced olives, for serving (optional)
2 tablespoons fresh basil, chiffonade, for serving (optional)
3 tablespoons balsamic vinegar, for serving (optional)

Directions:

Heat the olive oil in a large skillet over medium heat until it shimmers. Add the onions, bell pepper, and garlic and sauté for 5 minutes, stirring occasionally, until softened.

Stir in the zucchini slices, artichokes, and chickpeas and sauté for about 5 minutes until slightly tender.

Add the cooked farro and toss to combine until heated through. Sprinkle the salt and pepper to season.

Divide the mixture into bowls. Top each bowl evenly with feta cheese, olive slices, and basil and sprinkle with the balsamic vinegar, if desired.

Per Serving

calories: 366 | fat: 19.9g | protein: 9.3g | carbs: 50.7g

Vegetable and Tofu Scramble

Prep time: 5 minutes | **Cook time:** 10 minutes | **Serves:** 2

Ingredients:

2 tablespoons extra-virgin olive oil
½ red onion, finely chopped
1 cup chopped kale
8 ounces (227 g) mushrooms, sliced

2 garlic cloves, minced
Pinch red pepper flakes
½ teaspoon sea salt
⅛ teaspoon freshly ground black pepper
8 ounces (227 g) tofu, cut into pieces

Directions:

Heat the olive oil in a medium nonstick skillet over medium-high heat until shimmering.

Add the onion, kale, and mushrooms to the skillet and cook for about 5 minutes, stirring occasionally, or until the vegetables start to brown.

Add the tofu and stir-fry for 3 to 4 minutes until softened. Stir in the garlic, red pepper flakes, salt, and black pepper and cook for 30 seconds. Let the mixture cool for 5 minutes before serving.

Per Serving

calories: 233 | fat: 15.9g | protein: 13.4g | carbs: 11.9g

Zucchini Fritters

Prep time: 15 minutes | **Cook time:** 5 minutes
Makes 14 fritters

Ingredients:

4 cups grated zucchini
Salt, to taste
2 large eggs, lightly beaten
⅓ cup sliced scallions (green and white parts)

⅔ all-purpose flour
⅛ teaspoon black pepper
2 tablespoons olive oil

Directions:

Put the grated zucchini in a colander and lightly season with salt. Set aside to rest for 10 minutes. Squeeze out as much liquid from the grated zucchini as possible.

Pour the grated zucchini into a bowl. Fold in the beaten eggs, scallions, flour, salt, and pepper and stir until everything is well combined.

Heat the olive oil in a large skillet over medium heat until hot.

Drop 3 tablespoons mounds of the zucchini mixture onto the hot skillet to make each fritter, pressing them lightly into rounds and spacing them about 2 inches apart.

Cook for 2 to 3 minutes. Flip the zucchini fritters and cook for 2 minutes more, or until they are golden brown and cooked through.

Remove from the heat to a plate lined with paper towels. Repeat with the remaining zucchini mixture. Serve hot.

Per Serving (2 fritters)

calories: 113 | fat: 6.1g | protein: 4.0g | carbs: 12.2g

Vegetable and Red Lentil Stew

Prep time: 10 minutes | **Cook time:** 35 minutes | **Serves:** 6

Ingredients:

1 tablespoon extra-virgin olive oil
2 onions, peeled and finely diced
6½ cups water
2 zucchini, finely diced

4 celery stalks, finely diced
3 cups red lentils
1 teaspoon dried oregano
1 teaspoon salt, plus more as needed

Directions:

Heat the olive oil in a large pot over medium heat.

Add the onions and sauté for about 5 minutes, stirring constantly, or until the onions are softened.

Stir in the water, zucchini, celery, lentils, oregano, and salt and bring the mixture to a boil.

Reduce the heat to low and let simmer covered for 30 minutes, stirring occasionally, or until the lentils are tender.

Taste and adjust the seasoning as needed.

Per Serving

calories: 387 | fat: 4.4g | protein: 24.0g | carbs: 63.7g

Moroccan Tagine with Vegetables

Prep time: 20 minutes | **Cook time:** 40 minutes | **Serves:** 2

Ingredients:

2 tablespoons olive oil
½ onion, diced
1 garlic clove, minced
2 cups cauliflower florets
1 medium carrot, cut into 1-inch pieces
1 cup diced eggplant
1 (28-ounce / 794-g) can whole tomatoes with their juices
1 (15-ounce / 425-g) can chickpeas, drained and rinsed

2 small red potatoes, cut into 1-inch pieces
1 cup water
1 teaspoon pure maple syrup
½ teaspoon cinnamon
½ teaspoon turmeric
1 teaspoon cumin
½ teaspoon salt
1 to 2 teaspoons harissa paste

Directions:

In a Dutch oven, heat the olive oil over medium-high heat. Sauté the onion for 5 minutes, stirring occasionally, or until the onion is translucent.

Stir in the garlic, cauliflower florets, carrot, eggplant, tomatoes, and potatoes. Using a wooden spoon or spatula to break up the tomatoes into smaller pieces.

Add the chickpeas, water, maple syrup, cinnamon, turmeric, cumin, and salt and stir to incorporate. Bring the mixture to a boil.

Once it starts to boil, reduce the heat to medium-low. Stir in the harissa paste, cover, allow to simmer for about 40 minutes, or until the vegetables are softened. Taste and adjust seasoning as needed.

Let the mixture cool for 5 minutes before serving.

Per Serving

calories: 293 | fat: 9.9g | protein: 11.2g | carbs: 45.5g

Steamed Zucchini-Paprika (Italian)

Prep time: 15 minutes **Cook time:** 30 minutes **Servings:** 2

Ingredients:

4 tablespoons olive oil
3 medium-sized zucchinis, sliced thinly
A dash of paprika

3 cloves of garlic, minced
Salt and pepper to taste
1 onion, chopped

Directions:

Place all in the Instant Pot. Give a good stir to combine all . Close the lid and make sure that the steam release valve is set to "Venting."

Press the "Slow Cook" button and adjust the cooking time to 4 hours.

Halfway through the cooking time, open the lid and give a good stir to brown the other side.

Per Serving

Calories: 93; Carbs: 3.1g; Protein: 0.6g; Fat: 10.2g

Vegan Lentil Bolognese

Prep time: 15 minutes | **Cook time:** 50 minutes | **Serves:** 2

Ingredients:

1 medium celery stalk
1 large carrot
½ large onion
1 garlic clove
2 tablespoons olive oil
1 (28-ounce / 794-g) can crushed tomatoes

1 cup red wine
½ teaspoon salt, plus more as needed
½ teaspoon pure maple syrup
1 cup cooked lentils (prepared from ½ cup dry)

Directions:

Add the celery, carrot, onion, and garlic to a food processor and process until everything is finely chopped.

In a Dutch oven, heat the olive oil over medium-high heat. Add the chopped mixture and sauté for about 10 minutes, stirring occasionally, or until the vegetables are lightly browned.

Stir in the tomatoes, wine, salt, and maple syrup and bring to a boil.

Once the sauce starts to boil, cover, and reduce the heat to medium-low. Simmer for 30 minutes, stirring occasionally, or until the vegetables are softened.

Stir in the cooked lentils and cook for an additional 5 minutes until warmed through.

Taste and add additional salt, if needed. Serve warm.

Per Serving

calories: 367 | fat: 15.0g | protein: 13.7g | carbs: 44.

Grilled Vegetable Skewers

Prep time: 15 minutes | **Cook time:** 10 minutes | **Serves:** 4

Ingredients:

4 medium red onions, peeled and sliced into 6 wedges
4 medium zucchinis, cut into 1-inch-thick slices
2 beefsteak tomatoes, cut into quarters
4 red bell peppers, cut into 2-inch squares

2 orange bell peppers, cut into 2-inch squares
2 yellow bell peppers, cut into 2-inch squares
2 tablespoons plus 1 teaspoon olive oil, divided
Special Equipment:
4 wooden skewers, soaked in water for at least 30 minutes

Directions:

Preheat the grill to medium-high heat.

Skewer the vegetables by alternating between red onion, zucchini, tomatoes, and the different colored bell peppers. Brush them with 2 tablespoons of olive oil.

Oil the grill grates with 1 teaspoon of olive oil and grill the vegetable skewers for 5 minutes. Flip the skewers and grill for 5 minutes more, or until they are cooked to your liking.

Let the skewers cool for 5 minutes before serving.

Per Serving

calories: 115 | fat: 3.0g | protein: 3.5g | carbs: 18.7g

Stuffed Portobello Mushroom with Tomatoes

Prep time: 10 minutes | **Cook time:** 15 minutes | **Serves:**4

Ingredients:

4 large portobello mushroom caps
3 tablespoons extra-virgin olive oil
Salt and freshly ground black pepper, to taste
4 sun-dried tomatoes
1 cup shredded mozzarella cheese, divided
½ to ¾ cup low-sodium tomato sauce

Directions:

1. Preheat the broiler to High.
2. Arrange the mushroom caps on a baking sheet and drizzle with olive oil.
1. Sprinkle with salt and pepper.
2. Broil for 1o minutes, flipping the mushroom caps halfway through, until browned on the top.
3. Remove from the broil. Spoon 1 tomato, 2 tablespoons of cheese, and 2 to 3 tablespoons of sauce onto each mushroom cap.
4. Return the mushroom caps to the broiler and continue broiling for 2 to 3 minutes.
5. Cool for 5 minutes before serving.

Per Serving

calories: 217 | fat: 15.8g | protein: 11.2g | carbs: 11.7g

Stir-Fry Baby Bok Choy

Prep time: 12 minutes | **Cook time:** 10 to 13 minutes | **Serves:**6

Ingredients:

2 tablespoons coconut oil
1 large onion, finely diced
2 teaspoons ground cumin
1-inch piece fresh ginger, grated
1 teaspoon ground turmeric
½ teaspoon salt
12 baby bok choy heads, ends trimmed and sliced lengthwise
Water, as needed
3 cups cooked brown rice

Directions:

Heat the coconut oil in a large pan over medium heat.

Saut é the onion for 5 minutes, stirring occasionally, or until the onion is translucent. Fold in the cumin, ginger, turmeric, and salt and stir to coat well.

Add the bok choy and cook for 5 to 8 minutes, stirring occasionally, or until the bok choy is tender but crisp. You can add 1 tablespoon of water at a time, if the skillet gets dry until you finish sautéing. Transfer the bok choy to a plate and serve over the cooked brown rice.

Per Serving calories: 443 | fat: 8.8g | protein: 30.3g | carbs: 75.7g

Sweet Pepper Stew

Prep time: 20 minutes | **Cook time:** 50 minutes | **Serves:**2

Ingredients:

2 tablespoons olive oil
2 sweet peppers, diced (about 2 cups)
½ large onion, minced
1 garlic clove, minced
1 tablespoon gluten-free Worcestershire sauce
1 teaspoon oregano
1 cup low-sodium tomato juice
1 cup low-sodium vegetable stock
¼ cup brown rice
¼ cup brown lentils
Salt, to taste

Directions:

In a Dutch oven, heat the olive oil over medium-high heat.

Saut é the sweet peppers and onion for 10 minutes, stirring occasionally, or until the onion begins to turn golden and the peppers are wilted.

Stir in the garlic, Worcestershire sauce, and oregano and cook for 30 seconds more. Add the tomato juice, vegetable stock, rice, and lentils to the Dutch oven and stir to mix well. Bring the mixture to a boil and then reduce the heat to medium-low. Let it simmer covered for about 45 minutes, or until the rice is cooked through and the lentils are tender. Sprinkle with salt and serve warm.

Per Serving

calories: 378 | fat: 15.6g | protein: 11.4g | carbs: 52.8g

Cauliflower Rice Risotto with Mushrooms

Prep time: 5 minutes | **Cook time:** 10 minutes | **Serves:**4

Ingredients:

1 teaspoon extra-virgin olive oil
½ cup chopped portobello mushrooms
4 cups cauliflower rice
½ cup plain Greek yogurt
¼ cup low-sodium vegetable broth
1 cup shredded Parmesan cheese

Directions:

In a medium skillet, heat the olive oil over medium-low heat until shimmering.

Add the mushrooms and stir-fry for 3 minutes.

Stir in the cauliflower rice, yogurt, and vegetable broth. Cover and bring to a boil over high heat for 5 minutes, stirring occasionally.

Add the Parmesan cheese and stir to combine. Continue cooking for an additional 3 minutes until the cheese is melted.

Divide the mixture into four bowls and serve warm.

Per Serving

calories: 167 | fat: 10.7g | protein: 12.1g | carbs: 8.1g

Sautéed Cabbage with Parsley

Prep time: 10 minutes | **Cook time:** 12 to 14 minutes | **Serves:** 4 to 6

Ingredients:

1 small head green cabbage (about 1¼ pounds / 567 g), cored and sliced thin
2 tablespoons extra-virgin olive oil, divided
1½ teaspoons lemon juice
1 onion, halved and sliced thin
¾ teaspoon salt, divided
¼ teaspoon black pepper
¼ cup chopped fresh parsley

Directions:

Place the cabbage in a large bowl with cold water. Let sit for 3 minutes. Drain well. Heat 1 tablespoon of the oil in a skillet over medium-high heat until shimmering. Add the onion and ¼ teaspoon of the salt and cook for 5 to 7 minutes, or until softened and lightly browned. Transfer to a bowl. Heat the remaining 1 tablespoon of the oil in now-empty skillet over medium-high heat until shimmering. Add the cabbage and sprinkle with the remaining ½ teaspoon of the salt and black pepper. Cover and cook for about 3 minutes, without stirring, or until cabbage is wilted and lightly browned on bottom.

Stir and continue to cook for about 4 minutes, uncovered, or until the cabbage is crisp-tender and lightly browned in places, stirring once halfway through cooking. Off heat, stir in the cooked onion, parsley and lemon juice.

Transfer to a plate and serve.

Per Serving

calories: 117 | fat: 7.0g | protein: 2.7g | carbs: 13.4g

Grilled Romaine Lettuce

Prep time: 5 minutes | **Cook time:** 3 to 5 minutes | **Serves:** 4

Ingredients:

Romaine:
2 heads romaine lettuce, halved lengthwise
2 tablespoons extra-virgin olive oil
Dressing:
½ cup unsweetened almond milk
1 tablespoon extra-virgin olive oil
¼ bunch fresh chives, thinly chopped
1 garlic clove, pressed
1 pinch red pepper flakes

Directions:

Heat a grill pan over medium heat.

Brush each lettuce half with the olive oil. Place the lettuce halves, flat-side down, on the grill. Grill for 3 to 5 minutes, or until the lettuce slightly wilts and develops light grill marks. Meanwhile, whisk together all the ingredients for the dressing in a small bowl. Drizzle 2 tablespoons of the dressing over each romaine half and serve.

Per Serving

calories: 126 | fat: 11.0g | protein: 2.0g | carbs: 7.0g

Parmesan Stuffed Zucchini Boats

Prep time: 5 minutes | **Cook time:** 15 minutes | **Serves:** 4

Ingredients:

1 cup canned low-sodium chickpeas, drained and rinsed
1 cup no-sugar-added spaghetti sauce
2 zucchinis
¼ cup shredded Parmesan cheese

Directions:

Preheat the oven to 425ºF (220ºC).

In a medium bowl, stir together the chickpeas and spaghetti sauce.

Cut the zucchini in half lengthwise and scrape a spoon gently down the length of each half to remove the seeds.

Fill each zucchini half with the chickpea sauce and top with one-quarter of the Parmesan cheese. Place the zucchini halves on a baking sheet and roast in the oven for 15 minutes. Transfer to a plate. Let rest for 5 minutes before serving.

Per Serving

calories: 139 | fat: 4.0g | protein: 8.0g | carbs: 20.0g

Baby Kale and Cabbage Salad

Prep time: 10 minutes | **Cook time:** 0 minutes | **Serves:** 6

Ingredients:

2 bunches baby kale, thinly sliced
½ head green savoy cabbage, cored and thinly sliced
1 medium red bell pepper, thinly sliced
Dressing:
Juice of 1 lemon
¼ cup apple cider vinegar
1 teaspoon ground cumin
¼ teaspoon smoked paprika
1 garlic clove, thinly sliced
1 cup toasted peanuts

Directions:

In a large mixing bowl, toss together the kale and cabbage.

Make the dressing: Whisk together the lemon juice, vinegar, cumin and paprika in a small bowl.

Pour the dressing over the greens and gently massage with your hands. Add the pepper, garlic and peanuts to the mixing bowl. Toss to combine. Serve immediately.

Per Serving

calories: 199 | fat: 12.0g | protein: 10.0g | carbs: 17.0g

Braised Cauliflower with White Wine

Prep time: 10 minutes | **Cook time:** 12 to 16 minutes | **Serves:** 4 to 6

Ingredients:

3 tablespoons plus 1 teaspoon extra-virgin olive oil, divided
3 garlic cloves, minced
⅛ teaspoon red pepper flakes
1 head cauliflower (2 pounds / 907 g), cored and cut into 1½-inch florets

¼ teaspoon salt, plus more for seasoning
Black pepper, to taste
⅓ cup vegetable broth
⅓ cup dry white wine
2 tablespoons minced fresh parsley

Directions:

Combine 1 teaspoon of the oil, garlic and pepper flakes in small bowl.

Heat the remaining 3 tablespoons of the oil in a skillet over medium-high heat until shimmering. Add the cauliflower and ¼ teaspoon of the salt and cook for 7 to 9 minutes, stirring occasionally, or until florets are golden brown.

Push the cauliflower to sides of the skillet. Add the garlic mixture to the center of the skillet. Cook for about 30 seconds, or until fragrant. Stir the garlic mixture into the cauliflower.

Pour in the broth and wine and bring to simmer. Reduce the heat to medium-low. Cover and cook for 4 to 6 minutes, or until the cauliflower is crisp-tender. Off heat, stir in the parsley and season with salt and pepper. Serve immediately.

Per Serving

calories: 143 | fat: 11.7g | protein: 3.1g | carbs: 8.7g

Slow Cooked Buttery Mushrooms (Spanish)

Prep time: 10 minutes **Cooking Time:** 10 mins **Servings:** 2

Ingredients:

2 tablespoons butter
3 cloves of garlic, minced
Salt and pepper to taste
A dash of thyme

2 tablespoons olive oil
16 ounces fresh brown mushrooms, sliced
7 ounces fresh shiitake mushrooms, sliced

Directions:

Heat the butter and oil in a pot.

Sauté the garlic until fragrant, around 1 minute.

Stir in the rest of the and cook until soft, around 9 minutes.

Per Serving

Calories: 192; Carbs: 12.7g; Protein: 3.8g; Fat: 15.5g

Veggie Rice Bowls with Pesto Sauce

Prep time: 15 minutes | **Cook time:** 1 minute | **Serves:** 2

Ingredients:

2 cups water
1 cup arborio rice, rinsed
Salt and ground black pepper, to taste
2 eggs
1 cup broccoli florets
Lemon wedges, for serving

½ pound (227 g) Brussels sprouts
1 carrot, peeled and chopped
1 small beet, peeled and cubed
¼ cup pesto sauce

Directions:

Combine the water, rice, salt, and pepper in the Instant Pot. Insert a trivet over rice and place a steamer basket on top. Add the eggs, broccoli, Brussels sprouts, carrots, beet cubes, salt, and pepper to the steamer basket.

Lock the lid. Select the Manual mode and set the cooking time for 1 minute at High Pressure.

When the timer beeps, perform a natural pressure release for 10 minutes, then release any remaining pressure. Carefully open the lid. Remove the steamer basket and trivet from the pot and transfer the eggs to a bowl of ice water. Peel and halve the eggs. Use a fork to fluff the rice.

Divide the rice, broccoli, Brussels sprouts, carrot, beet cubes, and eggs into two bowls. Top with a dollop of pesto sauce and serve with the lemon wedges.

Per Serving

calories: 590 | fat: 34.1g | protein: 21.9g | carbs: 50.0g

Lentil and Tomato Collard Wraps

Prep time: 15 minutes | **Cook time:** 0 minutes | **Serves:** 4

Ingredients:

2 cups cooked lentils
5 Roma tomatoes, diced
½ cup crumbled feta cheese
10 large fresh basil leaves, thinly sliced
¼ cup extra-virgin olive oil
1 tablespoon balsamic vinegar

2 garlic cloves, minced
½ teaspoon raw honey
½ teaspoon salt
¼ teaspoon freshly ground black pepper
4 large collard leaves, stems removed

Directions:

Combine the lentils, tomatoes, cheese, basil leaves, olive oil, vinegar, garlic, honey, salt, and black pepper in a large bowl and stir until well blended.

Lay the collard leaves on a flat work surface. Spoon the equal-sized amounts of the lentil mixture onto the edges of the leaves. Roll them up and slice in half to serve.

Per Serving

calories: 318 | fat: 17.6g | protein: 13.2g | carbs: 27.5g

Zucchini Patties

Prep time: 15 minutes | **Cook time:** 5 minutes | **Serves:** 2

Ingredients:

2 medium zucchinis, shredded
1 teaspoon salt, divided
2 eggs
2 tablespoons chickpea flour
1 tablespoon chopped fresh mint
1 scallion, chopped
2 tablespoons extra-virgin olive oil

Directions:

Put the shredded zucchini in a fine-mesh strainer and season with ½ teaspoon of salt. Set aside.

Beat together the eggs, chickpea flour, mint, scallion, and remaining ½ teaspoon of salt in a medium bowl.

Squeeze the zucchini to drain as much liquid as possible. Add the zucchini to the egg mixture and stir until well incorporated. Heat the olive oil in a large skillet over medium-high heat.

Drop the zucchini mixture by spoonfuls into the skillet. Gently flatten the zucchini with the back of a spatula.

Cook for 2 to 3 minutes or until golden brown. Flip and cook for an additional 2 minutes.

Remove from the heat and serve on a plate.

Per Serving

calories: 264 | fat: 20.0g | protein: 9.8g | carbs: 16.1g

Creamy Sweet Potatoes and Collards

Prep time: 20 minutes | **Cook time:** 35 minutes | **Serves:** 2

Ingredients:

1 tablespoon avocado oil
3 garlic cloves, chopped
1 yellow onion, diced
½ teaspoon crushed red pepper flakes
1 large sweet potato, peeled and diced
2 bunches collard greens (about 2 pounds/907 g), stemmed, leaves chopped int
1-inch squares
1 (14.5-ounce / 411-g) can diced tomatoes with juice
1 (15-ounce / 425-g) can red kidney beans or chickpeas, drained and rinsed
1½ cups water
½ cup unsweetened coconut milk
Salt and black pepper, to taste

Directions:

In a large, deep skillet over medium heat, melt the avocado oil. Add the garlic, onion, and red pepper flakes and cook for 3 minutes. Stir in the sweet potato and collards.

Add the tomatoes with their juice, beans, water, and coconut milk and mix well. Bring the mixture just to a boil.

Reduce the heat to medium-low, cover, and simmer for about 30 minutes, or until softened.

Season to taste with salt and pepper and serve.

Per Serving calories: 445 fat: 9.6g protein: 18.1g carbs: 73.1g

Zucchini Crisp

Prep time: 10 minutes | **Cook time:** 20 minutes | **Serves:** 2

Ingredients:

4 zucchinis, sliced into ½-inch rounds
½ cup unsweetened almond milk
1 teaspoon fresh lemon juice
1 teaspoon arrowroot powder
½ teaspoon salt, divided
½ cup whole wheat bread crumbs
¼ cup nutritional yeast
¼ cup hemp seeds
½ teaspoon garlic powder
¼ teaspoon crushed red pepper
¼ teaspoon black pepper

Directions:

Preheat the oven to 375°F (190°C). Line two baking sheets with parchment paper and set aside.

Put the zucchini in a medium bowl with the almond milk, lemon juice, arrowroot powder, and ¼ teaspoon of salt. Stir to mix well.

In a large bowl with a lid, thoroughly combine the bread crumbs, nutritional yeast, hemp seeds, garlic powder, crushed red pepper and black pepper. Add the zucchini in batches and shake until the slices are evenly coated.

Arrange the zucchini on the prepared baking sheets in a single layer.

Bake in the preheated oven for about 20 minutes, or until the zucchini slices are golden brown. Season with the remaining ¼ teaspoon of salt before serving.

Per Serving

calories: 255 | fat: 11.3g | protein: 8.6g | carbs: 31.9g

Roasted Vegetables and Zucchini Pasta (Italian)

Preparation Time: 10 minutes **Cooking Time:** 7 minutes
Servings: 2

Ingredients:

¼ cup raw pine nuts
1 tablespoon extra-virgin olive oil
2 garlic cloves, minced
4 cups leftover vegetables
4 medium zucchinis, cut into long strips resembling noodles

Directions:

Heat oil in a large skillet over medium heat and sauté the garlic for 2 minutes.

Add the leftover vegetables and place the zucchini noodles on top. Let it cook for five minutes. Garnish with pine nuts.

Per Serving

Calories: 288; Carbs: 23.6g; Protein: 8.2g; Fat: 19.2g

Mediterranean Baked Chickpeas (Spanish)

Preparation Time: 15 minutes **Cooking Time:** 15 minutes
Servings: 6

Ingredients:

1 tablespoon extra-virgin olive oil

2 teaspoons smoked paprika

4 cups halved cherry tomatoes

1 cup crumbled feta

½ cup plain, unsweetened, full-fat Greek yogurt, for serving

½ medium onion, chopped

3 garlic cloves, chopped

¼ teaspoon ground cumin

2 (15-ounce) cans chickpeas, drained and rinsed

Directions:

Preheat the oven to 425°F.

In an oven-safe sauté pan or skillet, heat the oil over medium heat and sauté the onion and garlic. Cook for about 5 minutes, until softened and fragrant. Stir in the paprika and cumin and cook for 2 minutes. Stir in the tomatoes and chickpeas. Bring to a simmer for 5 to 10 minutes before placing in the oven.

Roast in oven for 25 to 30 minutes, until bubbling and thickened. To serve, top with Greek yogurt and feta.

Per Serving

Calories: 330; Carbs: 75.4g; Protein: 9.0g; Fat: 18.5g

Falafel Bites (Italian)

Preparation Time: 10 minutes **Cooking Time:** 15 minutes
Servings: 4

Ingredients:

1 2/3 cups falafel mix

1¼ cups water

1 tablespoon Pickled Onions (optional)

Turnips (optional)

Extra-virgin olive oil spray

1 tablespoon Pickled

2 tablespoons Tzatziki Sauce (optional)

Directions:

In a large bowl, carefully stir the falafel mix into the water. Mix well. Let stand 15 minutes to absorb the water. Form mixes into 1-inch balls and arrange on a baking sheet.

Preheat the broiler to high.

Take the balls and flatten slightly with your thumb (so they won't roll around on the baking sheet). Spray with olive oil, and then broil for 2 to 3 minutes on each side, until crispy and brown.

To fry the falafel, fill a pot with ½ inch of cooking oil and heat over medium-high heat to 375°F. Fry the balls for about 3 minutes, until brown and crisp. Drain on paper towels and serve with pickled onions, pickled turnips, and tzatziki sauce (if using).

Per Serving

Calories: 530; Carbs: 95.4g; Protein: 8.0g; Fat: 18.5g

Vegetable Hummus Wraps (Greek)

Prep time: 15 minutes **Cooking Time:** 10 minutes
Serving: 6

Ingredients:

1 large eggplant

½ cup extra-virgin olive oil

1 teaspoon salt

1 large onion

6 lavash wraps or large pita bread

1 cup hummus

Directions:

Preheat a grill, large grill pan, or lightly oiled large skillet on medium heat.

Slice the eggplant and onion into circles. Brush the vegetables with olive oil and sprinkle with salt.

Cook the vegetables on both sides, about 3 to 4 minutes each side.

To make the wrap, lay the lavash or pita flat. Spread about 2 tablespoons of hummus on the wrap.

Evenly divide the vegetables among the wraps, layering them along one side of the wrap. Gently fold over the side of the wrap with the vegetables, tucking them in and making a tight wrap.

Lay the wrap seam side-down and cut in half or thirds.

You can also wrap each sandwich with plastic wrap to help it hold its shape and eat it later.

Per Serving

calories: 362 | fat: 26g | protein: 15g | carbs: 28g

Summer Veggies in Instant Pot (Spanish)

Prep time: 10 minutes **Cooking Time:** 7 mins **Servings:** 6

Ingredients:

2 cups okra, sliced

1 cup mushroom, sliced

1 ½ cups onion, sliced

2 tablespoons basil, chopped 1 tablespoon thyme, chopped

1 cup grape tomatoes

2 cups bell pepper, sliced

2 ½ cups zucchini, sliced

½ cups balsamic vinegar

½ cups olive oil Salt and pepper

Directions:

Place all in the Instant Pot.

Stir the contents and close the lid.

Close the lid and press the Manual button.

Adjust the cooking time to 7 minutes.

Do quick pressure release.

Once cooled, evenly divide into serving size, keep in your preferred container, and refrigerate until ready to eat.

Per Serving

Calories: 233; Carbs: 7g; Protein: 3g; Fat: 18g

Peanut and Coconut Stuffed Eggplants

Prep time: 15 minutes | **Cook time:** 9 minutes | **Serves:**4

Ingredients:

1 tablespoon coriander seeds

½ teaspoon cumin seeds

½ teaspoon mustard seeds

2 to 3 tablespoons chickpea flour

2 tablespoons chopped peanuts

2 tablespoons coconut shreds

1-inch ginger, chopped

2 cloves garlic, chopped

1 hot green chili, chopped

A pinch of cinnamon

⅓ to ½ teaspoon cayenne

½ teaspoon turmeric

½ teaspoon raw sugar

½ to ¾ teaspoon salt

1 teaspoon lemon juice

Water as needed

4 baby eggplants

Fresh Cilantro for garnishing

½ teaspoon ground cardamom

Directions:

Add the coriander, mustard seeds and cumin in the instant pot.

Roast on Sauté function for 2 minutes.

Add the chickpea flour, nuts and coconut shred to the pot, and roast for 2 minutes.

Blend this mixture in a blender, then transfer to a medium-sized bowl. Roughly blend the ginger, garlic, raw sugar, chili, and all the spices in a blender.

Add the water and lemon juice to make a paste. Combine it with the dry flour mixture.

Cut the eggplants from one side and stuff with the spice mixture. Add 1 cup of water to the instant pot and place the stuffed eggplants inside.

Sprinkle some salt on top and secure the lid.

Cook on Manual for 5 minutes at High Pressure, then quick release the steam. Remove the lid and garnish with fresh cilantro, then serve hot.

Per Serving

calories: 207 | fat: 4.9g | protein: 7.9g | carbs: 39.6g

Mushroom, Potato, and Green Bean Mix

Prep time: 10 minutes | **Cook time:** 18 minutes | **Serves:**3

Ingredients:

1 tablespoon olive oil

½ carrot, peeled and minced

½ celery stalk, minced

½ small onion, minced

1 garlic clove, minced

½ teaspoon dried sage, crushed

½ teaspoon dried rosemary, crushed

4 ounces (113 g) fresh Portabella mushrooms, sliced

4 ounces (113 g) fresh white mushrooms, sliced

¼ cup red wine

1 Yukon Gold potato, peeled and diced

¾ cup fresh green beans, trimmed and chopped

1 cup tomatoes, chopped

½ cup tomato paste

½ tablespoon balsamic vinegar

3 cups water

Salt and freshly ground black pepper to taste

2 ounces (57 g) frozen peas

½ lemon juice

2 tablespoons fresh cilantro for garnishing, chopped

Directions:

1. Put the oil, onion, tomatoes and celery into the instant pot and Sauté for 5 minutes. Stir in the herbs and garlic and cook for 1 minute. Add the mushrooms and sauté for 5 minutes. Stir in the wine and cook for a further 2 minutes

2. Add the diced potatoes and mix. Cover the pot with a lid and let the potatoes cook for 2-3 minutes.

3. Now add the green beans, carrots, tomato paste, peas, salt, pepper, water and vinegar.

4. Secure the lid and cook on Manual function for 8 minutes at High Pressure with the pressure valve in the sealing position. Do a Quick release and open the pot, stir the veggies and then add lemon juice and cilantro, then serve with rice or any other of your choice.

Per Serving

calories: 238 | fat: 5.4g | protein: 8.3g | carbs: 42.7g

Rosemary Roasted Red Potatoes (Greek)

Preparation Time: 5 minutes **Cooking Time:** 20 minutes
Serving: 6

Ingredients:

1 pound (454 g) red potatoes, quartered	¼ cup olive oil
½ teaspoon kosher salt	1 garlic clove, minced
4 rosemary sprigs	¼ teaspoon black pepper

Directions:

Preheat the air fryer to 360°F (182°C).

In a large bowl, toss the potatoes with the olive oil, salt, pepper, and garlic until well coated.

Pour the potatoes into the air fryer basket and top with the sprigs of rosemary.

Roast for 10 minutes, then stir or toss the potatoes and roast for 10 minutes more.

Remove the rosemary sprigs and serve the potatoes. Season with additional salt and pepper, if needed.

Per Serving

calories: 133 | fat: 9g | protein: 1g | carbs: 12g

Savoy Cabbage with Coconut Cream Sauce (Spanish)

Prep time: 5 minutes **Cooking Time:** 20 mins **Servings:** 4

Ingredients:

1 tablespoons olive oil	2 cloves of garlic, minced
1 onion, chopped	1 bay leaf
1 head savoy cabbage, chopped finely	1 cup coconut milk, freshly squeezed
Salt and pepper to taste	2 tablespoons chopped parsley
2 cups bone broth	

Directions:

Heat oil in a pot for 2 minutes.

Stir in the onions, bay leaf, and garlic until fragrant, around 3 minutes.

Add the rest of the , except for the parsley and mix well.

Cover pot, bring to a boil, and let it simmer for 5 minutes or until cabbage is tender to taste.

Stir in parsley and serve.

Per Serving

Calories: 195; Carbs: 12.3g; Protein: 2.7g; Fat: 19.7g

Delicious Tomato Broth (Spanish)

Preparation Time: 10 minutes **Cooking Time:** 15 minutes
Servings: 2

Ingredients:

14 oz can fire-roasted tomatoes	½ tsp dried basil
½ cup heavy cream	½ tsp dried oregano Pepper
1 cup cheddar cheese, grated	½ cup parmesan cheese, grated
1 ½ cups vegetable stock	Salt
	¼ cup zucchini, grated

Directions:

Add tomatoes, stock, zucchini, oregano, basil, pepper, and salt into the instant pot and stir well.

Seal pot and cook on high pressure for 5 minutes.

Release pressure using quick release. Remove lid.

Set pot on sauté mode. Add heavy cream, parmesan cheese, and cheddar cheese and stir well and cook until cheese is melted.

Serve and enjoy.

Per Serving

460 Calories 35g Fat 24g Protein

Chapter 7
Poultry recipes & Meats Recipes

Herbed-Mustard-Coated Pork Tenderloin

Prep time: 10 minutes | **Cook time:** 15 minutes | **Serves:** 4

Ingredients:

3 tablespoons fresh rosemary leaves
¼ cup Dijon mustard
½ cup fresh parsley leaves
6 garlic cloves
½ teaspoon sea salt
¼ teaspoon freshly ground black pepper
1 tablespoon extra-virgin olive oil
1 (1½-pound / 680-g) pork tenderloin

Directions:

Preheat the oven to 400°F (205°C).

Put all the ingredients, except for the pork tenderloin, in a food processor. Pulse until it has a thick consistency.

Put the pork tenderloin on a baking sheet, then rub with the mixture to coat well.

Put the sheet in the preheated oven and bake for 15 minutes or until the internal temperature of the pork reaches at least 165°F (74°C). Flip the tenderloin halfway through the cooking time.

Transfer the cooked pork tenderloin to a large plate and allow to cool for 5 minutes before serving.

Per Serving
calories: 363 | fat: 18.1g | protein: 2.2g | carbs: 4.9g

Grilled Pork Chops

Prep time: 20 minutes | **Cook time:** 10 minutes | **Serves:** 4

Ingredients:

¼ cup extra-virgin olive oil
2 tablespoons fresh thyme leaves
1 teaspoon smoked paprika
1 teaspoon salt
4 pork loin chops, ½-inch-thick

Directions:

In a small bowl, mix together the olive oil, thyme, paprika, and salt. Put the pork chops in a plastic zip-top bag or a bowl and coat them with the spice mix. Let them marinate for 15 minutes.

Preheat the grill to high heat. Cook the pork chops for 4 minutes on each side until cooked through. Serve warm.

Per Serving
calories: 282 | fat: 23.0g | protein: 21.0g | carbs: 1.0g

Macadamia Pork

Prep time: 10 minutes | **Cook time:** 10 minutes | **Serves:** 4

Ingredients:

1 (1-pound / 454-g) pork tenderloin, cut into ½-inch slices and pounded thin
1 teaspoon sea salt, divided
1 tablespoon extra-virgin olive oil
¼ teaspoon freshly ground black pepper, divided
½ cup macadamia nuts
1 cup unsweetened coconut milk

Directions:

Preheat the oven to 400°F (205°C).

On a clean work surface, rub the pork with ½ teaspoon of the salt and ⅛ teaspoon of the ground black pepper. Set aside. Ground the macadamia nuts in a food processor, then combine with remaining salt and black pepper in a bowl. Stir to mix well and set aside.

Combine the coconut milk and olive oil in a separate bowl. Stir to mix well.

Dredge the pork chops into the bowl of coconut milk mixture, then dunk into the bowl of macadamia nut mixture to coat well. Shake the excess off.

Put the well-coated pork chops on a baking sheet, then bake for 10 minutes or until the internal temperature of the pork reaches at least 165°F (74°C). Transfer the pork chops to a serving plate and serve immediately.

Per Serving
calories: 436 | fat: 32.8g | protein: 33.1g | carbs: 5.9g

Lemon Beef (Spanish)

Preparation Time: 10 minutes **Cooking Time:** 6 hours
Servings: 4

Ingredients:

1 lb. beef chuck roast
1 teaspoon chili powder
1/2 teaspoon salt
1 garlic clove, crushed
2 cups lemon-lime soda
1 fresh lime juice

Directions:

Place beef chuck roast into the slow cooker. Season roast with garlic, chili powder, and salt. Pour lemon-lime soda over the roast.

Cover slow cooker with lid and cook on low for 6 hours. Shred the meat using fork.

Add lime juice over shredded roast and serve.

Per Serving
Calories 355 Fat 16.8 g Carbohydrates 14 g Sugar 11.3 g Protein 35.5 g Cholesterol 120 mg

Slow Cook Lamb Shanks with Cannellini Beans Stew

Prep time: 20 minutes | **Cook time:** 10 hours 15 minutes | Serves:12

Ingredients:

1 (19-ounce / 539-g) can cannellini beans, rinsed and drained
1 large yellow onion, chopped
2 medium-sized carrots, diced
1 large stalk celery, chopped
2 cloves garlic, thinly sliced

4 (1½-pound / 680-g) lamb shanks, fat trimmed
2 teaspoons tarragon
½ teaspoon sea salt
¼ teaspoon ground black pepper
1 (28-ounce / 794-g) can diced tomatoes, with the juice

Directions:

Combine the beans, onion, carrots, celery, and garlic in the slow cooker. Stir to mix well.

Add the lamb shanks and sprinkle with tarragon, salt, and ground black pepper.

Pour in the tomatoes with juice, then cover the lid and cook on high for an hour.

Reduce the heat to low and cook for 9 hours or until the lamb is super tender.

Transfer the lamb on a plate, then pour the bean mixture in a colander over a separate bowl to reserve the liquid.

Let the liquid sit for 5 minutes until set, then skim the fat from the surface of the liquid. Pour the bean mixture back to the liquid.

Remove the bones from the lamb heat and discard the bones. Put the lamb meat and bean mixture back to the slow cooker. Cover and cook to reheat for 15 minutes or until heated through.

Pour them on a large serving plate and serve immediately.

Per Serving

calories: 317 | fat: 9.7g | protein: 52.1g | carbs: 7.0g

Beef, Tomato, and Lentils Stew

Prep time: 10 minutes | **Cook time:** 10 minutes | **Serves:**4

Ingredients:

1 tablespoon extra-virgin olive oil
1 pound (454 g) extra-lean ground beef
1 onion, chopped
1 (14-ounce / 397-g) can chopped tomatoes with garlic and basil, drained

1 (14-ounce / 397-g) can lentils, drained
½ teaspoon sea salt
⅛ teaspoon freshly ground black pepper

Directions:

Heat the olive oil in a pot over medium-high heat until shimmering.

Add the beef and onion to the pot and sauté for 5 minutes or until the beef is lightly browned.

Add the remaining ingredients. Bring to a boil. Reduce the heat to medium and cook for 4 more minutes or until the lentils are tender. Keep stirring during the cooking.

Pour them in a large serving bowl and serve immediately.

Per Serving

calories: 460 | fat: 14.8g | protein: 44.2g | carbs: 36.9g

Beef Kebabs with Onion and Pepper

Prep time: 15 minutes | **Cook time:** 10 minutes | **Serves:**6

Ingredients:

2 pounds (907 g) beef fillet
1½ teaspoons salt
1 teaspoon freshly ground black pepper
½ teaspoon ground nutmeg

½ teaspoon ground allspice
⅓ cup extra-virgin olive oil
1 large onion, cut into 8 quarters
1 large red bell pepper, cut into 1-inch cubes

Directions:

Preheat the grill to high heat.

Cut the beef into 1-inch cubes and put them in a large bowl.

In a small bowl, mix together the salt, black pepper, allspice, and nutmeg.

Pour the olive oil over the beef and toss to coat. Evenly sprinkle the seasoning over the beef and toss to coat all pieces.

Skewer the beef, alternating every 1 or 2 pieces with a piece of onion or bell pepper.

To cook, place the skewers on the preheated grill, and flip every 2 to 3 minutes until all sides have cooked to desired doneness, 6 minutes for medium-rare, 8 minutes for well done. Serve hot.

Per Serving

calories: 485 | fat: 36.0g | protein: 35.0g | carbs: 4.0g

Chicken Bruschetta Burgers

Prep time: 10 minutes | **Cook time:** 16 minutes | **Serves:**2

Ingredients:

1 tablespoon olive oil
2 garlic cloves, minced
3 tablespoons finely minced onion
1 teaspoon dried basil
3 tablespoons minced sun-dried tomatoes packed in olive oil

8 ounces (227 g) ground chicken breast
¼ teaspoon salt
3 pieces small Mozzarella balls, minced

Directions:

Heat the olive oil in a nonstick skillet over medium-high heat. Add the garlic and onion and sauté for 5 minutes until tender. Stir in the basil. Remove from the skillet to a medium bowl. Add the tomatoes, ground chicken, and salt and stir until incorporated. Mix in the Mozzarella balls.

Divide the chicken mixture in half and form into two burgers, each about ¾-inch thick.

Heat the same skillet over medium-high heat and add the burgers. Cook each side for 5 to 6 minutes, or until they reach an internal temperature of 165ºF (74ºC).

Serve warm.

Per Serving

calories: 300 | fat: 17.0g | protein: 32.2g | carbs: 6.0g

Quick Chicken Salad Wraps

Prep time: 15 minutes | **Cook time:** 0 minutes | **Serves:**2

Ingredients:

Tzatziki Sauce:
½ cup plain Greek yogurt
1 tablespoon freshly squeezed lemon juice
Pinch garlic powder
1 teaspoon dried dill
Salt and freshly ground black pepper, to taste
1 scallion, chopped
¼ cup pitted black olives

Salad Wraps:
2 (8-inch) whole-grain pita bread
1 cup shredded chicken meat
2 cups mixed greens
2 roasted red bell peppers, thinly sliced
½ English cucumber, peeled if desired and thinly sliced

Directions:

Make the tzatziki sauce: In a bowl, whisk together the yogurt, lemon juice, garlic powder, dill, salt, and pepper until creamy and smooth.

Make the salad wraps: Place the pita bread on a clean work surface and spoon ¼ cup of the tzatziki sauce onto each piece of pita bread, spreading it all over. Top with the shredded chicken, mixed greens, red pepper slices, cucumber slices, black olives, finished by chopped scallion.

Roll the salad wraps and enjoy.

Per Serving

calories: 428 | fat: 10.6g | protein: 31.1g | carbs: 50.9g

Chicken Cacciatore

Prep time: 15 minutes | **Cook time:** 1 hour and 30 minutes
Serves:2

Ingredients:

1½ pounds (680 g) bone-in chicken thighs, skin removed and patted dry
Salt, to taste
2 tablespoons olive oil
½ large onion, thinly sliced
4 ounces (113 g) baby bella mushrooms, sliced
1 red sweet pepper, cut into 1-inch pieces

1 (15-ounce / 425-g) can crushed fire-roasted tomatoes
1 fresh rosemary sprig
½ cup dry red wine
1 teaspoon Italian herb seasoning
½ teaspoon garlic powder
3 tablespoons flour

Directions:

Season the chicken thighs with a generous pinch of salt.

Heat the olive oil in a Dutch oven over medium-high heat. Add the chicken and brown for 5 minutes per side.

Add the onion, mushrooms, and sweet pepper to the Dutch oven and sauté for another 5 minutes.

Add the tomatoes, rosemary, wine, Italian seasoning, garlic powder, and salt, stirring well.

Bring the mixture to a boil, then reduce the heat to low. Allow to simmer slowly for at least 1 hour, stirring occasionally, or until the chicken is tender and easily pulls away from the bone.

Measure out 1 cup of the sauce from the pot and put it into a bowl. Add the flour and whisk well to make a slurry.

Increase the heat to medium-high and slowly whisk the slurry into the pot. Stir until it comes to a boil and cook until the sauce is thickened.

Remove the chicken from the bones and shred it, and add it back to the sauce before serving, if desired.

Per Serving

calories: 520 | fat: 23.1g | protein: 31.8g | carbs: 37.0g

Parsley-Dijon Chicken and Potatoes

Prep time: 5 minutes | **Cook time:** 22 minutes | **Serves:**6

Ingredients:

1 tablespoon extra-virgin olive oil

1½ pounds (680 g) boneless, skinless chicken thighs, cut into 1-inch cubes, patted dry

1½ pounds (680 g) Yukon Gold potatoes, unpeeled, cut into ½-inch cubes

2 garlic cloves, minced

¼ cup dry white wine

1 cup low-sodium or no-salt-added chicken broth

1 tablespoon Dijon mustard

¼ teaspoon freshly ground black pepper

¼ teaspoon kosher or sea salt

1 cup chopped fresh flat-leaf (Italian) parsley, including stems

1 tablespoon freshly squeezed lemon juice

Directions:

In a large skillet over medium-high heat, heat the oil. Add the chicken and cook for 5 minutes, stirring only after the chicken has browned on one side. Remove the chicken and reserve on a plate.

Add the potatoes to the skillet and cook for 5 minutes, stirring only after the potatoes have become golden and crispy on one side. Push the potatoes to the side of the skillet, add the garlic, and cook, stirring constantly, for 1 minute. Add the wine and cook for 1 minute, until nearly evaporated. Add the chicken broth, mustard, salt, pepper, and reserved chicken. Turn the heat to high and bring to a boil. Once boiling, cover, reduce the heat to medium-low, and cook for 10 to 12 minutes, until the potatoes are tender and the internal temperature of the chicken measures 165°F (74°C) on a meat thermometer and any juices run clear. During the last minute of cooking, stir in the parsley. Remove from the heat, stir in the lemon juice, and serve.

Per Serving

calories: 324 | fat: 9.0g | protein: 16.0g | carbs: 45.0g

Herb Pork Roast (Spanish)

Preparation Time: 10 minutes **Cooking Time:** 14 hours **Servings:** 10

Ingredients:

4 lbs. pork roast boneless or bone-in

1 tablespoon dry herb mix

4 garlic cloves cut into slivers

1 tablespoon salt

Directions:

Using a sharp knife make small cuts all over meat then insert garlic slivers into the cuts.

In a small bowl, mix together Italian herb mix and salt and rub all over pork roast. Place pork roast in the crock pot. Cover and cook on low for 14 hours. Remove meat from crock pot and shred using a fork. Serve and enjoy.

Per Serving

Calories 327 Fat 8 g Carbohydrates 0.5 g Sugar 0 g Protein 59 g Cholesterol 166 mg

Potato Lamb and Olive Stew

Prep time: 20 minutes | **Cook time:** 3 hours 42 minutes | **Serves:**10

Ingredients:

4 tablespoons almond flour

¾ cup low-sodium chicken stock

1¼ pounds (567 g) small potatoes, halved

3 cloves garlic, minced

4 large shallots, cut into ½-inch wedges

3 sprigs fresh rosemary

1 tablespoon lemon zest

Coarse sea salt and black pepper, to taste

3½ pounds (1.6 kg) lamb shanks, fat trimmed and cut crosswise into 1½-inch pieces

2 tablespoons extra-virgin olive oil

½ cup dry white wine

1 cup pitted green olives, halved

2 tablespoons lemon juice

Directions:

Combine 1 tablespoon of almond flour with chicken stock in a bowl. Stir to mix well. Put the flour mixture, potatoes, garlic, shallots, rosemary, and lemon zest in the slow cooker. Sprinkle with salt and black pepper. Stir to mix well. Set aside.

Combine the remaining almond flour with salt and black pepper in a large bowl, then dunk the lamb shanks in the flour and toss to coat.

Heat the olive oil in a nonstick skillet over medium-high heat until shimmering.

Add the well-coated lamb and cook for 10 minutes or until golden brown. Flip the lamb pieces halfway through the cooking time. Transfer the cooked lamb to the slow cooker.

Pour the wine in the same skillet, then cook for 2 minutes or until it reduces in half. Pour the wine in the slow cooker.

Put the slow cooker lid on and cook on high for 3 hours and 30 minutes or until the lamb is very tender.

In the last 20 minutes of the cooking, open the lid and fold in the olive halves to cook.

Pour the stew on a large plate, let them sit for 5 minutes, then skim any fat remains over the face of the liquid.

Drizzle with lemon juice and sprinkle with salt and pepper. Serve warm.

Per Serving

calories: 309 | fat: 10.3g | protein: 36.9g | carbs: 16.1g

Roasted Chicken Thighs With Basmati Rice

Prep time: 15 minutes | **Cook time:** 50 to 55 minutes
Serves:2

Ingredients:

Chicken:
½ teaspoon cumin
½ teaspoon cinnamon
½ teaspoon paprika
¼ teaspoon ginger powder
¼ teaspoon garlic powder
¼ teaspoon coriander
¼ teaspoon salt
⅛ teaspoon cayenne pepper
¼ teaspoon salt

10 ounces (284 g) boneless, skinless chicken thighs (about 4 pieces)
Rice:
1 tablespoon olive oil
½ small onion, minced
½ cup basmati rice
2 pinches saffron
1 cup low-sodium chicken stock

Directions:
Make the Chicken

Preheat the oven to 350ºF (180ºC). Combine the cumin, cinnamon, paprika, ginger powder, garlic powder, coriander, salt, and cayenne pepper in a small bowl. Using your hands to rub the spice mixture all over the chicken thighs.

Transfer the chicken thighs to a baking dish. Roast in the preheated oven for 35 to 40 minutes, or until the internal temperature reaches 165ºF (74ºC) on a meat thermometer.

Meanwhile, heat the olive oil in a skillet over medium-high heat. Sauté the onion for 5 minutes until fragrant, stirring occasionally.

Stir in the basmati rice, saffron, chicken stock, and salt. Reduce the heat to low, cover, and bring to a simmer for 15 minutes, until light and fluffy.

Remove the chicken from the oven to a plate and serve with the rice.

Per Serving
calories: 400 | fat: 9.6g | protein: 37.2g | carbs: 40.7g

Roasted Pork Meat (Spanish)

Preparation Time: 5 minutes **Cooking Time:** 55 minutes
Servings: 6

Ingredients:

3 pounds of roast pork
Salt and pepper
1 sliced onion

1 tablespoon vegetable oil
2 cups of water

Directions:

Pour vegetable oil into the pot. Brown the pork on both sides in medium pressure over medium heat and then remove from the pot.

Pour the water into the pot. Put the pork on the rack of the pot. Season with salt, pepper and sliced onions.

Close and secure the lid. Place the pressure regulator on the vent tube and cook 55 minutes once the pressure regulator begins to rock slowly. Let the pressure decrease on its own.

Per Serving
Calories: 483, Carbohydrates: 0g, Fat: 27g, Protein: 53g, Cholesterol: 171mg,

Yogurt Chicken Breasts

Prep time: 10 minutes | **Cook time:** 10 minutes | **Serves:**4

Ingredients:

1 pound (454 g) boneless, skinless chicken breasts, cut into 2-inch strips
1 tablespoon extra-virgin olive oil
Yogurt Sauce:
½ cup plain Greek yogurt
2 tablespoons water

Pinch saffron (3 or 4 threads)
3 garlic cloves, minced
½ onion, chopped
2 tablespoons chopped fresh cilantro
Juice of ½ lemon
½ teaspoon salt

Directions:

Make the yogurt sauce: Place the yogurt, water, saffron, garlic, onion, cilantro, lemon juice, and salt in a blender, and pulse until completely mixed.

Transfer the yogurt sauce to a large bowl, along with the chicken strips. Toss to coat well.

Cover with plastic wrap and marinate in the refrigerator for at least 1 hour, or up to overnight. When ready to cook, heat the olive oil in a large skillet over medium heat.

Add the chicken strips to the skillet, discarding any excess marinade. Cook each side for 5 minutes, or until cooked through.

Let the chicken cool for 5 minutes before serving.

Per Serving
calories: 154 | fat: 4.8g | protein: 26.3g | carbs: 2.9g

Coconut Chicken Tenders

Prep time: 10 minutes | **Cook time:** 15 to 20 minutes | **Serves:**6

Ingredients:

4 chicken breasts, each cut lengthwise into 3 strips
½ teaspoon salt
¼ teaspoon freshly ground black pepper

½ cup coconut flour
2 eggs
2 tablespoons unsweetened plain almond milk
1 cup unsweetened coconut flakes

Directions:

Preheat the oven to 400ºF (205ºC). Line a baking sheet with parchment paper. On a clean work surface, season the chicken with salt and pepper.

In a small bowl, add the coconut flour. In a separate bowl, whisk the eggs with almond milk until smooth. Place the coconut flakes on a plate.

One at a time, roll the chicken strips in the coconut flour, then dredge them in the egg mixture, shaking off any excess, and finally in the coconut flakes to coat.

Arrange the coated chicken pieces on the baking sheet. Bake in the preheated oven for 15 to 20 minutes, flipping the chicken halfway through, or until the chicken is golden brown and cooked through. Remove from the oven and serve on plates.

Per Serving
calories: 215 | fat: 12.6g | protein: 20.2g | carbs: 8.9g

Sautéed Ground Turkey with Brown Rice

Prep time: 20 minutes | **Cook time:** 45 minutes | **Serves:**2

Ingredients:

1 tablespoon olive oil
½ medium onion, minced
2 garlic cloves, minced
8 ounces (227 g) ground
turkey breast
½ cup chopped roasted red
peppers, (about 2 jarred
peppers)

¼ cup sun-dried tomatoes,
minced
1¼ cups low-sodium
chicken stock
½ cup brown rice
1 teaspoon dried oregano
Salt, to taste
2 cups lightly packed baby
spinach

Directions:

In a skillet, heat the olive oil over medium heat. Sauté the onion for 5 minutes, stirring occasionally.

Stir in the garlic and sauté for 30 seconds more until fragrant.

Add the turkey breast and cook for about 7 minutes, breaking apart with a wooden spoon, until the turkey is no longer pink.

Stir in the roasted red peppers, tomatoes, chicken stock, brown rice, and oregano and bring to a boil.

When the mixture starts to boil, cover, and reduce the heat to medium- low. Bring to a simmer until the rice is tender, stirring occasionally, about 30 minutes. Sprinkle with the salt.

Add the baby spinach and keep stirring until wilted. Remove from the heat and serve warm.

Per Serving
calories: 445 | fat: 16.8g | protein: 30.2g | carbs: 48.9g

Baked Teriyaki Turkey Meatballs

Prep time: 20 minutes | **Cook time:** 20 minutes | **Serves:**6

Ingredients:

1 pound (454 g) lean ground
turkey
1 egg, whisked
¼ cup finely chopped
scallions, both white and
green parts
2 garlic cloves, minced

2 tablespoons reduced-
sodium tamari or gluten-free
soy sauce
1 teaspoon grated fresh
ginger
1 tablespoon honey
2 teaspoons mirin
1 teaspoon olive oil

Directions:

Preheat the oven to 400°F (205°C). Line a baking sheet with parchment paper and set aside.

Mix together the ground turkey, whisked egg, scallions, garlic, tamari, ginger, honey, mirin, and olive oil in a large bowl, and stir until well blended.

Using a tablespoon to scoop out rounded heaps of the turkey mixture, and then roll them into balls with your hands. Transfer the balls to the prepared baking sheet.

Bake in the preheated oven for 20 minutes, flipping the balls with a spatula halfway through, or until the meatballs are browned and cooked through.Serve warm.

Per Serving calories: 158 fat: 8.6g protein: 16.2g carbs: 4.0g

Ground Beef, Tomato, and Kidney Bean Chili

Prep time: 10 minutes | **Cook time:** 15 minutes | **Serves:**4

Ingredients:

1 tablespoon extra-virgin
olive oil
1 pound (454 g) extra-lean
ground beef
1 onion, chopped
2 (14-ounce / 397-g) cans
kidney beans

2 (28-ounce / 794-g) cans
chopped tomatoes, juice
reserved
Chili Spice:
1 teaspoon garlic powder
1 tablespoon chili powder
½ teaspoon sea salt

Directions:

Heat the olive oil in a pot over medium-high heat until shimmering.

Add the beef and onion to the pot and sauté for 5 minutes or until the beef is lightly browned and the onion is translucent.

Add the remaining ingredients. Bring to a boil. Reduce the heat to medium and cook for 10 more minutes. Keep stirring during the cooking.

Pour them in a large serving bowl and serve immediately.

Per Serving
calories: 891 | fat: 20.1g | protein: 116.3g | carbs: 62.9g

Ground Beef, Tomato, and Kidney Bean Chili

Prep time: 10 minutes | **Cook time:** 15 minutes | **Serves:**4

Ingredients:

1 tbsp extra-virgin olive oil
1 pound (454 g) extra-
lean ground beef
1 onion, chopped
2 (14-ounce / 397-g) cans
kidney beans

2 (28-ounce / 794-g) cans
chopped tomatoes, juice reserved
Chili Spice:
1 teaspoon garlic powder
1 tablespoon chili powder
½ teaspoon sea salt

Directions:

Heat the olive oil in a pot over medium-high heat until shimmering.

Add the beef and onion to the pot and sauté for 5 minutes or until the beef is lightly browned and the onion is translucent.

Add the remaining. Bring to a boil. Reduce the heat to medium and cook for 10 more minutes. Keep stirring during the cooking.

Pour them in a large serving bowl and serve immediately.

Per Serving
calories: 891 | fat: 20.1g | protein: 116.3g | carbs: 62.9g

Pork Ribs with Barbecue Sauce (Spanish)

Preparation Time: 5 minutes **Cooking Time:** 15 minutes
Servings: 6

Ingredients:

3 pounds of pork ribs in portions	1 cup of ketchup
½ cup of water	1 cup of water
¼ cup chopped onion	½ cup vinegar
1 teaspoon salt	¼ cup sugar
	1 teaspoon chili powder
	1 teaspoon celery seeds

Directions:

Put the ribs and water in the pot. Close and secure the lid. Place the pressure regulator on the vent tube and cook 5 minutes once the pressure regulator begins to rock slowly. Cool the pot quickly. Drain the liquid.

Mix the remaining and pour them over the ribs in the pot. Stir to cover the ribs.

Close and secure the lid. Place the pressure regulator on the vent tube and cook 10 minutes once the pressure regulator begins to rock slowly.

Let the pressure decrease on its own. Remove the ribs. Boil the sauce, without the lid, until the desired consistency is achieved.

Per Serving

Calories: 427, Carbohydrates: 0g, Fat: 27g, Protein: 47g, Sugar: 0g, Cholesterol: 107mg

Easy Pork Kabobs (Greek)

Preparation Time: 10 minutes
Cooking Time: 4 hours 20 minutes **Servings:** 6

Ingredients:

1 lbs. pork tenderloin, cut into 1-inch cubes	1 onion, chopped
½ cup olive oil	Pepper Salt
2 garlic cloves, chopped	2 tablespoon fresh parsley, chopped
½ cup red wine vinegar	

Directions:

In a large zip-lock bag, mix together red wine vinegar, parsley, garlic, onion, and oil.

Add meat to bag and marinate in the refrigerator for overnight.

Remove marinated pork from refrigerator and thread onto soaked wooden skewers. Season with pepper and salt.

Preheat the grill over high heat.

Grill pork for 3-4 minutes on each side. Serve and enjoy.

Per Serving

Calories 375 Fat 22 g Carbohydrates 2.5 g Sugar 1 g Protein 40 g Cholesterol 110 mg

Apricot Pork Meat (Spanish)

Preparation Time: 5 minutes **Cooking Time:** 60 minutes
Servings: 8

Ingredients:

3 pounds boneless rolled pork	½ cup ketchup
½ cup teriyaki sauce	1 teaspoon of paprika
¼ cup cider vinegar	1/3 Cup of canned apricots
1 large onion sliced	¼ cup dark brown sugar, packaged
1 teaspoon dried mustard	2 cups of water
¼ teaspoon black pepper	

Directions:

Put the creed meat in a large plastic bag or glass dish. Combine ketchup, teriyaki sauce, canned food, vinegar, brown sugar, paprika, mustard and pepper. Mix together and pour over pork. Refrigerate overnight.

Remove the pork from the marinade and keep the marinade. Brown pork on both sides in the pressure cooker over medium heat. Remove pork from the pot.

Place the pressure regulator on the vent tube and cook 60 minutes once the pressure regulator begins to rock slowly. Let the pressure decrease on its own. Put in a saucepan the marinade that it kept and boil until it thickens, stirring occasionally.

Remove the meat and onions from the pressure cooker. Add onions to the thickened marinade and serve with sliced pork. Onions can be stepped on before adding to the sauce and served with rice, if desired.

Per Serving

Calories: 332, Carbohydrates: 0g, Fat: 13g, Protein: 47g, Sugar: 0g, Cholesterol: 77mg

Feta Lamb Patties (Greek)

Preparation Time: 10 minutes **Cooking Time:** 12 minutes
Servings: 4

Ingredients:

1 lb. ground lamb	1/2 teaspoon garlic powder
1/4 cup mint leaves, chopped	1/2 cup feta cheese, crumbled
1/4 cup roasted red pepper, chopped	Pepper Salt
1/4 cup onion, chopped	

Directions:

Add all into the bowl and mix until well combined. Spray pan with cooking spray and heat over medium-high heat. Make small patties from meat mixture and place on hot pan and cook for 6-7 minutes on each side. Serve and enjoy.

Per Serving

Calories 270 Fat 12 g Carbohydrates 2.9 g Sugar 1.7 g Protein 34.9 g Cholesterol 119 mg

Grilled Chicken and Zucchini Kebabs

Prep time: 10 minutes | **Cook time:** 20 minutes | **Serves:** 4

Ingredients:

¼ cup extra-virgin olive oil
2 tablespoons balsamic vinegar
1 teaspoon dried oregano, crushed between your fingers
1 pound (454 g) boneless, skinless chicken breasts, cut into 1½-inch pieces

2 medium zucchinis, cut into 1-inch pieces
½ cup Kalamata olives, pitted and halved
2 tablespoons olive brine
¼ cup torn fresh basil leaves
Nonstick cooking spray

Special Equipment:

14 to 15 (12-inch) wooden skewers, soaked for at least 30 minutes

Directions:

Spray the grill grates with nonstick cooking spray. Preheat the grill to medium-high heat.

In a small bowl, whisk together the olive oil, vinegar, and oregano. Divide the marinade between two large plastic zip-top bags.

Add the chicken to one bag and the zucchini to another. Seal and massage the marinade into both the chicken and zucchini.

Thread the chicken onto 6 wooden skewers. Thread the zucchini onto 8 or 9 wooden skewers. Cook the kebabs in batches on the grill for 5 minutes, flip, and grill for 5 minutes more, or until any chicken juices run clear.

Remove the chicken and zucchini from the skewers to a large serving bowl. Toss with the olives, olive brine, and basil and serve.

Per Serving

calories: 283 | fat: 15.0g | protein: 11.0g | carbs: 26.0g

Slow Cooker Mediterranean Beef Stew (Greek)

Prep time: 10 mins **Cooking Time:** 10 hours **Servings:** 10

Ingredients:

Beef meat (for stew) 3 pounds Beef broth 2 cups 10 cloves Chopped onion Salt ½ tbsp.
2 tablespoons Tomato sauce 15 ounces Balsamic vinegar ½ cup
Pepper ½ tbsp

Baby mushrooms 16 ounces Garlic, minced 1 large Diced tomatoes in a can
14½ ounces Jar capers, drained 2 ounces Drained black olives
6 ounces Dried rosemary

Directions:

Put all the except the for garnishing in a 6-quart slow cooker and combine.

Cover the cooker and slow cook for 10 hours. Add pepper and salt as required. Garnish with parmesan and chopped parsley while serving.

Per Serving

Calories: 273 Carbohydrate: 16g Protein: 33g Sugars: 6g

Almond-Crusted Chicken Tenders with Honey

Prep time: 10 minutes | **Cook time:** 20 minutes | **Serves:** 4

Ingredients:

1 tablespoon honey
1 tablespoon whole-grain or Dijon mustard
¼ teaspoon freshly ground black pepper
¼ teaspoon kosher or sea salt

1 pound (454 g) boneless, skinless chicken breast tenders or tenderloins
1 cup almonds, roughly chopped
Nonstick cooking spray

Directions:

Preheat the oven to 425°F (220°C). Line a large, rimmed baking sheet with parchment paper. Place a wire cooling rack on the parchment-lined baking sheet, and spray the rack well with nonstick cooking spray.

In a large bowl, combine the honey, mustard, pepper, and salt. Add the chicken and toss gently to coat. Set aside.

Dump the almonds onto a large sheet of parchment paper and spread them out. Press the coated chicken tenders into the nuts until evenly coated on all sides. Place the chicken on the prepared wire rack.

Bake in the preheated oven for 15 to 20 minutes, or until the internal temperature of the chicken measures 165°F (74°C) on a meat thermometer and any juices run clear.

Cool for 5 minutes before serving.

Per Serving

calories: 222 | fat: 7.0g | protein: 11.0g | carbs: 29.0g

Greek-Style Lamb Burgers

Prep time: 10 minutes | **Cook time:** 10 minutes | **Serves:** 4

Ingredients:

1 pound (454 g) ground lamb
½ teaspoon salt
½ teaspoon freshly ground black pepper

4 tablespoons crumbled feta cheese
Buns, toppings, and tzatziki, for serving (optional)

Directions:

Preheat the grill to high heat. In a large bowl, using your hands, combine the lamb with the salt and pepper.

Divide the meat into 4 portions. Divide each portion in half to make a top and a bottom. Flatten each half into a 3-inch circle. Make a dent in the center of one of the halves and place 1 tablespoon of the feta cheese in the center. Place the second half of the patty on top of the feta cheese and press down to close the 2 halves together, making it resemble a round burger. Grill each side for 3 minutes, for medium-well. Serve on a bun with your favorite toppings and tzatziki sauce, if desired.

Per Serving

calories: 345 | fat: 29.0g | protein: 20.0g | carbs: 1.0g

Tender Lamb Chops (Greek)

Preparation Time: 10 minutes **Cooking Time:** 6 hours
Servings: 8

Ingredients:

8 lamb chops   ½ teaspoon dried thyme
1 teaspoon dried oregano   2 garlic cloves, minced
1 onion, sliced   Pepper and salt

Directions:

Add sliced onion into the slow cooker.

Combine together thyme, oregano, pepper, and salt. Rub over lamb chops.

Place lamb chops in slow cooker and top with garlic.

Pour ¼ cup water around the lamb chops.

Cover and cook on low for 6 hours.

Serve and enjoy.

Per Serving

Calories 40 Fat 1.9 g Carbohydrates 2.3 g Sugar 0.6 g Protein 3.4 g Cholesterol 0 mg

Sun-dried Tomato Chuck Roast (Italian)

Preparation Time: 10 minutes **Cooking Time:** 10 hours
Servings: 6

Ingredients:

1 lbs. beef chuck roast   1 teaspoon dried Italian
25 garlic cloves, peeled   seasoning, crushed
½ cup beef broth   2 tablespoon balsamic
¼ cup olives, sliced   vinegar
¼ cup sun-dried tomatoes,
chopped

Directions:

Place meat into the crock pot.

Pour remaining over meat.

Cover and cook on low for 10 hours.

Shred the meat using fork.

Serve and enjoy.

Per Serving

Calories 582 Fat 43 g Carbohydrates 5 g Sugar 0.5 g Protein 40g Cholesterol 156 mg 0.4 g Sugar 0.1 g Protein 42 g Cholesterol 132 mg

Herb Ground Beef (Spanish)

Preparation Time: 10 minutes **Cooking Time:** 15 minutes
Servings: 4

1 lb. ground beef   ½ teaspoon dried parsley
½ teaspoon dried basil   ½ teaspoon dried oregano
1 teaspoon garlic, minced   1 tablespoon olive oil
1 teaspoon pepper   ½ teaspoon dried thyme
¼ teaspoon nutmeg   ½ teaspoon dried rosemary
                                 1 teaspoon salt

Directions:

Heat oil in a pan over medium heat.

Add ground meat to the pan and fry until cooked.

Add remaining and stir well.

Serve and enjoy.

Per Serving

Calories 215 Fat 7.2 g Carbohydrates 1 g Sugar 0.2 g Protein 34 g Cholesterol 101 mg

Easy Beef Kofta (Spanish)

Preparation Time: 10 minutes **Cooking Time:** 10 minutes
Servings: 8

Ingredients:

1 lbs. ground beef   4 garlic cloves, minced
1 onion, minced   2 teaspoon cumin
1 cup fresh parsley,   ¼ teaspoon pepper
chopped
1 teaspoon salt

Directions:

Add all into the mixing bowl and mix until combined.

Roll meat mixture into the kabab shapes and cook in a hot pan for 4-6 minutes on each side or until cooked.

Serve and enjoy.

Per Serving

Calories 223 Fat 7.3 g Carbohydrates 2.5 g Sugar 0.7 g Protein 35 g Cholesterol 101 mg

Beef Stew with Beans and Zucchini

Prep time: 20 minutes | **Cook time:** 6 to 8 hours | **Serves:** 2

Ingredients:

1 (15-ounce / 425-g) can diced or crushed tomatoes with basil
1 teaspoon beef base
2 tablespoons olive oil, divided
8 ounces (227 g) baby bella (cremini) mushrooms, quartered
2 garlic cloves, minced
½ large onion, diced
1 pound (454 g) cubed beef stew meat
3 tablespoons flour
¼ teaspoon salt
Pinch freshly ground black pepper
¾ cup dry red wine
¼ cup minced brined olives
1 fresh rosemary sprig
1 (15-ounce / 425-g) can white cannellini beans, drained and rinsed
1 medium zucchini, cut in half lengthwise and then cut into 1-inch pieces.

Directions:

Place the tomatoes into a slow cooker and set it to low heat. Add the beef base and stir to incorporate.

Heat 1 tablespoon of olive oil in a large sauté pan over medium heat. Add the mushrooms and onion and sauté for 10 minutes, stirring occasionally, or until they're golden. Add the garlic and cook for 30 seconds more. Transfer the vegetables to the slow cooker.

In a plastic food storage bag, combine the stew meat with the flour, salt, and pepper. Seal the bag and shake well to combine. Heat the remaining 1 tablespoon of olive oil in the sauté pan over high heat.

Add the floured meat and sear to get a crust on the outside edges. Deglaze the pan by adding about half of the red wine and scraping up any browned bits on the bottom. Stir so the wine thickens a bit and transfer to the slow cooker along with any remaining wine.

Stir the stew to incorporate the ingredients. Stir in the olives and rosemary, cover, and cook for 6 to 8 hours on Low. About 30 minutes before the stew is finished, add the beans and zucchini to let them warm through. Serve warm.

Per Serving
calories: 389 | fat: 15.1g | protein: 30.8g | carbs: 25.0g

Greek Beef Kebabs

Prep time: 15 minutes | **Cook time:** 20 minutes | **Serves:** 2

Ingredients:

6 ounces (170 g) beef sirloin tip, trimmed of fat and cut into 2-inch pieces
3 cups of any mixture of vegetables: mushrooms, summer squash, zucchini, onions, red peppers, cherry tomatoes
½ cup olive oil
¼ cup freshly squeezed lemon juice
2 tablespoons balsamic vinegar
2 teaspoons dried oregano
1 teaspoon garlic powder
1 teaspoon salt
1 teaspoon minced fresh rosemary
Cooking spray

Directions:

Put the beef in a plastic freezer bag.

Slice the vegetables into similar-size pieces and put them in a second freezer bag.

Make the marinade: Mix the olive oil, lemon juice, balsamic vinegar, oregano, garlic powder, salt, and rosemary in a measuring cup. Whisk well to combine. Pour half of the marinade over the beef, and the other half over the vegetables.

Put the beef and vegetables in the refrigerator to marinate for 4 hours.

When ready, preheat the grill to medium-high heat and spray the grill grates with cooking spray.

Thread the meat onto skewers and the vegetables onto separate skewers.

Grill the meat for 3 minutes per side. They should only take 10 to 12 minutes to cook, depending on the thickness of the meat.

Grill the vegetables for about 3 minutes per side, or until they have grill marks and are softened. Serve hot.

Per Serving calories: 284 | fat: 18.2g | protein: 21.0g | carbs: 9.0g

Chapter 8
Fish Recipes & Seafood Recipes

Cioppino (Seafood Tomato Stew)

Prep time: 10 minutes | **Cook time:** 20 minutes | **Serves:** 2

Ingredients:

2 tablespoons olive oil
½ small onion, diced
½ green pepper, diced
2 teaspoons dried basil
2 teaspoons dried oregano
½ cup dry white wine
1 (14.5-ounce / 411-g) can diced tomatoes with basil
1 (8-ounce / 227-g) can no-salt-added tomato sauce

1 (6.5-ounce / 184-g) can minced clams with their juice
8 ounces (227 g) peeled, deveined raw shrimp
4 ounces (113 g) any white fish (a thick piece works best)
3 tablespoons fresh parsley
Salt and freshly ground black pepper, to taste

Directions:

In a Dutch oven, heat the olive oil over medium heat.

Saut é the onion and green pepper for 5 minutes, or until tender. Stir in the basil, oregano, wine, diced tomatoes, and tomato sauce and bring to a boil.

Once boiling, reduce the heat to low and bring to a simmer for 5 minutes.

Add the clams, shrimp, and fish and cook for about 10 minutes, or until the shrimp are pink and cooked through.

Scatter with the parsley and add the salt and black pepper to taste. Remove from the heat and serve warm.

Per Serving
calories: 221 | fat: 7.7g | protein: 23.1g | carbs: 10.9g

Fried Cod Fillets

Prep time: 5 minutes | **Cook time:** 10 minutes | **Serves:** 4

Ingredients:

½ cup all-purpose flour
1 teaspoon garlic powder
1 teaspoon salt

4 (4- to 5-ounce / 113- to 142-g) cod fillets
1 tablespoon extra-virgin olive oil

Directions:

Mix together the flour, garlic powder, and salt in a shallow dish. Dredge each piece of fish in the seasoned flour until they are evenly coated.

Heat the olive oil in a medium skillet over medium-high heat. Once hot, add the cod fillets and fry for 6 to 8 minutes, flipping the fish halfway through, or until the fish is opaque and flakes easily.

Remove from the heat and serve on plates.

Per Serving calories: 333 fat: 18.8g protein: 21.2g carbs: 20.0g

Lemon Grilled Shrimp

Prep time: 20 minutes | **Cook time:** 4 to 6 minutes | **Serves:** 4

Ingredients:

2 tablespoons garlic, minced
3 tablespoons fresh Italian parsley, finely chopped
¼ cup extra-virgin olive oil
½ cup lemon juice

1 teaspoon salt
2 pounds (907 g) jumbo shrimp (21 to 25), peeled and deveined
Special Equipment:
4 wooden skewers, soaked in water for at least 30 minutes

Directions:

Whisk together the garlic, parsley, olive oil, lemon juice, and salt in a large bowl.

Add the shrimp to the bowl and toss well, making sure the shrimp are coated in the marinade. Set aside to sit for 15 minutes.

When ready, skewer the shrimps by piercing through the center. You can place about 5 to 6 shrimps on each skewer. Preheat the grill to high heat.

Grill the shrimp for 4 to 6 minutes, flipping the shrimp halfway through, or until the shrimp are pink on the outside and opaque in the center. Serve hot.

Per Serving
calories: 401 | fat: 17.8g | protein: 56.9g | carbs: 3.9g

Dill Baked Sea Bass

Prep time: 10 minutes | **Cook time:** 10 to 15 minutes | **Serves:** 6

Ingredients:

¼ cup olive oil
2 pounds (907 g) sea bass
Sea salt and freshly ground pepper, to taste

1 garlic clove, minced
¼ cup dry white wine
3 teaspoons fresh dill
2 teaspoons fresh thyme

Directions:

Preheat the oven to 425°F (220°C).

Brush the bottom of a roasting pan with the olive oil. Place the fish in the pan and brush the fish with oil.

Season the fish with sea salt and freshly ground pepper. Combine the remaining ingredients and pour over the fish.

Bake in the preheated oven for 10 to 15 minutes, depending on the size of the fish. Serve hot.

Per Serving
calories: 224 | fat: 12.1g | protein: 28.1g | carbs: 0.9g

Baked Cod with Vegetables

Prep time: 15 minutes | **Cook time:** 25 minutes | **Serves:**2

Ingredients:

1 pound (454 g) thick cod fillet, cut into 4 even portions

¼ teaspoon onion powder (optional)

¼ teaspoon paprika

3 tablespoons extra-virgin olive oil

4 medium scallions

½ cup fresh chopped basil, divided

3 tablespoons minced garlic (optional)

2 teaspoons freshly ground black pepper

¼ teaspoon dry marjoram (optional)

6 sun-dried tomato slices

½ cup dry white wine

½ cup crumbled feta cheese

1 (15-ounce / 425-g) can oil-packed artichoke hearts, drained

1 lemon, sliced

1 cup pitted kalamata olives

1 teaspoon capers (optional)

4 small red potatoes, quartered

2 teaspoons salt

Directions:

Preheat the oven to 375°F (190°C).

Season the fish with paprika and onion powder (if desired).

Heat an ovenproof skillet over medium heat and sear the top side of the cod for about 1 minute until golden. Set aside.

Heat the olive oil in the same skillet over medium heat. Add the scallions, ¼ cup of basil, garlic (if desired), salt, pepper, marjoram (if desired), tomato slices, and white wine and stir to combine. Bring to a boil and remove from heat.

Evenly spread the sauce on the bottom of skillet. Place the cod on top of the tomato basil sauce and scatter with feta cheese. Place the artichokes in the skillet and top with the lemon slices.

Scatter with the olives, capers (if desired), and the remaining ¼ cup of basil. Remove from the heat and transfer to the preheated oven. Bake for 15 to 20 minutes, or until it flakes easily with a fork.

Meanwhile, place the quartered potatoes on a baking sheet or wrapped in aluminum foil. Bake in the oven for 15 minutes until fork-tender.

Cool for 5 minutes before serving.

Per Serving

calories: 1168 | fat: 60.0g | protein: 63.8g | carbs: 94.0g

Slow Cooker Salmon in Foil

Prep time: 5 minutes | **Cook time:** 2 hours | **Serves:**2

Ingredients:

2 (6-ounce / 170-g) salmon fillets

1 tablespoon olive oil

2 cloves garlic, minced

½ tablespoon lime juice

1 teaspoon finely chopped fresh parsley

¼ teaspoon black pepper

Directions:

Spread a length of foil onto a work surface and place the salmon fillets in the middle. Mix together the olive oil, garlic, lime juice, parsley, and black pepper in a small bowl. Brush the mixture over the fillets. Fold the foil over and crimp the sides to make a packet.

Place the packet into the slow cooker, cover, and cook on High for 2 hours, or until the fish flakes easily with a fork.

Serve hot.

Per Serving calories: 446 | fat: 20.7g | protein: 65.4g | carbs: 1.5g

Dill Chutney Salmon

Prep time: 5 minutes | **Cook time:** 3 minutes | **Serves:**2

Ingredients:

Chutney:

¼ cup fresh dill

¼ cup extra virgin olive oil

Juice from ½ lemon

Sea salt, to taste

Fish:

2 cups water

2 salmon fillets

Juice from ½ lemon

¼ teaspoon paprika

Salt and freshly ground pepper to taste

Directions:

Pulse all the chutney ingredients in a food processor until creamy. Set aside. Add the water and steamer basket to the Instant Pot. Place salmon fillets, skin-side down, on the steamer basket. Drizzle the lemon juice over salmon and sprinkle with the paprika. Secure the lid. Select the Manual mode and set the cooking time for 3 minutes at High Pressure.

Once cooking is complete, do a quick pressure release. Carefully open the lid. Season the fillets with pepper and salt to taste. Serve topped with the dill chutney.

Per Serving calories: 636 | fat: 41.1g | protein: 65.3g | carbs: 1.9g

Seared Salmon with Lemon Cream Sauce

Prep time: 10 minutes | **Cook time:** 20 minutes | **Serves:**4

Ingredients:

4 (5-ounce / 142-g) salmon fillets
Sea salt and freshly ground black pepper, to taste
1 tablespoon extra-virgin olive oil
½ cup low-sodium vegetable broth
Juice and zest of 1 lemon
1 teaspoon chopped fresh thyme
½ cup fat-free sour cream
1 teaspoon honey
1 tablespoon chopped fresh chives

Directions:

Preheat the oven to 400°F (205°C).

Season the salmon lightly on both sides with salt and pepper. Place a large ovenproof skillet over medium-high heat and add the olive oil.

Sear the salmon fillets on both sides until golden, about 3 minutes per side. Transfer the salmon to a baking dish and bake in the preheated oven until just cooked through, about 10 minutes.

Meanwhile, whisk together the vegetable broth, lemon juice and zest, and thyme in a small saucepan over medium-high heat until the liquid reduces by about one-quarter, about 5 minutes.

Whisk in the sour cream and honey.

Stir in the chives and serve the sauce over the salmon.

Per Serving

calories: 310 | fat: 18.0g | protein: 29.0g | carbs: 6.0g

Fennel Poached Cod with Tomatoes

Prep time: 10 minutes | **Cook time:** 20 minutes | **Serves:**4

Ingredients:

1 tablespoon olive oil
1 cup thinly sliced fennel
½ cup thinly sliced onion
1 tablespoon minced garlic
1 (15-ounce / 425-g) can diced tomatoes
2 cups chicken broth
½ cup white wine
Juice and zest of 1 orange
1 pinch red pepper flakes
1 bay leaf
1 pound (454 g) cod

Directions:

Heat the olive oil in a large skillet. Add the onion and fennel and cook for 6 minutes, stirring occasionally, or until translucent. Add the garlic and cook for 1 minute more. Add the tomatoes, chicken broth, wine, orange juice and zest, red pepper flakes, and bay leaf, and simmer for 5 minutes to meld the flavors.

Carefully add the cod in a single layer, cover, and simmer for 6 to 7 minutes. Transfer fish to a serving dish, ladle the remaining sauce over the fish, and serve.

Per Serving

calories: 336 | fat: 12.5g | protein: 45.1g | carbs:11.0g

Tuna and Zucchini Patties

Prep time: 10 minutes | **Cook time:** 12 minutes | **Serves:**4

Ingredients:

3 slices whole-wheat sandwich bread, toasted
2 (5-ounce / 142-g) cans tuna in olive oil, drained
1 cup shredded zucchini
1 large egg, lightly beaten
¼ cup diced red bell pepper
1 tablespoon dried oregano
1 teaspoon lemon zest
¼ teaspoon freshly ground black pepper
¼ teaspoon kosher or sea salt
1 tablespoon extra-virgin olive oil
Salad greens or 4 whole-wheat rolls, for serving (optional)

Directions:

Crumble the toast into bread crumbs with your fingers (or use a knife to cut into ¼-inch cubes) until you have 1 cup of loosely packed crumbs. Pour the crumbs into a large bowl. Add the tuna, zucchini, beaten egg, bell pepper, oregano, lemon zest, black pepper, and salt. Mix well with a fork. With your hands, form the mixture into four (½-cup-size) patties. Place them on a plate, and press each patty flat to about ¾-inch thick.

In a large skillet over medium-high heat, heat the oil until it's very hot, about 2 minutes.

Add the patties to the hot oil, then reduce the heat down to medium. Cook the patties for 5 minutes, flip with a spatula, and cook for an additional 5 minutes. Serve the patties on salad greens or whole-wheat rolls, if desired.

Per Serving

calories: 757 | fat: 72.0g | protein: 5.0g | carbs: 26.0g

Scallop Teriyaki

Prep time: 5 minutes | **Cook time:** 5 minutes | **Serves:**6

Ingredients:

2 pounds (907 g) jumbo sea scallops
2 tablespoons olive oil
6 tablespoons pure maple syrup
1 cup coconut aminos
1 teaspoon ground ginger
1 teaspoon garlic powder
1 teaspoon sea salt

Directions:

Add the olive oil to the Instant pot and heat it on the Sauté settings of your pot. Add the scallops to the pot and cook for a minute from each side.

Stir in all the remaining ingredients in the pot and mix them well. Secure the lid and select the Steam function to cook for 3 minutes. After the beep, do a Quick release then remove the lid. Serve hot.

Per Serving

calories: 228 | fat: 5.3g | protein: 23.4g | carbs: 21.4g

Baked Lemon Salmon

Prep time: 5 minutes | **Cook time:** 20 minutes | **Serves:**4

Ingredients:

¼ teaspoon dried thyme
Zest and juice of ½ lemon
¼ teaspoon salt
Nonstick cooking spray
½ teaspoon freshly ground
black pepper
1 pound (454 g) salmon
fillet

Directions:

Preheat the oven to 425°F (220°C). Coat a baking sheet with nonstick cooking spray.

Mix together the thyme, lemon zest and juice, salt, and pepper in a small bowl and stir to incorporate.

Arrange the salmon, skin-side down, on the coated baking sheet. Spoon the thyme mixture over the salmon and spread it all over.

Bake in the preheated oven for about 15 to 20 minutes, or until the fish flakes apart easily. Serve warm.

Per Serving calories: 162 | fat: 7.0g | protein: 23.1g | carbs:

Garlic Shrimp with Mushrooms

Prep time: 10 minutes | **Cook time:** 15 minutes | **Serves:**4

Ingredients:

1 pound (454 g) fresh
shrimp, peeled, deveined,
and patted dry
1 teaspoon salt
1 cup extra-virgin olive oil
8 large garlic cloves, thinly
sliced
4 ounces (113 g) sliced
mushrooms (shiitake, baby
bella, or button)
½ teaspoon red pepper
flakes
¼ cup chopped fresh flat-
leaf Italian parsley

Directions:

In a bowl, season the shrimp with salt. Set aside.

Heat the olive oil in a large skillet over medium-low heat.

Add the garlic and cook for 3 to 4 minutes until fragrant, stirring occasionally.

Sauté the mushrooms for 5 minutes, or until they start to exude their juices. Stir in the shrimp and sprinkle with red pepper flakes and sauté for 3 to 4 minutes more, or until the shrimp start to turn pink.

Remove the skillet from the heat and add the parsley. Stir to combine and serve warm.

Per Serving
calories: 619 | fat: 55.5g | protein: 24.1g | carbs: 3.7g

Lemony Shrimp with Orzo Salad

Prep time: 10 minutes | **Cook time:** 22 minutes | **Serves:**4

Ingredients:

1 cup orzo
1 hothouse cucumber,
deseeded and chopped
½ cup finely diced red
onion
2 tablespoons extra-virgin
olive oil
2 pounds (907 g) shrimp,
peeled and deveined
3 lemons, juiced
Salt and freshly ground
black pepper, to taste
¾ cup crumbled feta cheese
2 tablespoons dried dill
1 cup chopped fresh flat-
leaf parsley

Directions:

Bring a large pot of water to a boil. Add the orzo and cook covered for 15 to 18 minutes, or until the orzo is tender. Transfer to a colander to drain and set aside to cool.

Mix the cucumber and red onion in a bowl. Set aside.

Heat the olive oil in a medium skillet over medium heat until it shimmers.

Reduce the heat, add the shrimp, and cook each side for 2 minutes until cooked through.

Add the cooked shrimp to the bowl of cucumber and red onion. Mix in the cooked orzo and lemon juice and toss to combine. Sprinkle with salt and pepper. Scatter the top with the feta cheese and dill. Garnish with the parsley and serve immediately.

Per Serving
calories: 565 | fat: 17.8g | protein: 63.3g | carbs: 43.9g

Spicy Grilled Shrimp with Lemon Wedges

Prep time: 15 minutes | **Cook time:** 6 minutes | **Serves:**6

Ingredients:

1 large clove garlic, crushed
1 teaspoon coarse salt
1 teaspoon paprika
½ teaspoon cayenne pepper
2 teaspoons lemon juice
2 tablespoons plus
1 teaspoon olive oil, divided
2 pounds (907 g) large
shrimp, peeled and deveined
8 wedges lemon, for garnish

Directions:

Preheat the grill to medium heat.

Stir together the garlic, salt, paprika, cayenne pepper, lemon juice, and 2 tablespoons of olive oil in a small bowl until a paste forms. Add the shrimp and toss until well coated.

Grease the grill grates lightly with remaining 1 teaspoon of olive oil. Grill the shrimp for 4 to 6 minutes, flipping the shrimp halfway through, or until the shrimp is totally pink and opaque. Garnish the shrimp with lemon wedges and serve hot.

Per Serving
calories: 163 | fat: 5.8g | protein: 25.2g | carbs: 2.8g

Crispy Tilapia with Mango Salsa

Prep time: 5 minutes | **Cook time:** 10 minutes | **Serves:**2

Ingredients:
Salsa:
1 cup chopped mango
2 tablespoons chopped fresh cilantro
2 tablespoons chopped red onion
2 tablespoons freshly squeezed lime juice
½ jalapeño pepper, seeded and minced
Pinch salt
Tilapia:
1 tablespoon paprika
1 teaspoon onion powder
½ teaspoon dried thyme
½ teaspoon freshly ground black pepper
¼ teaspoon cayenne pepper
½ teaspoon garlic powder
¼ teaspoon salt
½ pound (227 g) boneless tilapia fillets
2 teaspoons extra-virgin olive oil
1 lime, cut into wedges, for serving

Directions:
Make the salsa: Place the mango, cilantro, onion, lime juice, jalapeño, and salt in a medium bowl and toss to combine. Set aside.

Make the tilapia: Stir together the paprika, onion powder, thyme, black pepper, cayenne pepper, garlic powder, and salt in a small bowl until well mixed. Rub both sides of fillets generously with the mixture.

Heat the olive oil in a large skillet over medium heat.

Add the fish fillets and cook each side for 3 to 5 minutes until golden brown and cooked through.

Divide the fillets among two plates and spoon half of the prepared salsa onto each fillet. Serve the fish alongside the lime wedges.

Per Serving
calories: 239 | fat: 7.8g | protein: 25.0g | carbs: 21.9g

Peppercorn-Seared Tuna Steaks

Prep time: 5 minutes | **Cook time:** 10 minutes | **Serves:**2

Ingredients:
2 (5-ounce / 142-g) ahi tuna steaks
1 teaspoon kosher salt
¼ teaspoon cayenne pepper
2 tablespoons olive oil
1 teaspoon whole peppercorns

Directions:
On a plate, Season the tuna steaks on both sides with salt and cayenne pepper.

In a skillet, heat the olive oil over medium-high heat until it shimmers.

Add the peppercorns and cook for about 5 minutes, or until they soften and pop.

Carefully put the tuna steaks in the skillet and sear for 1 to 2 minutes per side, depending on the thickness of the tuna steaks, or until the fish is cooked to the desired level of doneness. Cool for 5 minutes before serving.

Per Serving
calories: 260 | fat: 14.3g | protein: 33.4g | carbs: 0.2g

Mediterranean Grilled Sea Bass

Prep time: 20 minutes | **Cook time:** 20 minutes | **Serves:**6

Ingredients:
¼ teaspoon onion powder
¼ teaspoon garlic powder
¼ teaspoon paprika
Lemon pepper and sea salt to taste
2 pounds (907 g) sea bass
3 tablespoons extra-virgin olive oil, divided
2 large cloves garlic, chopped
1 tablespoon chopped Italian flat leaf parsley

Directions:
Preheat the grill to high heat.

Place the onion powder, garlic powder, paprika, lemon pepper, and sea salt in a large bowl and stir to combine.

Dredge the fish in the spice mixture, turning until well coated.

Heat 2 tablespoon of olive oil in a small skillet. Add the garlic and parsley and cook for 1 to 2 minutes, stirring occasionally. Remove the skillet from the heat and set aside. Brush the grill grates lightly with remaining 1 tablespoon olive oil.

Grill the fish for about 7 minutes. Flip the fish and drizzle with the garlic mixture and cook for an additional 7 minutes, or until the fish flakes when pressed lightly with a fork. Serve hot.

Per Serving
calories: 200 | fat: 10.3g | protein: 26.9g | carbs: 0.6g

Alfredo Tuscan Shrimp with Penne

Prep time: 5 minutes | **Cook time:** 5 minutes | **Serves:**3

Ingredients:
1 pound (454 g) shrimp
1 jar alfredo sauce
1½ cups fresh spinach
3 cups water
1 cup sun-dried tomatoes
1 box penne pasta
1½ teaspoons Tuscan seasoning

Directions:
Add the water and pasta to a pot over a medium heat, boil until it cooks completely. Then strain the pasta and keep it aside. Select the Sauté function on your Instant Pot and add the tomatoes, shrimp, Tuscan seasoning, and alfredo sauce into it.

Stir and cook until shrimp turn pink in color.

Now add the spinach leaves to the pot and cook for 5 minutes.

Add the pasta to the pot and stir well.

Serve hot.

Per Serving
calories: 1361 | fat: 70.1g | protein: 55.9g | carbs: 134.4g

Catfish and Shrimp Jambalaya

Prep time: 20 minutes | **Cook time:** 4 hours 45 minutes | **Serves:**

Ingredients:

4 ounces (113 g) catfish (cut into 1-inch cubes)	1 cup canned diced tomatoes
4 ounces (113 g) shrimp (peeled and deveined)	1 cup uncooked long-grain white rice
1 tablespoon olive oil	½ tablespoon Cajun seasoning
2 bacon slices, chopped	¼ teaspoon dried thyme
1¼ cups vegetable broth	¼ teaspoon cayenne pepper
¾ cup sliced celery stalk	½ teaspoon dried oregano
¼ teaspoon minced garlic	Salt and freshly ground black pepper, to taste
½ cup chopped onion	

Directions:

Select the Sauté function on your Instant Pot and add the oil into it.

Put the onion, garlic, celery, and bacon to the pot and cook for 10 minutes.

Add all the remaining ingredients to the pot except seafood. Stir well, then secure the cooker lid. Select the Slow Cook function on a medium mode. Keep the pressure release handle on venting position. Cook for 4 hours.

Once done, remove the lid and add the seafood to the gravy.

Secure the lid again, keep the pressure handle in the venting position.

Cook for another 45 minutes then serve.

Per Serving

calories: 437 | fat: 13.1g | protein: 21.3g | carbs: 56.7g

Balsamic-Honey Glazed Salmon

Prep time: 2 minutes | **Cook time:** 8 minutes | **Serves:**4

Ingredients:

½ cup balsamic vinegar	Sea salt and freshly ground pepper, to taste
1 tablespoon honey	
4 (8-ounce / 227-g) salmon fillets	1 tablespoon olive oil

Directions:

Heat a skillet over medium-high heat. Combine the vinegar and honey in a small bowl.

Season the salmon fillets with the sea salt and freshly ground pepper; brush with the honey-balsamic glaze.

Add olive oil to the skillet, and sear the salmon fillets, cooking for 3 to 4 minutes on each side until lightly browned and medium rare in the center.

Let sit for 5 minutes before serving.

Per Serving

calories: 454 | fat: 17.3g | protein: 65.3g | carbs: 9.7g

Salmon and Potato Casserole

Prep time: 20 minutes | **Cook time:** 8 hours | **Serves:**4

Ingredients:

½ tablespoon olive oil	3 tablespoons flour
8 ounces (227 g) cream of mushroom soup	1 (1-pound / 454-g) can salmon (drained and flaked)
¼ cup water	½ cup chopped scallion
3 medium potatoes (peeled and sliced)	¼ teaspoon ground nutmeg
	Salt and freshly ground black pepper, to taste

Directions:

Pour mushroom soup and water in a separate bowl and mix them well.

Add the olive oil to the Instant Pot and grease it lightly.

Place half of the potatoes in the pot and sprinkle salt, pepper, and half of the flour over it.

Now add a layer of half of the salmon over potatoes, then a layer of half of the scallions.

Repeat these layers and pour mushroom soup mix on top.

Top it with nutmeg evenly.

Secure the lid and set its pressure release handle to the venting position.

Select the Slow Cook function with Medium heat on your Instant Pot.

Let it cook for 8 hours then serve.

Per Serving

calories: 388 | fat: 11.6g | protein: 34.6g | carbs: 37.2g

Lemony Salmon

Prep time: 10 minutes | **Cook time:** 3 minutes | **Serves:**3

Ingredients:

1 cup water	1 teaspoon fresh lemon juice
3 lemon slices	
1 (5-ounce / 142-g) salmon fillet	Salt and ground black pepper, to taste
	Fresh cilantro to garnish

Directions:

Add the water to the Instant pot and place a trivet inside.

In a shallow bowl, place the salmon fillet. Sprinkle salt and pepper over it.

Squeeze some lemon juice on top then place a lemon slice over the salmon fillet.

Cover the lid and lock it. Set its pressure release handle to Sealing position.

Use Steam function on your cooker for 3 minutes to cook.

After the beep, do a Quick release and release the pressure.

Remove the lid, then serve with the lemon slice and fresh cilantro on top.

Per Serving

calories: 161 | fat: 5.0g | protein: 26.6g | carbs: 0.7g

Sardines and Plum Tomato Curry

Prep time: 10 minutes | **Cook time:** 8 hours 2 minutes | **Serves:**4

Ingredients:

1 tablespoon olive oil
1 pound (454 g) fresh sardines, cubed
2 plum tomatoes, chopped finely
½ large onion, sliced
1 garlic clove, minced
½ cup tomato purée
Salt and ground black pepper, to taste

Directions:

Select the Sauté function on your Instant pot then add the oil and sardines to it. Let it sauté for 2 minutes then add all the remaining ingredients.

Cover the lid and select Slow Cook function for 8 hours.

Remove the lid and stir the cooked curry. Serve warm.

Per Serving

calories: 292 | fat: 16.5g | protein: 28.9g | carbs: 6.0g

Salmon and Mushroom Hash with Pesto

Prep time: 15 minutes | **Cook time:** 20 minutes | **Serves:**6

Ingredients:

Pesto:
¼ cup extra-virgin olive oil
1 bunch fresh basil
Juice and zest of 1 lemon
⅓ cup water
¼ teaspoon salt, plus additional as needed

Hash:
2 tablespoons extra-virgin olive oil
6 cups mixed mushrooms (brown, white, shiitake, cremini, portobello, etc.), sliced
1 pound (454 g) wild salmon, cubed

Directions:

Make the pesto: Pulse the olive oil, basil, juice and zest, water, and salt in a blender or food processor until smoothly blended. Set aside.

Heat the olive oil in a large skillet over medium heat.

Stir-fry the mushrooms for 6 to 8 minutes, or until they begin to exude their juices.

Add the salmon and cook each side for 5 to 6 minutes until cooked through.

Fold in the prepared pesto and stir well. Taste and add additional salt as needed. Serve warm.

Per Serving

calories: 264 | fat: 14.7g | protein: 7.0g | carbs: 30.9g

Spiced Citrus Sole

Prep time: 10 minutes | **Cook time:** 10 minutes | **Serves:**4

Ingredients:

1 teaspoon garlic powder
1 teaspoon chili powder
½ teaspoon lemon zest
½ teaspoon lime zest
¼ teaspoon smoked paprika
2 teaspoons freshly squeezed lime juice
¼ teaspoon freshly ground black pepper Pinch sea salt
4 (6-ounce / 170-g) sole fillets, patted dry
1 tablespoon extra-virgin olive oil

Directions:

Preheat the oven to 450ºF (235ºC). Line a baking sheet with aluminum foil and set aside.

Mix together the garlic powder, chili powder, lemon zest, lime zest, paprika, pepper, and salt in a small bowl until well combined.

Arrange the sole fillets on the prepared baking sheet and rub the spice mixture all over the fillets until well coated. Drizzle the olive oil and lime juice over the fillets.

Bake in the preheated oven for about 8 minutes until flaky.

Remove from the heat to a plate and serve.

Per Serving

calories: 183 | fat: 5.0g | protein: 32.1g | carbs: 0g

Asian-Inspired Tuna Lettuce Wraps

Prep time: 10 minutes | **Cook time:** 0 minutes | **Serves:**2

Ingredients:

⅓ cup almond butter
1 tablespoon freshly squeezed lemon juice
1 teaspoon low-sodium soy sauce
1 teaspoon curry powder
½ teaspoon sriracha, or to taste
½ cup canned water chestnuts, drained and chopped
2 (2.6-ounce / 74-g) package tuna packed in water, drained
2 large butter lettuce leaves

Directions:

Stir together the almond butter, lemon juice, soy sauce, curry powder, sriracha in a medium bowl until well mixed. Add the water chestnuts and tuna and stir until well incorporated.

Place 2 butter lettuce leaves on a flat work surface, spoon half of the tuna mixture onto each leaf and roll up into a wrap. Serve immediately.

Per Serving

calories: 270 | fat: 13.9g | protein: 19.1g | carbs: 18.5g

Tasty Avocado Sauce over Zoodles (Italian)

Preparation Time: 10 minutes **Cooking Time:** 10 minutes
Servings: 2

Ingredients:

1 zucchini peeled and spiralized into 1/3 cup water
1 avocado peeled and pitted
12 sliced cherry tomatoes
Pepper and salt to taste
2 tablespoon lemon juice noodles
4 tablespoon pine nuts
1 1/4 cup basil

Directions:

Make the sauce in a blender by adding pine nuts, lemon juice, avocado, water, and basil. Pulse until smooth and creamy. Season with pepper and salt to taste. Mix well.

Place zoodles in salad bowl. Pour over avocado sauce and toss well to coat.

Add cherry tomatoes, serve, and enjoy.

Per Serving
Calories: 313; Protein: 6.8g; Carbs: 18.7g; Fat: 26.8g

Vegan Sesame Tofu and Eggplants (Greek)

Preparation Time: 10 minutes **Cooking Time:** 20 minutes
Servings: 4

Ingredients:

5 tablespoons olive oil
2 teaspoons Swerve sweetener
2 whole eggplants, sliced
Salt and pepper to taste
1 cup fresh cilantro, chopped
1-pound firm tofu, sliced
¼ cup soy sauce
3 tablespoons rice vinegar
¼ cup sesame seeds
4 tablespoons toasted sesame oil

Directions:

Heat the oil in a pan for 2 minutes.

Pan fry the tofu for 3 minutes on each side.

Stir in the rice vinegar, sweetener, eggplants, and soy sauce. Season with salt and pepper to taste.

Cover and cook for 5 minutes on medium fire. Stir and continue cooking for another 5 minutes.

Toss in the sesame oil, sesame seeds, and cilantro.

Serve and enjoy.

Per Serving
Calories: 616; Carbs: 27.4g; Protein: 23.9g; Fat: 49.2g

Simple Cod Piccata (Italian)

Preparation Time: 10 minutes **Cooking Time:** 15 minutes
Servings: 3

Ingredients:

¼ cup capers, drained
¾ cup chicken stock
1/3 cup almond flour
2 tablespoon fresh parsley, chopped
2 tablespoon grapeseed oil
½ teaspoon salt
1-pound cod fillets, patted dry
3 tablespoon extra-virgin oil
3 tablespoon lemon juice

Directions:

In a bowl, combine the almond flour and salt.

Dredge the fish in the almond flour to coat. Set aside.

Heat a little bit of olive oil to coat a large skillet. Heat the skillet over medium high heat. Add grapeseed oil. Cook the cod for 3 minutes on each side to brown. Remove from the plate and place on a paper towel- lined plate.

In a saucepan, mix together the chicken stock, capers and lemon juice. Simmer to reduce the sauce to half. Add the remaining grapeseed oil.

Drizzle the fried cod with the sauce and sprinkle with parsley.

Per Serving
Calories: 277.1; Fat: 28.3 g; Protein: 1.9 g; Carbs: 3.7 g

Yummy Salmon Panzanella (Italian)

Preparation Time: 10 minutes **Cooking Time:** 10 minutes
Servings: 4

Ingredients:

¼ cup thinly sliced fresh basil
¼ teaspoon freshly ground pepper, divided
1 lb. center cut salmon, skinned and cut into 4 equal portions
1 medium cucumber, peeled, seeded, and cut into 1-inch slices
2 thick slices day old whole grain bread, sliced into 1-inch cubes
¼ cup thinly sliced red onion
½ teaspoon salt
3 tablespoon virgin olive oil
2 large tomatoes, cut into 1-inch pieces
1 tablespoon capers, rinsed and chopped
8 Kalamata olives, pitted and chopped
3 tablespoon red wine vinegar

Directions:

Grease grill grate and preheat grill to high.

In a large bowl, whisk 1/8 teaspoon pepper, capers, vinegar, and olives. Add oil and whisk well.

Stir in basil, onion, cucumber, tomatoes, and bread.

Season both sides of salmon with remaining pepper and salt.Grill on high for 4 minutes per side. Into 4 plates, evenly divide salad, top with grilled salmon, and serve.

Per Serving
Calories: 383; Fat: 20.6g; Protein: 34.8g; Carbs: 13.6g

Avocado Shrimp Ceviche

Prep time: 15 minutes | **Cook time:** 0 minutes | **Serves:**4

Ingredients:

1 pound (454 g) fresh shrimp, peeled, deveined, and cut in half lengthwise
1 small red or yellow bell pepper, cut into ½-inch chunks
½ small red onion, cut into thin slivers
½ English cucumber, peeled and cut into ½-inch chunks
¼ cup chopped fresh cilantro

⅓ cup freshly squeezed lime juice
2 tablespoons freshly squeezed clementine juice
2 tablespoons freshly squeezed lemon juice
1 teaspoon salt
½ teaspoon freshly ground black pepper
2 ripe avocados, peeled, pitted, and cut into ½-inch chunks
½ cup extra-virgin olive oil

Directions:

Place the shrimp, bell pepper, red onion, cucumber, and cilantro in a large bowl and toss to combine.

In a separate bowl, stir together the olive oil, lime, clementine, and lemon juice, salt, and black pepper until smooth. Pour the mixture into the bowl of shrimp and vegetable mixture and toss until they are completely coated.

Cover the bowl with plastic wrap and transfer to the refrigerator to marinate for at least 2 hours, or up to 8 hours.

When ready, stir in the avocado chunks and toss to incorporate. Serve immediately.

Per Serving
calories: 496 | fat: 39.5g | protein: 25.3g | carbs: 13.8g

Baked Salmon with Basil and Tomato

Prep time: 10 minutes | **Cook time:** 20 minutes | **Serves:**2

Ingredients:

2 (6-ounce / 170-g) boneless salmon fillets
1 tablespoon dried basil
1 tomato, thinly sliced

1 tablespoon olive oil
2 tablespoons grated Parmesan cheese
Nonstick cooking spray

Directions:

Preheat the oven to 375°F (190°C). Line a baking sheet with a piece of aluminum foil and mist with nonstick cooking spray.

Arrange the salmon fillets onto the aluminum foil and scatter with basil. Place the tomato slices on top and drizzle with olive oil. Top with the grated Parmesan cheese.

Bake for about 20 minutes, or until the flesh is opaque and it flakes apart easily.

Remove from the oven and serve on a plate.

Per Serving
calories: 403 | fat: 26.5g | protein: 36.3g | carbs: 3.8g

Cod with Parsley Pistou

Prep time: 15 minutes | **Cook time:** 10 minutes | **Serves:**4

Ingredients:

1 cup packed roughly chopped fresh flat-leaf Italian parsley
Zest and juice of 1 lemon
1 to 2 small garlic cloves, minced
1 teaspoon salt

½ teaspoon freshly ground black pepper
1 cup extra-virgin olive oil, divided
1 pound (454 g) cod fillets, cut into 4 equal-sized pieces

Directions:

Make the pistou: Place the parsley, lemon zest and juice, garlic, salt, and pepper in a food processor until finely chopped. With the food processor running, slowly drizzle in ¾ cup of olive oil until a thick sauce forms. Set aside.

Heat the remaining ¼ cup of olive oil in a large skillet over medium-high heat.

Add the cod fillets, cover, and cook each side for 4 to 5 minutes, until browned and cooked through.

Remove the cod fillets from the heat to a plate and top each with generous spoonfuls of the prepared pistou. Serve immediately.

Per Serving
calories: 580 | fat: 54.6g | protein: 21.1g | carbs: 2.8g

Mediterranean Braised Cod with Vegetables

Prep time: 10 minutes | **Cook time:** 18 minutes | **Serves:**2

Ingredients:

1 tablespoon olive oil
½ medium onion, minced
2 garlic cloves, minced
1 teaspoon oregano
1 (15-ounce / 425-g) can artichoke hearts in water, drained and halved

1 (15-ounce / 425-g) can diced tomatoes with basil
¼ cup pitted Greek olives, drained
10 ounces (284 g) wild cod
Salt and freshly ground black pepper, to taste

Directions:

In a skillet, heat the olive oil over medium-high heat.

Sauté the onion for about 5 minutes, stirring occasionally, or until tender. Stir in the garlic and oregano and cook for 30 seconds more until fragrant.

Add the artichoke hearts, tomatoes, and olives and stir to combine. Top with the cod. Cover and cook for 10 minutes, or until the fish flakes easily with a fork and juices run clean. Sprinkle with the salt and pepper. Serve warm.

Per Serving
calories: 332 | fat: 10.5g | protein: 29.2g | carbs: 30.7g

Shrimps with Broccoli

Prep time: 5 minutes | **Cook time:** 10 minutes | **Serves:** 2

Ingredients:

2 teaspoons vegetable oil
2 tablespoons corn starch
1 cup broccoli florets
¼ cup chicken broth
8 ounces (227 g) large shrimp, peeled and deveined
¼ cup soy sauce
¼ cup water
¼ cup sliced carrots
3 tablespoons rice vinegar
2 teaspoons sesame oil
1 tablespoon chili garlic sauce
Coriander leaves to garnish
Boiled rice or noodles, for serving

Directions:

Add 1 tablespoon of corn starch and shrimp to a bowl. Mix them well then set it aside.

In a small bowl, mix the remaining corn starch, chicken broth, carrots, chili garlic sauce, rice vinegar and soy sauce together. Keep the mixture aside.

Select the Sauté function on your Instant pot, add the sesame oil and broccoli florets to the pot and sauté for 5 minutes. Add the water to the broccoli, cover the lid and cook for 5 minutes. Stir in shrimp and vegetable oil to the broccoli, sauté it for 5 minutes. Garnish with coriander leaves on top. Serve with rice or noodles.

Per Serving

calories: 300 | fat: 16.5g | protein: 19.6g | carbs: 17.1g

Salmon with Lemon & Dill (Spanish)

Prep time: 15 minutes **Cooking Time:** 2 hours **Servings:** 4

Ingredients:

Cooking spray
1 tablespoon fresh dill, chopped
Salt and pepper to taste
1 teaspoon olive oil
1 clove garlic, minced
1 lemon, sliced
2 lb. salmon

Directions:

Spray your slow cooker with oil.

Brush both sides of salmon with olive oil.

Season the salmon with salt, pepper, dill and garlic

Add to the slow cooker.

Put the lemon slices on top.

Cover the pot and cook on high for 2 hours.

Per Serving

Calories 313 Fat 15.2g Carbohydrate 0.7g Protein 44.2g Sugars 0g

Shrimp and Tomato Creole

Prep time: 20 minutes | **Cook time:** 7 hours 10 minutes | **Serves:** 4

Ingredients:

1 pound (454 g) shrimp (peeled and deveined)
1 tablespoon olive oil
1 (28-ounce / 794-g) can crush whole tomatoes
1 cup celery stalk (sliced)
¾ cup chopped white onion
½ cup green bell pepper (chopped)
1 (8-ounce / 227-g) can tomato sauce
½ teaspoon minced garlic
¼ teaspoon ground black pepper
1 tablespoon Worcestershire sauce
4 drops hot pepper sauce
Salt, to taste
White rice for serving

Directions:

Put the oil to the Instant Pot along with all the ingredients except the shrimp. Secure the cooker lid and keep the pressure handle valve turned to the venting position.

Select the Slow Cook function on your cooker and set it on medium heat. Let the mixture cook for 6 hours.

Remove the lid afterwards and add the shrimp to the pot.

Stir and let the shrimp cook for another 1 hour on Slow Cook function. Keep the lid covered with pressure release handle in the venting position. To serve, pour the juicy shrimp creole over steaming white rice.

Per Serving

calories: 231 | fat: 4.8g | protein: 27.6g | carbs: 23.8g

Tuna with Shirataki Noodles

Prep time: 5 minutes | **Cook time:** 4 minutes | **Serves:** 2

Ingredients:

½ can tuna, drained
8 ounces (227 g) Shirataki noodles
½ cup frozen peas
1 (14-ounce / 397-g) can cream mushroom soup
2 ounces (57 g) shredded Cheddar cheese
1½ cups water

Directions:

Add the water with noodles to the base of your Instant Pot.

Place the tuna and peas over it. Then pour the mushroom soup on top.

Secure the lid and cook with the Manual function at High Pressure for 4 minutes.

After the beep, do a Quick release then remove the lid.

Stir in shredded cheese to the tuna mix.

Serve warm.

Per Serving

calories: 362 | fat: 11.1g | protein: 19.5g | carbs: 46.5g

Shrimp and Spaghetti Squash Bowls

Prep time: 5 minutes | **Cook time:** 25 minutes | **Serves:** 4

Ingredients:

½ cup dry white wine
¼ teaspoon crushed red pepper flakes
1 large shallot, finely chopped
1 pound (454 g) jumbo shrimp, peeled and deveined

1 (28-ounce / 794-g) can crushed tomatoes
2 cloves garlic, minced
2½ pounds (1.1 kg) spaghetti squash
1 teaspoon olive oil
Salt and pepper, to taste
Parsley leaves (garnish)

Directions:

At first, sprinkle some salt and pepper over the shrimp and keep them in a refrigerator until further use.

Hit the Sauté function on your Instant Pot, then add the olive oil and red pepper flakes into it. Sauté for 1 minute.

Add the shallot and cook for 3 minutes. Then add the garlic, cook for 1 minute.

Add the dry wine, tomatoes, and whole spaghetti squash in the pot. Select Manual settings with medium pressure for 20 minutes. After the beep, do a Natural release. Remove the lid and the spaghetti squash.

Cut squash in half, remove its seed and stab with a fork to form spaghetti strands out of it. Keep them aside.

Select the Sauté function on your instant pot again, stir in shrimp. Mix well the shrimp with sauce. To serve, top the spaghetti squash with shrimp and sauce. Garnish it with parsley.

Per Serving

calories: 222 | fat: 4.4g | protein: 19.3g | carbs: 30.1g

Asparagus Smoked Salmon (Spanish)

Preparation Time: 15 minutes **Cooking Time:** 5 hours **Servings:** 6

Ingredients:

1 tablespoon extra-virgin olive oil
2 teaspoons chopped fresh dill, plus additional for garnish
¼ teaspoon freshly ground black pepper
6 ounces smoked salmon, flaked
½ teaspoon kosher salt

1 cup heavy (whipping) cream
6 large eggs
12 ounces asparagus, trimmed and sliced
1 1/2 cups shredded Havarti or Monterey Jack cheese

Directions:

Brush butter into a cooker

Whisk in the heavy cream with eggs, dill, salt, and pepper.

Stir in the cheese and asparagus.

Gently fold in the salmon and then pour the mixture into the prepared insert. Cover and cook on low or 3 hours on high. Serve warm, garnished with additional fresh dill.

Per Serving

Calories 388 Fat 19 Carbs 1.0 Protein 21

Grits with Shrimp

Prep time: 5 minutes | **Cook time:** 15 minutes | **Serves:** 8

Ingredients:

1 tablespoon oil
2 cups quick grits
12 ounces (340 g) Parmesan cheese, shredded
2 cups heavy cream

24 ounces (680 g) tail-on shrimp
2 tablespoons Old Bay seasoning
A pinch of ground black pepper
4 cups water

Directions:

Add a tablespoon of oil to the Instant Pot. Select the Sauté function for cooking.

Add the shrimp to the oil and drizzle old bay seasoning over it.

Cook the shrimp for 3-4 minutes while stirring then set them aside.

Now add the water, cream, and quick grits to the pot. Select the Manual function for 3 minutes at High Pressure.

After the beep, do a Quick release then remove the lid.

Add the shredded cheese to the grits then stir well.

Take a serving bowl, first pour in the creamy grits mixture then top it with shrimp.

Sprinkle black pepper on top then serve hot.

Per Serving

calories: 528 | fat: 38.6g | protein: 30.7g | carbs: 15.2g

Grilled Salmon (Spanish)

Prep time: 15 minutes **Cooking Time:** 16 mins **Servings:** 6

Ingredients:

1 1/2 pounds salmon fillet
Pepper to taste
1/3 cup of brown sugar
1/3 cup of water

Garlic powder to taste
1/3 cup soy sauce
1/4 cup vegetable oil

Directions:

Season the salmon fillets with lemon pepper, salt, and garlic powder.

Mix the soy sauce, brown sugar, water, and vegetable oil in a small bowl until the sugar is dissolved. Place the fish in a big resealable plastic bag with the soy sauce mixture, seal, and let marinate for at least 2 hours.

Preheat the grill on medium heat.

Lightly oil the grill. Place the salmon on the preheated grill and discard the marinade. Cook salmon 6 to 8 minutes per side or until the fish flakes easily with a fork.

Per Serving

318 calories 20.1 grams of fat 13.2 g carbohydrates 20.5 g of protein 56 mg cholesterol

Fish Tacos (Italian)

Preparation Time: 40 minutes **Cooking Time:** 15 minutes
Servings: 8

Ingredients:

1 cup flour	2 tablespoons corn flour
1 teaspoon baking powder	1 egg
1/2 teaspoon of salt	1 liter of oil for frying
1 cup of beer	1/2 cup of yogurt
1/2 cup of mayonnaise	1 jalapeño pepper, minced
1 lime, juice	1 cup Finely chopped
1/2 teaspoon ground cumin	capers
1/2 teaspoon dried dill	1/2 teaspoon dried oregano
1 teaspoon ground cayenne	1 pound of cod fillets, 2-3
pepper	ounces each
1/2 medium cabbage, finely	8 corn tortillas
shredded	

Directions:

Prepare beer dough: combine flour, corn flour, baking powder and salt in a large bowl. Mix the egg and the beer and stir in the flour mixture quickly.

To make a white sauce: combine yogurt and mayonnaise in a medium bowl. Gradually add fresh lime juice until it is slightly fluid — season with jalapeño, capers, oregano, cumin, dill, and cayenne pepper.

Heat the oil in a frying pan.

Lightly sprinkle the fish with flour. Dip it in the beer batter and fry until crispy and golden brown. Drain on kitchen paper. Heat the tortillas. Place the fried fish in a tortilla and garnish with grated cabbage and white sauce.

Per Serving

409 calories 18.8 g of fat 43 grams of carbohydrates 17.3 g of protein 54 mg cholesterol.

Leftover Salmon Salad Power Bowls (Greek)

Preparation Time: 10 minutes **Cooking Time:** 10 minutes
Servings: 1

Ingredients:

½ cup raspberries	½ cup zucchini, sliced
1 tablespoon balsamic glaze	4 cups seasonal greens
2 sprigs of thyme, chopped	1 lemon, juice squeezed
2 tablespoon olive oil	4 ounces leftover grilled
Salmon Salt and pepper to	
taste	

Directions:

Heat oil in a skillet over medium flame and sauté the zucchini. Season with salt and pepper to taste.

In a mixing bowl, mix all together.

Toss to combine everything.

Sprinkle with nut cheese.

Per Serving

Calories: 450.3; Fat: 35.5 g; Protein: 23.4g; Carbs: 9.3 g

Grilled Tilapia with Mango Salsa (Spanish)

Preparation Time: 45 minutes **Cooking Time:** 10 minutes
Servings: 2

Ingredients:

1/3 cup extra virgin olive oil	1 tablespoon chopped fresh parsley
1 tablespoon lemon juice	1 clove of garlic, minced
1 teaspoon dried basil	1 teaspoon ground black
1/2 teaspoon salt	pepper
2 tilapia fillets (1 oz. each)	1 large ripe mango, peeled,
1/2 red pepper, diced	pitted and diced
2 tablespoons chopped red onion	1 tablespoon chopped fresh coriander
2 tablespoons lime juice	1 jalapeño pepper, seeded
Salt and pepper to taste	and minced
1 tablespoon lemon juice	

Directions:

Mix extra virgin olive oil, 1 tablespoon lemon juice, parsley, garlic, basil, 1 teaspoon pepper, and 1/2 teaspoon salt in a bowl, then pour into a resealable plastic bag. Add the tilapia fillets, cover with the marinade, remove excess air, and close the bag. Marinate in the fridge for 1 hour.

Prepare the mango salsa by combining the mango, red pepper, red onion, coriander, and jalapeño pepper in a bowl. Add the lime juice and 1 tablespoon lemon juice and mix well. Season with salt and pepper and keep until serving.

Preheat a grill over medium heat and lightly oil. Remove the tilapia from the marinade and remove the excess. Discard the rest of the marinade. Grill the fillets until the fish is no longer translucent in the middle and flake easily with the fork for 3 to 4 minutes on each side, depending on the thickness of the fillets. Serve the tilapia topped with mango salsa.

Per Serving

634 calories 40.2 grams of fat 33.4 g carbohydrates 36.3 g of protein 62 mg cholesterol

One-Pot Seafood Chowder (Greek)

Prep time: 10 minutes **Cooking Time:** 10 mins **Servings:** 3

Ingredients:

3 cans coconut milk	1 tablespoon garlic, minced
1 can corn, drained	Salt and pepper to taste
3 cans clams, chopped	1 package fresh shrimps,
2 cans shrimps, canned	shelled and deveined
4 large potatoes, diced	2 carrots, peeled and chopped
	2 celery stalks, chopped

Directions:

Place all in a pot and give a good stir to mix everything. Close the lid and turn on the heat to medium.

Bring to a boil and allow to simmer for 10 minutes. Place in individual containers. Put a label and store in the fridge. Allow to warm at room temperature before heating in the microwave oven.

Per Serving Calories: 532; Carbs: 92.5g; Protein: 25.3g

Herbed Salmon Loaf with Sauce (Italian)

Preparation Time: 5 minutes **Cooking Time:** 5 hours
Servings: 4

Ingredients:

For the Salmon Meatloaf:
1cup fresh bread crumbs
1/3 cup whole milk
1 egg
1/4 cup scallions, chopped
1 teaspoon ground
coriander
1/2 teaspoon fenugreek
1/4 teaspoon white pepper
1/2 cup cucumber,
chopped
Salt, to taste

1 can (7 1/2 ounce) salmon,
drained
1 tablespoon fresh lemon
juice 1 teaspoon dried
rosemary
1 teaspoon mustard seed
1/2 teaspoon salt
1/2 teaspoon dill weed
1/2 cup reduced-fat plain
yogurt

Directions:

Line your crock pot with a foil.

Mix all for the salmon meatloaf until everything is well incorporated; form into loaf and place in the crock pot.

Cover with a suitable lid and cook on low heat setting 5 hours.

Combine all of the for the sauce; whisk to combine.

Serve your meatloaf with prepared sauce.

Per Serving
Calories: 145 Fat: 11 g Carbs: 2 g Protein: 11 g

Scallops in Wine 'n Olive Oil (Greek)

Preparation Time: 10 minutes **Cooking Time:** 8 minutes
Servings: 4

Ingredients:

¼ teaspoon salt
1 ½ lbs. large sea scallops
2 tablespoon olive oil
Black pepper – optional

½ cup dry white wine
1 ½ teaspoon chopped
fresh tarragon

Directions:

On medium high fire, place a large nonstick fry pan and heat oil.

Add scallops and fry for 3 minutes per side or until edges are lightly browned. Transfer to a serving plate.

On same pan, add salt, tarragon and wine while scraping pan to loosen browned bits.

Turn off fire.

Pour sauce over scallops and serve.

Per Serving
Calories: 205.2; Fat: 8 g; Protein: 28.6 g; Carbohydrates: 4.7 g

Warm Caper Tapenade on Cod (Greek)

Preparation Time: 10 minutes **Cooking Time:** 30 minutes
Servings: 4

Ingredients:

¼ cup chopped cured olives
1 cup halved cherry
tomatoes
1 ½ teaspoon chopped
fresh oregano
1 teaspoon balsamic vinegar
1 tablespoon capers, rinsed
and chopped

¼ teaspoon freshly ground
pepper
1 tablespoon minced shallot
1 lb. cod fillet
3 teaspoon extra virgin olive
oil, divided

Directions:

Grease baking sheet with cooking spray and preheat oven to 450 F.

Place cod on prepared baking sheet. Rub with 2 teaspoon oil and season with pepper.

Roast in oven for 15 to 20 minutes or until cod is flaky.

While waiting for cod to cook, on medium fire, place a small fry pan and heat 1 teaspoon oil.

Sauté shallots for a minute.

Add tomatoes and cook for two minutes or until soft.

Add capers and olives. Sauté for another minute.

Add vinegar and oregano. Turn off fire and stir to mix well.

Evenly divide cod into 4 serving and place on a plate.

1 To serve, top cod with Caper-Olive-Tomato Tapenade and enjoy.

Per Serving
Calories: 107; Fat: 2.9g; Protein: 17.6g; Carbs: 2.0g

Tomato Basil Cauliflower Rice (Spanish)

Preparation Time: 5 minutes **Cooking Time:** 10 minutes
Servings: 4

Ingredients:

Salt and pepper to taste
Dried parsley for garnish
½ teaspoon garlic, minced
½ teaspoon marjoram
1 large head of cauliflower
1 teaspoon oil

¼ cup tomato paste
1 teaspoon dried oregano
½ teaspoon onion powder
1 ½ teaspoon dried basil

Directions:

Cut the cauliflower into florets and place in the food processor.

Pulse until it has a coarse consistency similar with rice. Set aside.

In a skillet, heat the oil and sauté the garlic and onion for three minutes. Add the rest of the . Cook for 8 minutes.

Per Serving
Calories: 106; Carbs: 15.1g; Protein: 3.3g; Fat: 5.0g

Berries and Grilled Calamari (Spanish)

Preparation Time: 10 minutes **Cooking Time:** 5 minutes **Servings:** 4

Ingredients:

¼ cup dried cranberries
¼ cup olive oil
½ lemon, juiced
1 ½ pounds calamari tube, cleaned
1 granny smith apple, sliced thinly
Sea salt to taste
Freshly grated pepper to taste
¼ cup extra virgin olive oil
¼ cup sliced almonds
¾ cup blueberries
2 tablespoons apple cider vinegar
6 cups fresh spinach
1 tablespoon fresh lemon juice

Directions:

In a small bowl, make the vinaigrette by mixing well the tablespoon of lemon juice, apple cider vinegar, and extra virgin olive oil. Season with pepper and salt to taste. Set aside.

Turn on the grill to medium fire and let the grates heat up for a minute or two.

In a large bowl, add olive oil and the calamari tube. Season calamari generously with pepper and salt.

Place seasoned and oiled calamari onto heated grate and grill until cooked or opaque. This is around two minutes per side.

As you wait for the calamari to cook, you can combine almonds, cranberries, blueberries, spinach, and the thinly sliced apple in a large salad bowl. Toss to mix.

Remove cooked calamari from grill and transfer on a chopping board. Cut into ¼-inch thick rings and throw into the salad bowl.

Drizzle with vinaigrette and toss well to coat salad.

Serve and enjoy!

Per Serving

Calories: 567; Fat: 24.5g; Protein: 54.8g; Carbs: 30.6g

Dill Relish on White Sea Bass (Greek)

Prep time: 10 mins **Cooking Time:** 12 minutes **Servings:** 4

Ingredients:

1 ½ tablespoon chopped white onion
1 teaspoon Dijon mustard
1 ½ teaspoon chopped fresh dill
1 lemon, quartered
1 teaspoon lemon juice
1 teaspoon pickled baby capers, drained
4 pieces of 4-oz white sea bass fillets

Directions:

Preheat oven to 375oF.

Mix lemon juice, mustard, dill, capers and onions in a small bowl.

Prepare four aluminum foil squares and place 1 fillet per foil.

Squeeze a lemon wedge per fish.

Evenly divide into 4 the dill spread and drizzle over fillet.

Close the foil over the fish securely and pop in the oven.

Bake for 10 to 12 minutes or until fish is cooked through.

Remove from foil and transfer to a serving platter, serve and enjoy.

Per Serving

Calories: 115; Protein: 7g; Fat: 1g; Carbs: 12g

Sweet Potatoes Oven Fried (Spanish)

Preparation Time: 10 minutes **Cooking Time:** 30 minutes **Servings:** 7

Ingredients:

1 small garlic clove, minced
1 teaspoon grated orange rind
¼ teaspoon pepper
1 tablespoon fresh parsley, chopped finely
1 tablespoon olive oil
¼ teaspoon salt
4 medium sweet potatoes, peeled and sliced to ¼-inch thickness

Directions:

In a large bowl mix well pepper, salt, olive oil and sweet potatoes.

In a greased baking sheet, in a single layer arrange sweet potatoes.

Pop in a preheated 400oF oven and bake for 15 minutes, turnover potato slices and return to oven. Bake for another 15 minutes or until tender.

Meanwhile, mix well in a small bowl garlic, orange rind and parsley, sprinkle over cooked potato slices and serve.

You can store baked sweet potatoes in a lidded container and just microwave whenever you want to eat it. Do consume within 3 days.

Per Serving

Calories: 176; Carbs: 36.6g; Protein: 2.5g; Fat: 2.5g

Baked Fish with Pistachio Crust

Prep time: 10 minutes | **Cook time:** 15 to 20 minutes | Serves:4

Ingredients:

½ cup extra-virgin olive oil, divided
1 pound (454 g) flaky white fish (such as cod, haddock, or halibut), skin removed
½ cup shelled finely chopped pistachios
½ cup ground flaxseed
Zest and juice of 1 lemon, divided
1 teaspoon ground cumin
1 teaspoon ground allspice
½ teaspoon salt
¼ teaspoon freshly ground black pepper

Directions:

Preheat the oven to 400°F (205°C).

Line a baking sheet with parchment paper or aluminum foil and drizzle 2 tablespoons of olive oil over the sheet, spreading to evenly coat the bottom.

Cut the fish into 4 equal pieces and place on the prepared baking sheet. In a small bowl, combine the pistachios, flaxseed, lemon zest, cumin, allspice, salt, and pepper. Drizzle in ¼ cup of olive oil and stir well.

Divide the nut mixture evenly on top of the fish pieces. Drizzle the lemon juice and remaining 2 tablespoons of olive oil over the fish and bake until cooked through, 15 to 20 minutes, depending on the thickness of the fish.

Cool for 5 minutes before serving.

Per Serving

calories: 509 | fat: 41.0g | protein: 26.0g | carbs: 9.0g

Haddock with Cucumber Sauce

Prep time: 10 minutes | **Cook time:** 10 minutes | Serves:4

Ingredients:

¼ cup plain Greek yogurt
½ scallion, white and green parts, finely chopped
½ English cucumber, grated, liquid squeezed out
2 teaspoons chopped fresh mint
1 teaspoon honey
Sea salt and freshly ground black pepper, to taste
4 (5-ounce / 142-g) haddock fillets, patted dry
Nonstick cooking spray

Directions:

In a small bowl, stir together the yogurt, cucumber, scallion, mint, honey, and a pinch of salt. Set aside.

Season the fillets lightly with salt and pepper.

Place a large skillet over medium-high heat and spray lightly with cooking spray.

Cook the haddock, turning once, until it is just cooked through, about 5 minutes per side.

Remove the fish from the heat and transfer to plates.

Serve topped with the cucumber sauce.

Per Serving

calories: 164 | fat: 2.0g | protein: 27.0g | carbs: 4.0g

Sole Piccata with Capers

Prep time: 10 minutes | **Cook time:** 17 minutes | **Serves:**4

Ingredients:

1 teaspoon extra-virgin olive oil
4 (5-ounce / 142-g) sole fillets, patted dry
3 tablespoons almond butter
2 teaspoons minced garlic
2 tablespoons all-purpose flour
2 cups low-sodium chicken broth
Juice and zest of ½ lemon
2 tablespoons capers

Directions:

Place a large skillet over medium-high heat and add the olive oil.

Sear the sole fillets until the fish flakes easily when tested with a fork, about 4 minutes on each side. Transfer the fish to a plate and set aside.

Return the skillet to the stove and add the butter.

Sauté the garlic until translucent, about 3 minutes.

Whisk in the flour to make a thick paste and cook, stirring constantly, until the mixture is golden brown, about 2 minutes.

Whisk in the chicken broth, lemon juice and zest.

Cook for about 4 minutes until the sauce is thickened.

Stir in the capers and serve the sauce over the fish.

Per Serving

calories: 271 | fat:13.0g | protein: 30.0g | carbs: 7.0g

Crispy Herb Crusted Halibut

Prep time: 10 minutes | **Cook time:** 20 minutes | **Serves:**4

Ingredients:

4 (5-ounce / 142-g) halibut fillets, patted dry
Extra-virgin olive oil, for brushing
½ cup coarsely ground unsalted pistachios
Pinch freshly ground black pepper
1 tablespoon chopped fresh parsley
1 teaspoon chopped fresh basil
1 teaspoon chopped fresh thyme
Pinch sea salt

Directions:

Preheat the oven to 350°F (180°C). Line a baking sheet with parchment paper.

Place the fillets on the baking sheet and brush them generously with olive oil.

In a small bowl, stir together the pistachios, parsley, basil, thyme, salt, and pepper.

Spoon the nut mixture evenly on the fish, spreading it out so the tops of the fillets are covered.

Bake in the preheated oven until it flakes when pressed with a fork, about 20 minutes. Serve immediately.

Per Serving calories: 262 fat: 11.0g protein: 32.0g carbs: 4.0g

Chapter 9
Fruits Recipes and Desserts Recipes

Rice Pudding with Roasted Orange

Prep time: 10 minutes | **Cook time:** 19 to 20 minutes | **Serves:** 6

Ingredients:

2 medium oranges
2 teaspoons extra-virgin olive oil
⅛ teaspoon kosher salt
2 large eggs
2 cups unsweetened almond milk
1 cup orange juice
1 cup uncooked instant brown rice
¼ cup honey
½ teaspoon ground cinnamon
1 teaspoon vanilla extract
Cooking spray

Directions:

Preheat the oven to 450°F (235°C). Spritz a large, rimmed baking sheet with cooking spray. Set aside.

Slice the unpeeled oranges into ¼-inch rounds. Brush with the oil and sprinkle with salt. Place the slices on the baking sheet and roast for 4 minutes. Flip the slices and roast for 4 more minutes, or until they begin to brown. Remove from the oven and set aside.

Crack the eggs into a medium bowl. In a medium saucepan, whisk together the milk, orange juice, rice, honey and cinnamon. Bring to a boil over medium-high heat, stirring constantly. Reduce the heat to medium- low and simmer for 10 minutes, stirring occasionally.

Using a measuring cup, scoop out ½ cup of the hot rice mixture and whisk it into the eggs. While constantly stirring the mixture in the pan, slowly pour the egg mixture back into the saucepan.

Cook on low heat for 1 to 2 minutes, or until thickened, stirring constantly. Remove from the heat and stir in the vanilla. Let the pudding stand for a few minutes for the rice to soften. The rice will be cooked but slightly chewy. For softer rice, let stand for another half hour. Top with the roasted oranges. Serve warm or at room temperature.

Per Serving

calories: 204 | fat: 6.0g | protein: 5.0g | carbs: 34.0g

Cherry Walnut Brownies

Prep time: 10 minutes | **Cook time:** 20 minutes | **Serves:** 9

Ingredients:

2 large eggs
½ cup 2% plain Greek yogurt
½ cup sugar ⅓ cup honey
¼ cup extra-virgin olive oil
1 teaspoon vanilla extract
½ cup whole-wheat pastry flour
⅓ cup unsweetened dark chocolate cocoa powder
¼ teaspoon baking powder
¼ teaspoon salt
⅓ cup chopped walnuts
9 fresh cherries, stemmed and pitted
Cooking spray

Directions:

Preheat the oven to 375°F (190°C) and set the rack in the middle of the oven. Spritz a square baking pan with cooking spray. In a large bowl, whisk together the eggs, yogurt, sugar, honey, oil and vanilla.

In a medium bowl, stir together the flour, cocoa powder, baking powder and salt. Add the flour mixture to the egg mixture and whisk until all the dry ingredients are incorporated. Fold in the walnuts.

Pour the batter into the prepared pan. Push the cherries into the batter, three to a row in three rows, so one will be at the center of each brownie once you cut them into squares. Bake the brownies for 20 minutes, or until just set. Remove from the oven and place on a rack to cool for 5 minutes. Cut into nine squares and serve.

Per Serving

calories: 154 | fat: 6.0g | protein: 3.0g | carbs: 24.0g

Watermelon and Blueberry Salad

Prep time: 5 minutes | **Cook time:** 0 minutes
Serves: 6 to 8

Ingredients:

1 medium watermelon
1 cup fresh blueberries
⅓ cup honey
2 tablespoons lemon juice
2 tablespoons finely chopped fresh mint leaves

Directions:

Cut the watermelon into 1-inch cubes. Put them in a bowl.

Evenly distribute the blueberries over the watermelon.

In a separate bowl, whisk together the honey, lemon juice and mint. Drizzle the mint dressing over the watermelon and blueberries. Serve cold.

Per Serving

calories: 238 | fat: 1.0g | protein: 4.0g | carbs: 61.0g

Berry and Rhubarb Cobbler

Prep time: 15 minutes | **Cook time:** 35 minutes | **Serves:**8

Ingredients:
Cobbler:
1 cup fresh raspberries
2 cups fresh blueberries
1 cup sliced (½-inch) rhubarb pieces
1 tablespoon arrowroot powder
¼ cup unsweetened apple juice
¼ cup raw honey

Topping:
1 cup almond flour
1 tablespoon arrowroot powder
½ cup shredded coconut
¼ cup raw honey
½ cup coconut oil
2 tablespoons melted coconut oil

Directions:
Make the Cobbler

Preheat the oven to 350°F (180°C). Grease a baking dish with melted coconut oil.

Combine the ingredients for the cobbler in a large bowl. Stir to mix well.

Spread the mixture in the single layer on the baking dish. Set aside.

Make the Topping

Combine the almond flour, arrowroot powder, and coconut in a bowl. Stir to mix well.

Fold in the honey and coconut oil. Stir with a fork until the mixture crumbled.

Spread the topping over the cobbler, then bake in the preheated oven for 35 minutes or until frothy and golden brown.

Serve immediately.

Per Serving
calories: 305 | fat: 22.1g | protein: 3.2g | carbs: 29.8g

Chocolate, Almond, and Cherry Clusters

Prep time: 15 mins | **Cook time:** 3 mins | Makes 10 clusters

Ingredients:
1 cup dark chocolate (60% cocoa or higher), chopped
1 tablespoon coconut oil
½ cup dried cherries
1 cup roasted salted almonds

Directions:
Line a baking sheet with parchment paper.

Melt the chocolate and coconut oil in a saucepan for 3 minutes. Stir constantly.

Turn off the heat and mix in the cherries and almonds.

Drop the mixture on the baking sheet with a spoon. Place the sheet in the refrigerator and chill for at least 1 hour or until firm.

Serve chilled.

Per Serving
calories: 197 | fat: 13.2g | protein: 4.1g | carbs: 17.8g

Citrus Cranberry and Quinoa Energy Bites

Prep time: 25 minutes | **Cook time:** 0 mins | Makes 12 bites

Ingredients:
2 tablespoons almond butter
2 tablespoons maple syrup
¾ cup cooked quinoa
1 tablespoon dried cranberries
1 tablespoon chia seeds
¼ cup ground almonds
¼ cup sesame seeds, toasted
Zest of 1 orange
½ teaspoon vanilla extract

Directions:
Line a baking sheet with parchment paper.

Combine the butter and maple syrup in a bowl. Stir to mix well.

Fold in the remaining ingredients and stir until the mixture holds together and smooth.

Divide the mixture into 12 equal parts, then shape each part into a ball.

Arrange the balls on the baking sheet, then refrigerate for at least 15 minutes.

Serve chilled.

Per Serving (1 bite)
calories: 110 | fat: 10.8g | protein: 3.1g | carbs: 4.9g

Coconut Blueberries with Brown Rice

Prep time: 55 minutes | **Cook time:** 10 minutes | **Serves:**4

Ingredients:
1 cup fresh blueberries
2 cups unsweetened coconut milk
1 teaspoon ground ginger
¼ cup maple syrup
Sea salt, to taste
2 cups cooked brown rice

Directions:
Put all the ingredients, except for the brown rice, in a pot. Stir to combine well.

Cook over medium-high heat for 7 minutes or until the blueberries are tender.

Pour in the brown rice and cook for 3 more minute or until the rice is soft. Stir constantly.

Serve immediately.

Per Serving
calories: 470 | fat: 24.8g | protein: 6.2g | carbs: 60.1g

Apple Compote

Prep time: 15 minutes | **Cook time:** 10 minutes | **Serves:** 4

Ingredients:

6 apples, peeled, cored, and chopped
¼ cup raw honey

1 teaspoon ground cinnamon
¼ cup apple juice
Sea salt, to taste

Directions:

Put all the ingredients in a stockpot. Stir to mix well, then cook over medium-high heat for 10 minutes or until the apples are glazed by honey and lightly saucy. Stir constantly. Serve immediately.

Per Serving calories: 246 | fat: 0.9g | protein: 1.2g | carbs: 66.3g

Peanut Butter and Chocolate Balls

Prep time: 45 minutes | **Cook time:** 0 mins | **Serves:** 15 balls

Ingredients:

¾ cup creamy peanut butter
¼ cup unsweetened cocoa powder
2 tablespoons softened almond butter

½ teaspoon vanilla extract
1¾ cups maple syrup

Directions:

Line a baking sheet with parchment paper.

Combine all the ingredients in a bowl. Stir to mix well.

Divide the mixture into 15 parts and shape each part into a 1-inch ball. Arrange the balls on the baking sheet and refrigerate for at least 30 minutes, then serve chilled.

Per Serving (1 ball)
calories: 146 | fat: 8.1g | protein: 4.2g | carbs: 16.9g

Spiced Sweet Pecans

Prep time: 4 minutes | **Cook time:** 17 minutes | **Serves:** 4

Ingredients:

1 cup pecan halves
3 tablespoons almond butter
1 teaspoon ground cinnamon

½ teaspoon ground nutmeg
¼ cup raw honey
¼ teaspoon sea salt

Directions:

Preheat the oven to 350ºF (180ºC). Line a baking sheet with parchment paper. Combine all the ingredients in a bowl. Stir to mix well, then spread the mixture in the single layer on the baking sheet with a spatula. Bake in the preheated oven for 16 minutes or until the pecan halves are well browned.

Serve immediately.

Per Serving calories: 324 | protein: 3.2g | carbs: 13.9g

Greek Yogurt Affogato with Pistachios

Prep time: 5 minutes | **Cook time:** 0 minutes | **Serves:** 4

Ingredients:

24 ounces (680 g) vanilla Greek yogurt
2 teaspoons sugar
4 shots hot espresso

4 tablespoons chopped unsalted pistachios
4 tablespoons dark chocolate chips

Directions:

Spoon the yogurt into four bowls or tall glasses.

Mix ½ teaspoon of sugar into each of the espresso shots.

Pour one shot of the hot espresso over each bowl of yogurt.

Top each bowl with 1 tablespoon of the pistachios and 1 tablespoon of the chocolate chips and serve.

Per Serving
calories: 190 | fat: 6.0g | protein: 20.0g | carbs: 14.0g

Grilled Peaches with Whipped Ricotta

Prep time: 5 minutes | **Cook time:** 14 to 22 minutes | **Serves:** 4

Ingredients:

4 peaches, halved and pitted
2 teaspoons extra-virgin olive oil
¾ cup whole-milk Ricotta cheese

1 tablespoon honey
¼ teaspoon freshly grated nutmeg
4 sprigs mint
Cooking spray

Directions:

Spritz a grill pan with cooking spray. Heat the grill pan to medium heat.

Place a large, empty bowl in the refrigerator to chill.

Brush the peaches all over with the oil. Place half of the peaches, cut-side down, on the grill pan and cook for 3 to 5 minutes, or until grill marks appear.

Using tongs, turn the peaches over. Cover the grill pan with aluminum foil and cook for 4 to 6 minutes, or until the peaches are easily pierced with a sharp knife. Set aside to cool. Repeat with the remaining peaches.

Remove the bowl from the refrigerator and add the Ricotta. Using an electric beater, beat the Ricotta on high for 2 minutes. Add the honey and nutmeg and beat for 1 more minute. Divide the cooled peaches among 4 serving bowls. Top with the Ricotta mixture and a sprig of mint and serve.

Per Serving
calories: 176 | fat: 8.0g | protein: 8.0g | carbs: 20.0g

Walnut and Date Balls

Prep time: 5 minutes | **Cook time:** 8 to 10 minutes | **Serves:** 6 to 8

Ingredients:

1 cup walnuts
1 cup unsweetened shredded coconut
14 medjool dates, pitted
8 tablespoons almond butter

Directions:

Preheat the oven to 350ºF (180ºC).

Put the walnuts on a baking sheet and toast in the oven for 5 minutes.

Put the shredded coconut on a clean baking sheet. Toast for about 3 to 5 minutes, or until it turns golden brown. Once done, remove it from the oven and put it in a shallow bowl.

In a food processor, process the toasted walnuts until they have a medium chop. Transfer the chopped walnuts into a medium bowl.

Add the dates and butter to the food processor and blend until the dates become a thick paste. Pour the chopped walnuts into the food processor with the dates and pulse just until the mixture is combined, about 5 to 7 pulses.

Remove the mixture from the food processor and scrape it into a large bowl.

To make the balls, spoon 1 to 2 tablespoons of the date mixture into the palm of your hand and roll around between your hands until you form a ball. Put the ball on a clean, lined baking sheet. Repeat until all the mixture is formed into balls.

Roll each ball in the toasted coconut until the outside of the ball is coated. Put the ball back on the baking sheet and repeat.

Put all the balls into the refrigerator for 20 minutes before serving. Store any leftovers in the refrigerator in an airtight container.

Per Serving

calories: 489 | fat: 35.0g | protein: 5.0g | carbs: 48.0g

Apple and Berries Ambrosia

Prep time: 15 minutes | **Cook time:** 0 minutes | **Serves:** 4

Ingredients:

2 cups unsweetened coconut milk, chilled
2 tablespoons raw honey
1 apple, peeled, cored, and chopped
2 cups fresh raspberries
2 cups fresh blueberries

Directions:

Spoon the chilled milk in a large bowl, then mix in the honey. Stir to mix well.

Then mix in the remaining ingredients. Stir to coat the fruits well and serve immediately.

Per Serving calories: 386 fat: 21.1g protein: 4.2g carbs: 45.9g

Banana, Cranberry, and Oat Bars

Prep time: 15 mins | **Cook time:** 40 mins | Makes 16 bars

Ingredients:

2 tablespoon extra-virgin olive oil
2 medium ripe bananas, mashed
½ cup almond butter
½ cup maple syrup
⅓ cup dried cranberries
1½ cups old-fashioned rolled oats
¼ cup oat flour
¼ cup ground flaxseed
¼ teaspoon ground cloves
½ cup shredded coconut
½ teaspoon ground cinnamon
1 teaspoon vanilla extract

Directions:

Preheat the oven to 400ºF (205ºC). Line a 8-inch square pan with parchment paper, then grease with olive oil.

Combine the mashed bananas, almond butter, and maple syrup in a bowl. Stir to mix well.

Mix in the remaining ingredients and stir to mix well until thick and sticky.

Spread the mixture evenly on the square pan with a spatula, then bake in the preheated oven for 40 minutes or until a toothpick inserted in the center comes out clean.

Remove them from the oven and slice into 16 bars to serve.

Per Serving

calories: 145 | fat: 7.2g | protein: 3.1g | carbs: 18.9g

Chocolate and Avocado Mousse

Prep time: 40 minutes | **Cook time:** 5 mins | **Serves:** 4 to 6

Ingredients:

8 ounces (227 g) dark chocolate (60% cocoa or higher), chopped
¼ cup unsweetened coconut milk
2 ripe avocados, deseeded
¼ cup raw honey
Sea salt, to taste
2 tablespoons coconut oil

Directions:

Put the chocolate in a saucepan. Pour in the coconut milk and add the coconut oil.

Cook for 3 minutes or until the chocolate and coconut oil melt. Stir constantly.

Put the avocado in a food processor, then drizzle with honey and melted chocolate. Pulse to combine until smooth.

Pour the mixture in a serving bowl, then sprinkle with salt. Refrigerate to chill for 30 minutes and serve.

Per Serving

calories: 654 | fat: 46.8g | protein: 7.2g | carbs: 55.9g

Blueberry and Oat Crisp

Prep time: 15 minutes | **Cook time:** 20 minutes | **Serves:**4

Ingredients:

2 tablespoons coconut oil, melted, plus more for greasing
4 cups fresh blueberries
Juice of ½ lemon
2 teaspoons lemon zest

¼ cup maple syrup
1 cup gluten-free rolled oats
½ cup chopped pecans
½ teaspoon ground cinnamon
Sea salt, to taste

Directions:

Preheat the oven to 350ºF (180ºC). Grease a baking sheet with coconut oil.

Combine the blueberries, lemon juice and zest, and maple syrup in a bowl. Stir to mix well, then spread the mixture on the baking sheet.

Combine the remaining ingredients in a small bowl. Stir to mix well. Pour the mixture over the blueberries mixture.

Bake in the preheated oven for 20 minutes or until the oats are golden brown.

Serve immediately with spoons.

Per Serving
calories: 496 | fat: 32.9g | protein: 5.1g | carbs: 50.8g

Glazed Pears with Hazelnuts

Prep time: 10 minutes | **Cook time:** 20 minutes | **Serves:**4

Ingredients:

4 pears, peeled, cored, and quartered lengthwise
1 cup apple juice

1 tablespoon grated fresh ginger
½ cup pure maple syrup
¼ cup chopped hazelnuts

Directions:

Put the pears in a pot, then pour in the apple juice. Bring to a boil over medium-high heat, then reduce the heat to medium-low. Stir constantly.

Cover and simmer for an additional 15 minutes or until the pears are tender.

Meanwhile, combine the ginger and maple syrup in a saucepan. Bring to a boil over medium-high heat. Stir frequently. Turn off the heat and transfer the syrup to a small bowl and let sit until ready to use.

Transfer the pears in a large serving bowl with a slotted spoon, then top the pears with syrup.

Spread the hazelnuts over the pears and serve immediately.

Per Serving
calories: 287 | fat: 3.1g | protein: 2.2g | carbs: 66.9g

Lemony Blackberry Granita

Prep time: 10 minutes | **Cook time:** 0 minutes | **Serves:**4

Ingredients:

1 pound (454 g) fresh blackberries
1 teaspoon chopped fresh thyme

½ cup raw honey
½ cup water
¼ cup freshly squeezed lemon juice

Directions:

Put all the ingredients in a food processor, then pulse to purée.

Pour the mixture through a sieve into a baking dish. Discard the seeds remain in the sieve.

Put the baking dish in the freezer for 2 hours. Remove the dish from the refrigerator and stir to break any frozen parts.

Return the dish back to the freezer for an hour, then stir to break any frozen parts again.

Return the dish to the freezer for 4 hours until the granita is completely frozen.

Remove it from the freezer and mash to serve.

Per Serving
calories: 183 | fat: 1.1g | protein: 2.2g | carbs: 45.9g

Lemony Tea and Chia Pudding

Prep time: 30 minutes | **Cook time:** 0 minutes
Serves:3 to 4

Ingredients:

2 teaspoons matcha green tea powder (optional)
2 tablespoons ground chia seeds

1 to 2 dates
2 cups unsweetened coconut milk
Zest and juice of 1 lime

Directions:

Put all the ingredients in a food processor and pulse until creamy and smooth.

Pour the mixture in a bowl, then wrap in plastic. Store in the refrigerator for at least 20 minutes, then serve chilled.

Per Serving
calories: 225 | fat: 20.1g | protein: 3.2g | carbs: 5.9g:

Chapter 10
Sauces Recipes, Dips Recipes, & Dressings Recipes

Creamy Cucumber Dip

Prep time: 10 minutes | **Cook time:** 0 minutes | **Serves:**6

Ingredients:

1 medium cucumber, peeled and grated
¼ teaspoon salt
1 cup plain Greek yogurt
2 garlic cloves, minced
1 tablespoon extra-virgin olive oil
1 tablespoon freshly squeezed lemon juice
¼ teaspoon freshly ground black pepper

Directions:

Place the grated cucumber in a colander set over a bowl and season with salt. Allow the cucumber to stand for 10 minutes. Using your hands, squeeze out as much liquid from the cucumber as possible. Transfer the grated cucumber to a medium bowl.

Add the yogurt, garlic, olive oil, lemon juice, and pepper to the bowl and stir until well blended.

Cover the bowl with plastic wrap and refrigerate for at least 2 hours to blend the flavors.

Serve chilled.

Per Serving (¼ cup)

calories: 47 | fat: 2.8g | protein: 4.2g | carbs: 2.7g

Italian Dressing

Prep time: 5 minutes | **Cook time:** 0 minutes | **Serves:**12

Ingredients:

½ cup extra-virgin olive oil
¼ cup red wine vinegar
1 teaspoon dried Italian seasoning
1 teaspoon Dijon mustard
¼ teaspoon salt
¼ teaspoon freshly ground black pepper
1 garlic clove, minced

Directions:

Place all the ingredients in a mason jar and cover. Shake vigorously for 1 minute until completely mixed.

Store in the refrigerator for up to 1 week.

Per Serving (1 tablespoon)

calories: 80 | fat: 8.6g | protein: 0g | carbs: 0g

Ranch-Style Cauliflower Dressing

Prep time: 10 minutes | **Cook time:** 0 minutes | **Serves:**8

Ingredients:

2 cups frozen cauliflower, thawed
½ cup unsweetened plain almond milk
2 tablespoons apple cider vinegar
2 tablespoons extra-virgin olive oil
1 garlic clove, peeled
2 teaspoons finely chopped fresh parsley
2 teaspoons finely chopped scallions (both white and green parts)
1 teaspoon finely chopped fresh dill
½ teaspoon onion powder
½ teaspoon Dijon mustard
½ teaspoon salt
¼ teaspoon freshly ground black pepper

Directions:

Place all the ingredients in a blender and pulse until creamy and smooth.

Serve immediately, or transfer to an airtight container to refrigerate for up to 3 days.

Per Serving (2 tablespoons)

calories: 41 | fat: 3.6g | protein: 1.0g | carbs: 1.9g

Asian-Inspired Vinaigrette

Prep time: 5 minutes | **Cook time:** 0 minutes | **Serves:**2

Ingredients:

¼ cup extra-virgin olive oil
3 tablespoons apple cider vinegar
1 garlic clove, minced
1 tablespoon peeled and grated fresh ginger
1 tablespoon chopped fresh cilantro
1 tablespoon freshly squeezed lime juice
½ teaspoon sriracha

Directions:

Add all the ingredients in a small bowl and stir to mix well.

Serve immediately, or store covered in the refrigerator and shake before using.

Per Serving

calories: 251 | fat: 26.8g | protein: 0g | carbs: 1.8g

Guacamole

Prep time: 10 minutes | **Cook time:** 0 minutes | **Serves:**6

Ingredients:

2 large avocados
¼ white onion, finely diced
1 small, firm tomato, finely diced
¼ cup finely chopped fresh cilantro

2 tablespoons freshly squeezed lime juice
¼ teaspoon salt
Freshly ground black pepper, to taste

Directions:

Slice the avocados in half and remove the pits. Using a large spoon to scoop out the flesh and add to a medium bowl.

Mash the avocado flesh with the back of a fork, or until a uniform consistency is achieved. Add the onion, tomato, cilantro, lime juice, salt, and pepper to the bowl and stir to combine.

Serve immediately, or transfer to an airtight container and refrigerate until chilled.

Per Serving (¼ cup)

calories: 81 | fat: 6.8g | protein: 1.1g | carbs: 5.7g

Lentil-Tahini Dip

Prep time: 10 minutes | **Cook time:** 15 mins | Makes 3 cups

Ingredients:

1 cup dried green or brown lentils, rinsed
2½ cups water, divided

⅓ cup tahini
1 garlic clove
½ teaspoon salt, plus more as needed

Directions:

Add the lentils and 2 cups of water to a medium saucepan and bring to a boil over high heat.

Once it starts to boil, reduce the heat to low, and then cook for 14 minutes, stirring occasionally, or the lentils become tender but still hold their shape. You can drain any excess liquid.

Transfer the lentils to a food processor, along with the remaining water, tahini, garlic, and salt and process until smooth and creamy.

Taste and adjust the seasoning if needed. Serve immediately.

Per Serving (¼ cup)

calories: 100 | fat: 3.9g | protein: 5.1g | carbs: 10.7g

Lemon-Dill Cashew Dip

Prep time: 10 minutes | **Cook time:** 0 mins | Makes 1 cup

Ingredients:

¾ cup cashews, soaked in water for at least
4 hours and drained well
¼ cup water

Juice and zest of 1 lemon
2 tablespoons chopped fresh dill
¼ teaspoon salt, plus more as needed

Directions:

Put the cashews, water, lemon juice and zest in a blender and blend until smooth.

Add the dill and salt to the blender and blend again.

Taste and adjust the seasoning, if needed.

Transfer to an airtight container and refrigerate for at least 1 hour to blend the flavors.

Serve chilled.

Per Serving (1 tablespoon)

calories: 37 | fat: 2.9g | protein: 1.1g | carbs: 1.9g

Homemade Blackened Seasoning

Prep time: 10 minutes | **Cook time:** 0 minutes | Makes about ½ cup

Ingredients:

2 tablespoons smoked paprika
2 tablespoons garlic powder
2 tablespoons onion powder
1 tablespoon sweet paprika

1 teaspoon dried dill
1 teaspoon freshly ground black pepper
½ teaspoon ground mustard
¼ teaspoon celery seeds

Directions:

Add all the ingredients to a small bowl and mix well.

Serve immediately, or transfer to an airtight container and store in a cool, dry and dark place for up to 3 months.

Per Serving (1 tablespoon)

calories: 22 | fat: 0.9g | protein: 1.0g | carbs: 4.7g

Garlic Lemon-Tahini Dressing

Prep time: 5 minutes | **Cook time:** 0 mins | **Serves:** 8 to 10

Ingredients:

½ cup tahini
¼ cup extra-virgin olive oil
¼ cup freshly squeezed lemon juice
1 garlic clove, finely minced
2 teaspoons salt

Directions:

In a glass mason jar with a lid, combine the tahini, olive oil, lemon juice, garlic, and salt. Cover and shake well until combined and creamy.

Store in the refrigerator for up to 2 weeks.

Per Serving

calories: 121 | fat: 12.0g | protein: 2.0g | carbs: 3.0g

Creamy Grapefruit and Tarragon Dressing

Prep time: 5 minutes | **Cook time:** 0 mins | **Serves:** 4 to 6

Ingredients:

½ cup avocado oil mayonnaise
2 tablespoons Dijon mustard
1 teaspoon dried tarragon or 1 tablespoon chopped fresh tarragon
½ teaspoon salt
Zest and juice of ½ grapefruit
¼ teaspoon freshly ground black pepper
1 to 2 tablespoons water (optional)

Directions:

In a large mason jar with a lid, combine the mayonnaise, Dijon, tarragon, grapefruit zest and juice, salt, and pepper and whisk well with a fork until smooth and creamy. If a thinner dressing is preferred, thin out with water.

Serve immediately or refrigerate until ready to serve.

Per Serving

calories: 86 | fat: 7.0g | protein: 1.0g | carbs: 6.0g

Vinaigrette

Prep time: 5 minutes | **Cook time:** 0 minutes | Makes 1 cup

Ingredients:

½ cup extra-virgin olive oil
¼ cup red wine vinegar
1 tablespoon Dijon mustard
1 teaspoon dried rosemary
½ teaspoon salt
½ teaspoon freshly ground black pepper

Directions:

In a cup or a mansion jar with a lid, combine the olive oil, vinegar, mustard, rosemary, salt, and pepper and shake until well combined.

Serve chilled or at room temperature.

Per Serving

calories: 124 | fat: 14.0g | protein: 0g | carbs: 1.0g

Ginger Teriyaki Sauce

Prep time: 5 minutes | **Cook time:** 0 minutes | **Serves:** 2

Ingredients:

¼ cup pineapple juice
¼ cup low-sodium soy sauce
2 tablespoons packed coconut sugar
1 tablespoon grated fresh ginger
1 tablespoon arrowroot powder or cornstarch
1 teaspoon garlic powder

Directions:

Whisk the pineapple juice, soy sauce, coconut sugar, ginger, arrowroot powder, and garlic powder together in a small bowl.

Store in an airtight container in the fridge for up to 5 days.

Per Serving

calories: 37 | fat: 0.1g | protein: 1.1g | carbs: 12.0g

Aioli

Prep time: 5 minutes | **Cook time:** 0 mins | Makes ½ cup

Ingredients:

½ cup plain Greek yogurt
2 teaspoons Dijon mustard
½ teaspoon hot sauce
¼ teaspoon raw honey
Pinch salt

Directions:

In a small bowl, whisk together the yogurt, mustard, hot sauce, honey, and salt.

Serve immediately or refrigerate in an airtight container for up to 3 days.

Per Serving

calories: 47 | fat: 2.5g | protein: 2.1g | carbs: 3.5g

Parsley Vinaigrette

Prep time: 5 minutes | **Cook time:** 0 minutes | Makes about ½ cup

Ingredients:

½ cup lightly packed fresh parsley, finely chopped
⅓ cup extra-virgin olive oil
3 tablespoons red wine vinegar
1 garlic clove, minced
¼ teaspoon salt, plus additional as needed

Directions:

Place all the ingredients in a mason jar and cover. Shake vigorously for 1 minute until completely mixed.

Taste and add additional salt as needed.

Serve immediately or serve chilled.

Per Serving (1 tablespoon)

calories: 92 | fat: 10.9g | protein: 0g | carbs: 0g

Not Old Bay Seasoning

Prep time: 10 minutes | **Cook time:** 0 minutes
Makes about ½ cup

Ingredients:

3 tablespoons sweet paprika
1 tablespoon mustard seeds
2 tablespoons celery seeds
2 teaspoons freshly ground black pepper
1½ teaspoons cayenne pepper

1 teaspoon red pepper flakes
½ teaspoon ground ginger
½ teaspoon ground nutmeg
½ teaspoon ground cinnamon
¼ teaspoon ground cloves

Directions:

Mix together all the ingredients in an airtight container until well combined.

You can store it in a cool, dry, and dark place for up to 3 months.

Per Serving (1 tablespoon)
calories: 26 | fat: 1.9g | protein: 1.1g | carbs: 3.6g

Tzatziki

Prep time: 15 minutes | **Cook time:** 0 mins | **Serves:** 4 to 6

Ingredients:

½ English cucumber, finely chopped
1 teaspoon salt, divided
1 cup plain Greek yogurt
8 tablespoons olive oil, divided

1 garlic clove, finely minced
1 to 2 tablespoons chopped fresh dill
1 teaspoon red wine vinegar
½ teaspoon freshly ground black pepper

Directions:

In a food processor, pulse the cucumber until puréed. Place the cucumber on several layers of paper towels lining the bottom of a colander and sprinkle with ½ teaspoon of salt. Allow to drain for 10 to 15 minutes. Using your hands, squeeze out any remaining liquid.

In a medium bowl, whisk together the cucumber, yogurt, 6 tablespoons of olive oil, garlic, dill, vinegar, remaining ½ teaspoon of salt, and pepper until very smooth.

Drizzle with the remaining 2 tablespoons of olive oil. Serve immediately or refrigerate until ready to serve.

Per Serving calories: 286 | fat: 29.0g | protein: 3.0g

Harissa Sauce

Prep time: 10 minutes | **Cook time:** 20 minutes
Makes 3 to 4 cups

Ingredients:

1 large red bell pepper, deseeded, cored, and cut into chunks
1 yellow onion, cut into thick rings
4 garlic cloves, peeled
1 cup vegetable broth

2 tablespoons tomato paste
1 tablespoon tamari
1 teaspoon ground cumin
1 tablespoon Hungarian paprika

Directions:

Preheat the oven to 450°F (235°C). Line a baking sheet with parchment paper.

Place the bell pepper on the prepared baking sheet, flesh-side up, and space out the onion and garlic around the pepper.

Roast in the preheated oven for 20 minutes. Transfer to a blender.

Add the vegetable broth, tomato paste, tamari, cumin, and paprika. Purée until smooth. Served chilled or warm.

Per Serving (¼ cup)
calories: 15 | fat: 1.0g | protein: 1.0g | carbs: 3.0g

Pineapple Salsa

Prep time: 10 minutes | **Cook time:** 0 mins | **Serves:** 6 to 8

Ingredients:

1 pound (454 g) fresh or thawed frozen pineapple, finely diced, juices reserved
1 white or red onion, finely diced

1 bunch cilantro or mint, leaves only, chopped
1 jalapeño, minced (optional)
Salt, to taste

Directions:

Stir together the pineapple with its juice, onion, cilantro, and jalapeño (if desired) in a medium bowl. Season with salt to taste and serve.

The salsa can be refrigerated in an airtight container for up to 2 days.

Per Serving
calories: 55 | fat: 0.1g | protein: 0.9g | carbs: 12.7g

Chapter 11
Dinner Recipes

Salad Skewers (Greek)

Preparation Time: 10 minutes **Cooking Time:** 0 minutes
Servings: 1

Ingredients:

1 wooden skewers, soaked in water for 30 minutes before use
1 yellow pepper, cut into eight squares.
For the dressing:
1 tbsp. extra-virgin olive oil.
Juice of ½ lemon.
3.5-oz. (about 10cm) cucumber, cut into four slices and halved. oz. feta, cut into 8 cubes.
A right amount of salt and freshly ground black pepper

8 cherry tomatoes.
. 8 large black olives.
. Few leaves oregano,chppd
½ red onion, chopped in half and separated into eight pieces.
1 tsp. balsamic vinegar.
Few leaves basil, finely chopped (or ½ tsp dried mixed herbs to replace basil and oregano).
½ clove garlic, peeled and crushed

Directions:

Thread each skewer in the order with salad olive, tomato, yellow pepper, red onion, cucumber, feta, basil, olive, yellow pepper, red ointment, cucumber, feta. Put all the ingredients of the dressing in a small bowl and blend well together. Pour over the spoils.

Per Serving

Calories: 315 g. Fat: 30 g. Protein: 56 g. Carbs: 45 g.
Cholesterol: 230 mg. Sugar: 0 g.

Creamy Strawberry & Cherry Smoothie (Greek)

Prep time: 10 minutes **Cooking Time:** 15 mins **Servings:** 1

Ingredients:

1 ½ oz. strawberries.
1 tbsp. plain full-fat yogurt..

oz. frozen pitted cherries.
oz. unsweetened soya milk

Directions:

Place the ingredients into a blender then process until smooth. Serve and enjoy.

Per Serving

Calories: 132 g. Fat: 30 g. Protein: 56 g. Carbs: 45 g.
Cholesterol: 230 mg. Sugar: 0 g.

Italian Style Ground Beef (Italian)

Preparation Time: 10 minutes **Cooking Time:** 20 minutes
Servings: 4

Ingredients:

2 lbs. ground beef
Salt
3 tbsp olive oil
1/2 tsp dried sage
2 tsp thyme

eggs, lightly beaten
1/4 tsp dried basil
1 1/2 tsp dried parsley
1 tsp oregano
1 tsp rosemary Pepper

Directions:

Pour 1 1/2 cups of water into the instant pot then place the trivet in the pool.

Spray loaf pan with cooking spray.Add all ingredients into the mixing bowl and mix until well combined.

Transfer meat mixture into the prepared loaf pan and place loaf pan on top of the trivet in the pot.

Seal pot with lid and cook on high for 35 minutes. Once done, allow to release pressure naturally for 10 minutes then release remaining using quick release. Remove lid. Serve and enjoy.

Per Serving

Calories 365 Fat 18 Sugar 0.1 g Protein 47.8 g

Turkey With Cauliflower Couscous (Italian)

Preparation Time: 20 minutes **Cooking Time:** 50 minutes
Servings: 1

Ingredients:

3 oz. turkey.
1 tsp. fresh ginger.
1 pepper Bird's Eye.
1 clove of garlic.
oz. dried tomatoes.
0.3-oz. parsley.
¼ fresh lemon juice.

1- oz. cauliflower.
3 tbsps. extra virgin olive oil.
2 tsps. turmeric.
Dried sage to taste.
1 tbsp. capers.
2 oz. red onion.

Directions:

Blend the raw cauliflower tops and cook them in a tsp. of extra virgin olive oil, garlic, red onion, chili pepper, ginger, and a tsp. of turmeric.

Leave to flavor on the fire for a minute, then add the chopped sun-dried tomatoes and 5 g of parsley. Season the turkey slice with a tsp. of extra virgin olive oil, the dried sage, and cook it in another tsp. of extra virgin olive oil. Once ready, season with a tbsp. of capers, ¼ of lemon juice, 5 g of parsley, a tbsp. of water and add the cauliflower.

Per Serving

Calories: 120 g. Fat: 10 g. Protein: 56 g. Carbs: 45 g.
Cholesterol: 230 mg. Sugar: 0 g.

One-Pan Tuscan Chicken (Italian)

Preparation Time: 10 minutes **Cooking Time:** 25 minutes
Servings: 6

Ingredients:

¼ cup extra-virgin olive oil, divided	1 onion
1 red bell pepper	1 lb. boneless chicken
3 garlic cloves	½ cup dry white wine
1 (14 oz.) can white beans	2 (14 oz.) can tomatoes
½ tsp. sea salt	1 tbsp Italian seasoning
1/8 tsp. red pepper flakes	1/8 tsp. freshly ground black pepper
¼ cup fresh basil leaves, chopped	

Directions:

In a huge skillet over medium-high heat, preheat 2 tbsps. of olive oil. Add the chicken and cook for 6 minutes, stirring. Take out the chicken and set it aside on a platter, tented with aluminum foil to keep warm.

Return the skillet to heat and heat the remaining 2 tbsps. of olive oil. Add the onion and red bell pepper. Cook for 5 minutes.

Cook the garlic for 30 seconds. Stir in the wine. Cook for 1 minute, stirring.

Add the crushed and chopped tomatoes, white beans, Italian seasoning, sea salt, pepper, and red pepper flakes. Bring to a simmer and reduce the heat to medium. Cook for 5 minutes, stirring occasionally.

Take the chicken and any juices that have collected back to the skillet. Cook for 1–2 minutes. Pull out from the heat and stir in the basil before serving.

Per Serving
Calories: 271 Protein: 14 g. Fat: 0.1 g.

Mediterranean Rice and Sausage (Italian)

Preparation Time: 15 minutes **Cooking Time:** 8 hours
Servings: 6

Ingredients:

1 ½ lb. Italian sausage, crumbled	2 tbsps. steak sauce
2 cups long-grain rice, uncooked	1 medium onion, chopped
½ cup water	1 (14 oz.) can diced tomatoes with juice
	1 medium green pepper, diced Olive oil

Directions:

Spray your slow cooker with olive oil or nonstick cooking spray.

Add the sausage, onion, and steak sauce to the slow cooker. Cook on low for 8–10 hours.

After 8 hours, add the rice, tomatoes, water, and green pepper. Stir to combine thoroughly. Cook for 20–25 minutes.

Per Serving
Calories: 650 Fat: 36 g. Protein: 22 g.

Chicken Kapama (Spanish)

Preparation Time: 10 minutes **Cooking Time:** 90 minutes
Servings: 4

Ingredients:

1 (32 oz.) can tomatoes, chopped	¼ cup dry white wine
3 tbsps. extra-virgin olive oil	2 tbsps. tomato paste
½ tsp. dried oregano	¼ tsp. red pepper flakes
½ tsp. sea salt	1 cinnamon stick
4 boneless, skinless chicken breast halves	1/8 tsp. black pepper
	2 whole cloves

Directions:

In a pot over medium-high heat, mix the tomatoes, wine, tomato paste, olive oil, red pepper flakes, allspice, oregano, cloves, cinnamon stick, sea salt, and pepper. Bring to a simmer, stirring occasionally. Adjust the heat to medium-low and simmer for 30 minutes, stirring occasionally. Remove and discard the whole cloves and cinnamon stick from the sauce and let the sauce cool.

Preheat the oven to 350°F.

Place the chicken in a 9-by-13-inch baking dish. Drizzle sauce over the chicken and cover the pan with aluminum foil. Bake for 45 minutes.

Per Serving
Calories: 220 Protein: 8 g. Fat: 14 g.

Spinach and Feta-Stuffed Chicken Breasts (Greek)

Preparation Time: 10 minutes **Cooking Time:** 45 minutes
Servings: 4

Ingredients:

2 tbsps. extra-virgin olive oil	3 garlic cloves, minced
1 lb. fresh baby spinach	1 lemon zest
½ tsp. sea salt	1/8 tsp. freshly ground black pepper
4 chicken breast halves	
½ cup Feta cheese, crumbled	

Directions:

Preheat the oven to 350°F.

Preheat the oil and skillet over medium-high heat.

Cook the spinach for 3–4 minutes. Cook the garlic, lemon zest, sea salt, and pepper. Cool slightly and mix in the cheese.

Spread the spinach and cheese mixture in an even layer over the chicken pieces and roll the breast around the filling. Hold closed with toothpicks or butcher's twine.

Place the breasts in a 9-by-13-inch baking dish and bake for 30–40 minutes. Take away from the oven and let rest for 5 minutes before slicing and serving.

Per Serving
Calories: 263 Protein: 17 g. Fat: 20 g.

Roasted Trout Stuffed with Veggies (Greek)

Preparation Time: 10 minutes **Cooking Time:** 25 minutes
Servings: 2

Ingredients:

1 (8 oz.) whole trout fillets	¼ tsp. salt
1 tbsp. extra-virgin olive oil	1 poblano pepper
1/8 tsp. black pepper	1 small onion, thinly sliced
½ red bell pepper	2–3 shiitake mushrooms,
Cooking spray	sliced 1 lemon, sliced

Directions:

Set the oven to 425ºF (220°C). Coat the baking sheet with nonstick cooking spray.

Rub both trout fillets, inside and out, with olive oil. Season with salt and pepper.

Mix the onion, bell pepper, poblano pepper, and mushrooms in a large bowl. Stuff half of this mix into the cavity of each fillet. Top the mixture with 2–3 lemon slices inside each fillet.

Place the fish on the prepared baking sheet side by side. Roast in the preheated oven for 25 minutes.

Pull out from the oven and serve on a plate.

Per Serving
Calories: 453 Fat: 22 g. Protein: 49 g.

Chicken Gyros with Tzatziki (Italian)

Preparation Time: 10 minutes **Cooking Time:** 80 minutes
Servings: 6

Ingredients:

1 lb. ground chicken breast	2 tbsps. dried rosemary
1 onion	1 tbsp. dried marjoram
½ tsp. sea salt	¼ tsp. freshly ground black
6 garlic cloves, minced	pepper Tzatziki Sauce

Directions:

Preheat the oven to 350°F.

In a stand mixer, blend the chicken, onion, rosemary, marjoram, garlic, sea salt, and pepper.

Press the mixture into a loaf pan. Bake for 1 hour. Pull out from the oven and set it aside for 20 minutes before slicing.

Slice the gyro and spoon the tzatziki sauce over the top.

Per Serving
Calories: 289 Protein: 50 g. Fat: 1 g.

Veal Pot Roast (Spanish)

Preparation Time: 20 minutes **Cooking Time:** 5 hours
Servings: 6–8

Ingredients:

1 tbsps. olive oil	2 lbs. boneless veal roast
Salt and pepper	4 medium carrots, peeled
2 parsnips, peeled and halved	2 white turnips, peeled and quartered
2 sprigs of fresh thyme	1 orange, scrubbed and zested
10 garlic cloves, peeled	1 cup chicken or veal stock

Directions:

Heat a large skillet over medium-high heat.

Coat veal roast all over with olive oil, then season with salt and pepper.

When the skillet is hot, add the veal roast and sear on all sides.

Once the veal roast is cooked on all sides, transfer it to the slow cooker.

Toss the carrots, parsnips, turnips, and garlic into the skillet. Stir and cook for 5 minutes—not all the way through, just to get some of the brown bits from the veal and give them a bit of color.

Transfer the vegetables to the slow cooker, placing them all around the meat.

Top the veal roast with the thyme and the zest from the orange. Slice orange in half and squeeze the juice over the top of the meat.

Add the chicken stock, then cook the veal roast on LOW for 5 hours.

Per Serving
Calories: 426 Fat: 12.8 g. Protein: 48.8 g.

Slow Cooker Salmon in Foil (Italian)

Preparation Time: 5 minutes **Cooking Time:** 2 hours
Servings: 2

Ingredients:

1 (6 oz./170 g.) salmon fillets	2 garlic cloves, minced
½ tbsp. lime juice	1 tbsp. olive oil
¼ tsp. black pepper	1 tsp. fresh parsley, finely chopped

Directions:

Spread a length of foil onto a work surface and place the salmon fillets in the middle.

Blend the olive oil, garlic, lime juice, parsley, and black pepper. Brush the mixture over the fillets. Fold the foil over and crimp the sides to make a packet.

Place the packet into the slow cooker, cover, and cook on HIGH for 2 hours. Serve hot.

Per Serving
Calories: 446 Fat: 21 g. Protein: 65 g.

Spicy Chicken Shawarma (Greek)

Preparation Time: 15 minutes **Cooking Time:** 6 minutes
Servings: 4

Ingredients:

1 lb. chicken breast	4 (6-inch) halved pitas
½ cup plum tomato, chopped	½ cup cucumber, chopped
¼ cup red onion, chopped	5 tbsps. plain low-fat
2 tbsps. lemon juice, divided	Greek-style yogurt, divided
2 tbsps. parsley, finely	1 tbsp. Tahini
chopped	2 tbsps. extra-virgin olive oil
½ tsp. salt	½ tsp. crushed red pepper
¼ tsp. ground cumin	¼ tsp. ground ginger
1/8 tsp. ground coriander	

Directions:

Combine the parsley, salt, red pepper, ginger, cumin, coriander, 1 tbsp. yogurt, 1 tbsp. juice, and 2 cloves of garlic. Add the chicken, stir to coat. Preheat the oil in a nonstick pan over medium-high heat. Add the chicken mixture to the pan and cook for 6 minutes.

In the meantime, combine the remaining 1 tbsp. lemon juice, the remaining ¼ cup of yogurt, the remaining 1 clove of garlic, and the tahini, mixing well. Put 1 ½ tsp. the tahini mixture inside each half of the pita, divide the chicken between the pita halves. Fill each half of the pita with 1 tbsp. cucumber, 1 tbsp. tomato, and 1 ½ tsp. onion.

Per Serving
Calories: 440 Protein: 37 g. Fat: 19 g.

Parmesan Honey Pork Loin Roast (Italian)

Preparation Time: 10 minutes **Cooking Time:** 5 hours
Servings: 8

Ingredients:

3 lbs. pork loin	2/3 cup grated parmesan
1 tbsp. oregano	cheese
½ cup honey	3 tbsps. soy sauce
1 tbsp. basil	2 tbsps. garlic, chopped
½ tsp. salt	2 tbsps. cornstarch
¼ cup chicken broth	Olive oil or nonstick
2 tbsps. olive oil	cooking spray

Directions:

Spray your slow cooker with olive oil or nonstick cooking spray.

Place the pork loin in the slow cooker. In a small mixing bowl, combine the cheese, honey, soy sauce, oregano, basil, garlic, olive oil, and salt. Stir with a fork to mix well, then pour over the pork loin. Cook on low for 5–6 hours.

Remove the pork loin and put it on a serving platter.

Pour the juices from the slow cooker into a small saucepan. Create a slurry by mixing the cornstarch into the chicken broth and whisking until smooth. Bring the contents of the saucepan to a boil, then whisk in the slurry and let simmer until thickened. Pour over the pork loin and serve.

Per Serving
Calories: 449 Fat: 15 g. Protein: 55 g.

Fried Whole Tilapia (Spanish)

Preparation Time: 10 minutes **Cooking Time:** 25 minutes
Servings: 2

Ingredients:

10-oz. tilapia.	5 garlic cloves, mince.
4 large onions, chopped.	1 tsp. cumin powder.
2 tbsps. red chili powder.	2 tbsps. oil.
1 tsp. coriander powder.	Black pepper to taste.
Salt to taste.	2 tbsps. soy sauce.
2 tbsps. fish sauce.	1 tsp. turmeric powder

Directions:

Take the tilapia fish and clean it well without taking off the skin. You need to fry it whole, so you have to be careful about cleaning the gut inside.

Cut few slits on the skin so the seasoning gets inside well.

Marinate the fish with fish sauce, soy sauce, red chili powder, cumin powder, turmeric powder, coriander powder, salt, and pepper.

Coat half of the onions in the same mixture too.

Let them marinate for 1 hour.

In a skillet heat the oil. Fry the fish for 8 minutes on each side.

Transfer the fish to a serving plate.

Fry the marinated onions until they become crispy.

Add the remaining raw onions on top and serve hot.

Per Serving
Calories: 368 g. Fats: 30.1 g. Carbs: 9.2 g. Proteins: 16.6 g.

Artichoke Petals Bites (Spanish)

Preparation Time: 10 minutes **Cooking Time:** 10 minutes
Servings: 8

Ingredients:

8 oz. artichoke petals,	½ cup almond flour.
boiled, drained, without salt.	4 oz. Parmesan, grated
	2 tbsps. almond butter,
	melted.

Directions:

In the mixing bowl, mix up together almond flour and grated Parmesan.

Preheat the oven to 355º F.

Dip the artichoke petals in the almond butter and then coat in the almond flour mixture.

Place them in the tray.

Transfer the tray to the preheated oven and cook the petals for 10 minutes.

Chill the cooked petal bites a little before serving.

Per Serving
Calories: 140 g. Fat: 6.4 g Carbs: 14.6 g. Protein: 10 g.

Steamed Trout with Lemon Herb Crust (Spanish)

Preparation Time: 10 minutes **Cooking Time:** 15 minutes
Servings: 2

Ingredients:

3 tbsps. olive oil
1 tbsp. fresh mint, chopped
2 tbsps. fresh lemon juice
¼ tsp. dried ground thyme
1 tsp. sea salt

3 garlic cloves, chopped
1 tbsp. fresh parsley, chopped
1 lb. (454 g.) fresh trout (2 pieces) 2 cups fish stock

Directions:

Blend the olive oil, garlic, lemon juice, mint, parsley, thyme, and salt. Brush the marinade onto the fish.

Insert a trivet in the electric pressure cooker. Fill in the fish stock and place the fish on the trivet.

Secure the lid. Select the STEAM mode and set the cooking time for 15 minutes at high pressure.

Once cooking is complete, do a quick pressure release. Carefully open the lid. Serve warm.

Per Serving
Calories: 477 Fat: 30 g. Protein: 52 g.

Lamb with String Beans (Spanish)

Preparation Time: 10 minutes **Cooking Time:** 1 hour
Servings: 6

Ingredients:

¼ cup extra-virgin olive oil
6 lamb chops
½ tsp. black pepper
1 ½ cups hot water
2 tomatoes

1 tsp. sea salt
2 tbsps. tomato paste
1 lb. green beans
1 onion

Directions:

In a skillet at medium-high heat, pour 2 tbsps. of olive oil.

Season the lamb chops with ½ tsp. sea salt and 1/8 tsp. pepper. Cook the lamb in the hot oil for 4 minutes. Transfer the meat to a platter and set it aside.

Put back to the heat then put the 2 tbsps. of olive oil. Heat until it shimmers.

Blend the tomato paste and the hot water. Mix to the hot skillet along with the green beans, onion, tomatoes, and the remaining ½ tsp. sea salt and ¼ tsp. pepper. Bring to a simmer.

Return the lamb chops to the pan. Bring to boil and reduce the heat to medium-low. Simmer for 45 minutes until the beans are soft, adding additional water as needed to adjust the thickness of the sauce.

Per Serving
Calories: 439 Protein: 50 g. Fat: 22 g.

Chicken Piccata (Italian)

Preparation Time: 10 minutes **Cooking Time:** 10 minutes
Servings: 6

Ingredients:

½ cup whole-wheat flour
1/8 tsp. freshly ground black pepper
1 ½ lb. boneless
½ cup dry white wine
¼ cup capers, drained and rinsed
1 lemon juice

½ tsp. sea salt
3 tbsps. extra-virgin olive oil
1 cup unsalted chicken broth
1 lemon zest
¼ cup fresh parsley leaves, chopped

Directions:

In a shallow dish, whisk the flour, sea salt, and pepper. Dredge the chicken in the flour and tap off any excess.

Heat the olive oil in a pan over medium-high heat.

Add the chicken and cook for 4 minutes. Remove the chicken from the pan and set aside, tented with aluminum foil to keep warm.

Return to the heat and mix the broth, wine, lemon juice, and lemon zest, and capers. Simmer for 3–4 minutes, stirring. Remove the skillet from the heat and return the chicken to the pan. Turn to coat. Stir in the parsley and serve.

Per Serving
Calories: 153 Protein: 8 g. Fat: 9 g.

Chicken and Tzatziki Pitas (Greek)

Preparation Time: 10 minutes **Cooking Time:** 0 minutes
Servings: 8

Ingredients:

2 pita breads
8 teaspoons tzatziki sauce

10 oz chicken fillet, grilled
1 cup lettuce, chopped

Directions:

Cut every pita bread on the halves to get 8 pita pockets.

Then fill every pita pocket with chopped lettuce and sprinkle greens with tzatziki sauce.

Chop chicken fillet and add it in the pita pockets too.

Per Serving
calories 106, fat 3.8, carbs 6.1, protein 11

Olive Feta Beef (Greek)

Preparation Time: 10 minutes **Cooking Time:** 6 hours
Servings: 8

Ingredients:

1 lbs. beef stew meat, cut into half-inch pieces	30 oz. can tomato, diced
½ cup feta cheese, crumbled.	½ tsp. salt.
	¼ tsp. pepper.
	1 cup olives, pitted, and cut in half.

Directions:

Add all ingredients into the crockpot and stir well.

Cover and cook on high for 6 hours.

Season with pepper and salt.Stir well and serve.

Per Serving
Calories: 370 g. Fat: 12 g. Carbs: 10 g. Protein: 50 g.

African Chicken Curry (Greek)

Prep time: 10 minutes **Cooking Time:** 30 mins **Servings:** 4

Ingredients:

1 lb. whole chicken.	½ onion.
½ cup coconut milk.	½ bay leaf.
1 ½ tsps. olive oil.	½ cup peeled tomatoes.
1 clove garlic	1 tsp. curry powder.
½ lemon, juiced..	1 tsp. salt.

Directions:

Keep the skin of the chicken.

Cut your chicken into 8 pieces. It looks good when you keep the size not too small or not too big.

Discard the skin of the onion and garlic and mince the garlic and dice the onion.

Cut the tomato wedges.

Now in a pot add the olive oil and heat over medium heat.

Add the garlic and fry until it becomes brown.

Add the diced onion and caramelize it.

Add the bay leaf, and chicken pieces.

Fry the chicken pieces until they are golden.

Add the curry powder, coconut milk, and salt.

Cover and cook for 10 minutes on high heat.

Lower the heat to medium-low and add the lemon juice.

Add the tomato wedges and coconut milk.

Cook for another 10 minutes.

Serve hot with rice or tortilla.

Per Serving
Calories: 354 g. Fats: 10 g. Proteins: 18 g. Carbs: 17 g.

Prawn Arrabbiata (Greek)

Preparation Time: 10 minutes **Cooking Time:** 40 minutes
Servings: 1

Ingredients:

Raw or cooked prawns (Ideally king prawns). oz. buckwheat pasta.	1 tbsp. extra-virgin olive oil. For the arrabbiata sauce:
Red onion, finely chopped.	1 tsp. dried mixed herbs.
1.2-oz. celery, finely chopped.	1 garlic clove, finely chopped
1 Bird's eye chili, finely chopped.	1 tbsp. chopped parsley.
14-oz. tinned chopped tomatoes	1 tsp. extra-virgin olive oil.
	2 tbsps. white wine (optional).

Directions:

Firstly, fry the onion, garlic, celery, and chili over medium-low heat and dry herbs in the oil for 1–2 minutes. Switch the flame to medium, then add the wine and cook for 1 minute. Add the tomatoes and leave the sauce to cook for 20–30 minutes over medium-low heat until it has a nice rich consistency. If you feel the sauce becomes too thick, add some water.

While the sauce is cooking, boil a pan of water, and cook the pasta as directed by the packet. Drain, toss with the olive oil when cooked to your liking, and keep in the pan until needed.

Add the raw prawns to the sauce and cook for another 3–4 minutes until they have turned pink and opaque, then attach the parsley and serve. If you use cooked prawns add the parsley, bring the sauce to a boil and eat.

Add the cooked pasta to the sauce, blend well, and serve gently.

Per Serving
Calories: 185 g. Fat: 30 g. Protein: 56 g. Carbs: 45 g. Cholesterol: 230 mg. Sugar: 0 g.

Lime Chicken with Black Beans (Spanish)

Preparation Time: 15 minutes **Cooking Time:** 30 minutes
Servings: 8

Ingredients:

8 chicken thighs (boneless and skinless)	1 cup black beans
1 cup canned tomatoes	3 tablespoons lime juice
	4 teaspoons garlic powder

Directions:

Marinate the chicken in a mixture of lime juice and garlic powder.

Add the chicken to the Instant Pot. Pour the tomatoes on top of the chicken. Seal the pot. Set it to manual. Cook at high pressure for 10 minutes. Release the pressure naturally. Stir in the black beans. Press sauté to simmer until black beans are cooked.

Per Serving
Calories 370; Total Fat 11.2g; Saturated Fat 3.1g; Cholesterol 130mg

Coated Cauliflower Head (Spanish)

Preparation Time: 10 minutes **Cooking Time:** 40 minutes
Servings: 6

Ingredients:

2-lb. cauliflower head.	1 tbsp. butter softened.
3 tbsps. olive oil.	1 tsp. salt.
1 egg, whisked.	1 tsp. dried cilantro.
1 tsp. Tahini paste.	1 tsp. dried oregano.
1 tsp. ground coriander.	

Directions:

Trim cauliflower head if needed.

Preheat oven to 350° F.

In the mixing bowl, mix up together olive oil, softened butter, ground coriander, salt, whisked egg, dried cilantro, dried oregano, and tahini paste.

Then brush the cauliflower head with this mixture generously and transfer it to the tray.

Bake the cauliflower head for 40 minutes.

Brush it with the remaining oil mixture every 10 minutes.

Per Serving
Calories: 131 g. Fat: 10.3 g. Carbs: 8.4 g. Protein: 4.1 g.

Chicken Sausage and Peppers (Spanish)

Preparation Time: 10 minutes **Cooking Time:** 20 minutes
Servings: 6

Ingredients:

1 tbsps. extra-virgin olive oil	1 red bell pepper
6 Italian chicken sausage links	pepper Pinch red pepper flakes
1 green bell pepper	3 garlic cloves, minced
½ cup dry white wine	½ tsp. sea salt
¼ tsp. freshly ground black	1 onion

Directions:

Heat the olive oil in a skillet at medium-high heat.

Add the sausages and cook for 5–7 minutes, turning occasionally, until browned, and they reach an internal temperature of 165°F. With tongs, remove the sausage from the pan and set it aside on a platter, tented with aluminum foil to keep warm.

Put the skillet back to heat and add the onion, red bell pepper, and green bell pepper. Cook them for 5–7 minutes.

Cook the garlic for 30 seconds, stirring constantly.

Stir in the wine, sea salt, pepper, and red pepper flakes. Scrape and fold in any browned bits from the bottom. Simmer for 4 minutes more. Spoon the peppers over the sausages and serve.

Per Serving
Calories: 173 Protein: 22 g. Fat: 5 g.

Chicken Merlot with Mushrooms (Spanish)

Prep time: 10 minutes **Cooking Time:** 40 mins **Servings:** 2

Ingredients:

6 boneless, skinless chicken breasts, cubed.	1 large red onion, chopped.
¾ cup chicken broth.	2 cloves garlic, minced.
¼ cup Merlot.	1 (6 oz.) can tomato paste.
2 tbsps. basil, chopped finely.	3 tbsps. chia seeds.
1 (10 oz.) package buckwheat ramen noodles, cooked.	Salt and pepper to taste
	3 cups mushrooms, sliced..
	2 tbsps. Parmesan, shaved.
	2 tsps. sugar

Directions:

Rinse chicken; set aside.

Add mushrooms, onion, and garlic to the crockpot and mix.

Place chicken cubes on top of the vegetables and do not mix.

In a large bowl, combine broth, tomato paste, wine, chia seeds, basil, sugar, salt, and pepper. Pour over the chicken.

Cover and cook on low for 7–8 hours or on high for 3 ½–4 hours.

To serve, spoon chicken, mushroom mixture, and sauce over hot cooked buckwheat ramen noodles. Top with shaved Parmesan.

Per Serving
Calories: 213 g. Fat: 10 g. Protein: 56 g. Carbs: 45 g. Cholesterol: 230 mg. Sugar: 0 g.

Garlic Herb Grilled Chicken Breast (Greek)

Prep time: 7 minutes **Cooking Time:** 20 mins **Servings:** 4

Ingredients:

1 ¼ lb. chicken breasts, skinless and boneless.	1 tbsp. garlic & herb seasoning blend.
2 tsps. olive oil.	Salt and Pepper.

Directions:

Pat dries the chicken breasts, coat it with olive oil, and season it with salt and pepper on both sides.

Season the chicken with garlic and herb seasoning or any other seasoning of your choice.

Turn the grill on and oil the grate.

Place the chicken on the hot grate and let it grill till the sides turn white.

Flip them over and let them cook again.

When the internal temperature is about 160° F, it is most likely cooked.

Set aside for 15 minutes. Chop into pieces.

Per Serving
Calories: 187 g. Fats: 6 g. Protein: 32 g. Carbs: 5 g.

Appendix 1   Measurement Conversion Chart

VOLUME EQUIVALENTS(DRY)

US STANDARD	METRIC (APPROXIMATE)
1/8 teaspoon	0.5 mL
1/4 teaspoon	1 mL
1/2 teaspoon	2 mL
3/4 teaspoon	4 mL
1 teaspoon	5 mL
1 tablespoon	15 mL
1/4 cup	59 mL
1/2 cup	118 mL
3/4 cup	177 mL
1 cup	235 mL
2 cups	475 mL
3 cups	700 mL
4 cups	1 L

VOLUME EQUIVALENTS(LIQUID)

US STANDARD	US STANDARD (OUNCES)	METRIC (APPROXIMATE)
2 tablespoons	1 fl.oz.	30 mL
1/4 cup	2 fl.oz.	60 mL
1/2 cup	4 fl.oz.	120 mL
1 cup	8 fl.oz.	240 mL
1 1/2 cup	12 fl.oz.	355 mL
2 cups or 1 pint	16 fl.oz.	475 mL
4 cups or 1 quart	32 fl.oz.	1 L
1 gallon	128 fl.oz.	4 L

TEMPERATURES EQUIVALENTS

FAHRENHEIT(F)	CELSIUS(C) (APPROXIMATE)
225 °F	107 °C
250 °F	120 °C
275 °F	135 °C
300 °F	150 °C
325 °F	160 °C
350 °F	180 °C
375 °F	190 °C
400 °F	205 °C
425 °F	220 °C
450 °F	235 °C
475 °F	245 °C
500 °F	260 °C

WEIGHT EQUIVALENTS

US STANDARD	METRIC (APPROXIMATE)
1 ounce	28 g
2 ounces	57 g
5 ounces	142 g
10 ounces	284 g
15 ounces	425 g
16 ounces (1 pound)	455 g
1.5 pounds	680 g
2 pounds	907 g

Appendix 2   Dirty Dozen and Clean Fifteen

The Environmental Working Group (EWG) is a nonprofit, nonpartisan organization dedicated to protecting human health and the environment Its mission is to empower people to live healthier lives in a healthier environment. This organization publishes an annual list of the twelve kinds of produce, in sequence, that have the highest amount of pesticide residue-the Dirty Dozen-as well as a list of the fifteen kinds ofproduce that have the least amount of pesticide residue-the Clean Fifteen.

THE DIRTY DOZEN

- The 2016 Dirty Dozen includes the following produce. These are considered among the year's most important produce to buy organic:

Strawberries	Spinach
Apples	Tomatoes
Nectarines	Bell peppers
Peaches	Cherry tomatoes
Celery	Cucumbers
Grapes	Kale/collard greens
Cherries	Hot peppers

- *The Dirty Dozen list contains two additional itemskale/collard greens and hot peppers-because they tend to contain trace levels of highly hazardous pesticides.*

THE CLEAN FIFTEEN

- The least critical to buy organically are the Clean Fifteen list. The following are on the 2016 list:

Avocados	Papayas
Corn	Kiw
Pineapples	Eggplant
Cabbage	Honeydew
Sweet peas	Grapefruit
Onions	Cantaloupe
Asparagus	Cauliflower
Mangos	

- *Some of the sweet corn sold in the United States are made from genetically engineered (GE) seedstock. Buy organic varieties of these crops to avoid GE produce.*

Appendix 3
Index

Leave a Review

As an independent author with a small marketing budget, reviews are my livelihood on this platform. If you enjoyed this book, I'd appreciate it if you could leave your honest feedback.

I read EVERY single review because I love the feedback from MY readers!

Thank you for staying with me.

Made in United States
North Haven, CT
07 December 2022

27125018R00063